Digital contention in a divided society

Manchester University Press

Digital contention in a divided society

Social media, parades and protests in Northern Ireland

PAUL REILLY

Manchester University Press

Copyright © Paul Reilly 2021

The right of Paul Reilly to be identified as the author of this work has been asserted by them in accordance with the Copyright, Designs and Patents Act 1988.

Published by Manchester University Press
Oxford Road, Manchester M13 9PL

www.manchesteruniversitypress.co.uk

British Library Cataloguing-in-Publication Data
A catalogue record for this book is available from the British Library

ISBN 978 0 7190 8707 3 hardback
ISBN 978 15261 7875 6 paperback

First published 2021

The publisher has no responsibility for the persistence or accuracy of URLs for any external or third-party internet websites referred to in this book, and does not guarantee that any content on such websites is, or will remain, accurate or appropriate.

Typeset
by Sunrise Setting Ltd, Brixham

Contents

List of figures and tables   *page* vi

Acknowledgements   ix

List of abbreviations   x

Introduction   1

1 Social media, contentious politics and social movements   24

2 Too many cyberwarriors? The case of Loyalist Peaceful
   Protest Updater   47

3 "You can't eat a flag": Northern Ireland Twitter responds
   to the flag protests   74

4 PSNIRA vs peaceful protesters? YouTube, sousveillance
   and the policing of the flag protests   102

5 Parody of esteem? LAD and the rise of 'silly citizenship'   129

6 Twitter, affective publics and public demonstrations:
   the 2014 and 2015 Ardoyne parade disputes   156

   Conclusion   184

   Appendix 1 Content analysis of newspaper coverage
   of flag protests   205

   Appendix 2 Content analysis of newspaper coverage
   of the Ardoyne parade disputes   220

   Afterword   227

   Bibliography   240

   Index   261

Figures and tables

Figures

1.1	IssueCrawler network for Northern Irish political blogs, 2014	*page* 37
2.1	Number of flag protest articles in main Northern Irish newspapers, December 2012–February 2013	54
2.2	Number of comments posted on LPPU and LPPUB page, 3 January–17 February 2013	59
2.3	Main themes in threads on LPPU and LPPUB, January 2013	62
3.1	Tweets with flag protest response hashtags, 14–31 January 2013	80
3.2	Number of tweets tagged #flegs, January–February 2013	81
3.3	Classification of #flegs tweets	82
3.4	Top 50 #flegs tweeters by actor type	83
3.5	#Flegs tweeters by actor type	84
3.6	Authors of retweeted content in #flegs	85
5.1	Number of comments posted on LAD Facebook page, December 2012–February 2013	135
5.2	Main themes in threads on LAD Facebook page, December 2012–February 2013	136
5.3	Number of tweets from LAD Twitter account, October–November 2013	143
5.4	Themes in posts retweeted by LAD, October–November 2013	144
6.1	Tweets mentioning Ardoyne, 12 July 2014 and 13 July 2015	166

6.2   Classification of 'Ardoyne' tweets   166
6.3   Top 50 'Ardoyne' tweeters by actor type   167
6.4   Ardoyne tweeters by actor type   168
6.5   Authors of retweeted content in #Ardoyne   169

Appendix 1

A1.1   Main themes in *Belfast Telegraph* coverage of
        flag protests, December 2012–February 2013   217
A1.2   Main themes in *Irish News* coverage of flag
        protests, December 2012–February 2013   217
A1.3   Main themes in *News Letter* coverage of flag
        protests, December 2012–February 2013   218
A1.4   Actors quoted in *Irish News* coverage of flag protests,
        December 2012–February 2013   218
A1.5   Actors quoted in *News Letter* coverage of protests,
        December 2012–February 2013   219

Tables

2.1   Characteristics of three subsamples taken from
        LPPU and LPPUB   60
4.1   Characteristics of flag protest videos, 21 December
        2012–10 March 2013   114

Appendix 1

A1.1   Number of articles from three newspapers analysed,
        December 2012–February 2013   205
A1.2   Actors quoted in *Belfast Telegraph/Sunday Life*
        coverage of protests, December 2012   206
A1.3   Actors quoted in *Belfast Telegraph/Sunday Life*
        coverage of protests, January 2013   208
A1.4   Actors quoted in *Belfast Telegraph/Sunday Life*
        coverage of protests, February 2013   210
A1.5   Actors quoted in *Irish News* coverage of protests,
        December 2012   210
A1.6   Actors quoted in *Irish News* coverage of protests,
        January 2013   212

A1.7   Actors quoted in *Irish News* coverage of protests,
        February 2013   214
A1.8   Actors quoted in *News Letter* coverage of protests,
        December 2012   215
A1.9   Actors quoted in *News Letter* coverage of protests,
        January 2013   216
A1.10 Actors quoted in *News Letter* coverage of protests,
        February 2013   216

Appendix 2

A2.1   Newspaper articles addressing Ardoyne parade
        dispute, 8–14 July 2014   220
A2.2   Actors quoted in newspaper coverage of Ardoyne
        dispute, 8–14 July 2014   222
A2.3   Newspaper articles addressing Ardoyne parade
        dispute, 8–15 July 2015   223
A2.4   Actors quoted in newspaper coverage of Ardoyne
        dispute, 8–15 July 2015   225

Acknowledgements

This book draws on nearly ten years of work and could not have been completed without the support of my colleagues, students and friends in Glasgow, Leicester and Sheffield. Part of this research was funded by a small grant from the British Academy and I am grateful to the anonymous reviewers from First Monday for feedback on previous iterations of Chapters 4 and 6. Many thanks to my interviewees and all those who provided help with the social media data collection and analysis. In particular, I would like to express my gratitude to Caitlin Shayda Jones and Miruna Sfăt (Vîrtopeanu); without their support this work would have been much inferior.

This undertaking could not have been realised without the inspiration of research collaborators such as Dima Atanasova, John Coster, Faith Gordon, Darren Lilleker, Rebecca Stevenson, Ioanna Tantanasi, Giuliana Tiripelli, Filippo Trevisan, Anastasia Veneti and Stefania Vicari. A special mention is due to my researchers and those who took my Activism and Protest in the Information Age and Digital Advocacy modules, from whom I have learnt a lot over the past decade. Thanks also to Rob Byron, Lucy Burns and the team at Manchester University Press for their support and assistance in bringing this book to fruition.

Writing a book is very much a marathon rather than a sprint. In this endeavour, I have been fortunate to have the same support team that helped me write 'Framing the Troubles Online'. Thanks to Dad, Mum, Emma, Mark, Colin, Jack and Lucia for everything. However, this book must surely be dedicated to Sarah. It would not have been possible without her love, support, indefatigability and the occasional grammar check. Needless to say, any mistakes in the text are all mine, not hers.

Abbreviations

CARA	Crumlin Ardoyne Residents Association
DUP	Democratic Unionist Party
GARC	Greater Ardoyne Residents' Collective
NIUG	Northern Ireland Unionist Collective Group
PC	Protestant Coalition
PIRA	Provisional Irish Republican Army
PSNI	Police Service of Northern Ireland
PUP	Progressive Unionist Party
RUC	Royal Ulster Constabulary
SDLP	Social Democratic and Labour Party
TUV	Traditional Unionist Voice
UDA	Ulster Defence Association
UKIP	UK Independence Party
UPF	Ulster People's Forum
UPRG	Ulster Political Research Group
UPV	United Protestant Voice
UUP	Ulster Unionist Party
UVF	Ulster Volunteer Force

Introduction

How are platforms such as Facebook and Twitter[1] used by citizens to frame contentious parades and protests in 'post-conflict' Northern Ireland?[2] Do these 'affective publics' appear to escalate or de-escalate the tensions caused by these hybrid media events? What do these contentious episodes tell us about the potential of information and communication technologies (ICTs) to promote positive intergroup contact within deeply divided societies? Certainly, there has been no shortage of political contention within Northern Ireland in recent times. Most notably, the Stormont Assembly was suspended for three years (January 2017–January 2020) in the wake of scandals such as 'Irisgate' and the renewable heating incentive scheme.[3] At the same time, the New Irish Republican Army murder of journalist Lyra McKee in Derry/Londonderry in April 2019 illustrated the continued threat to the peace process from violent dissidents on both sides.[4] Intercommunal tensions were further exacerbated by the referendum held in June 2016 over the United Kingdom's future membership of the European Union (EU). Northern Ireland faced the prospect of leaving the EU despite the fact that 56 per cent of voters in the contested entity had voted to remain.[5] The only parties in the region to campaign for 'Brexit' were the Democratic Unionist Party (DUP) and Traditional Unionist Voice (TUV); the former eventually struck a confidence and supply arrangement with the Conservative Party in order to keep Prime Minister Theresa May in office after she failed to win a majority in the 2017 UK General Election. The UK-wide referendum campaign was mired in controversy in no small part due to the use of online platforms to circulate misinformation, the sharing of false information without harmful intent, and disinformation, the "deliberate sharing of false information to cause harm to others" (Wardle, 2017). For example, pro-Brexit groups such as Vote Leave circulated false claims on Facebook that Turkey was about to join the EU and that the UK government was powerless to place caps on immigration from other member states.[6] This raised further questions about the responsibility of online platforms to take stronger action to remove 'fake news', which was said to have had a modest but potentially significant impact upon voting behaviour during Donald Trump's unexpected victory in the 2016 US Presidential Election (Allcott and Gentzkow, 2017).

This book contextualises contemporary debates about digital contention by exploring how social media users responded to controversial public demonstrations in Northern Ireland between 2012–2016. In doing so, it is congruent with the agenda for digital politics research advanced by Karpf (2020), which acknowledges the temporality of social media, how platforms and their uses evolve, and the importance of analysing how online platforms are utilised during specific periods in time. It provides the first in-depth qualitative exploration of how social media were used during the union flag protests (December 2012–March 2013) and the Ardoyne parade disputes (July 2014 and July 2015). *The Flag Dispute: Anatomy of a Protest* written by Paul Nolan and his colleagues from Queen's University Belfast (Nolan et al., 2014: 19) notes that the former was "utterly typical" of the crises that had occurred in nearly every decade since Northern Ireland was founded in 1921. Together with the long-running dispute between the nationalist Ardoyne residents and the Orange Order over the route of an annual Twelfth parade, it could be viewed as a manifestation of the 'symbolic contestation' that has continued unabated throughout both the conflict and 'post-conflict' phases of what is colloquially known as the 'Troubles'. Hayward and Komarova (2014) suggest that this stalemate over how to commemorate the past is symptomatic of the political failure to establish a common civic culture in Northern Ireland. However, unlike its antecedents, these contentious public demonstrations were experienced by many citizens through platforms such as Facebook, Twitter and YouTube. Whereas previously news media projected a limited number of interpretations of these protests, social media 'presenced' under-represented viewpoints and 'discursively rendered' publics through framing devices such as hashtags (Couldry, 2012; Papacharissi, 2014).

Whether these viewpoints are listened to or not remains to be seen. Previous work in this field focused on how digital media relates to the territorial strategies of rival interface communities (O'Dochartaigh, 2007), as well as how loyalists and republicans used the Internet to frame the 1998 Belfast Agreement (sometimes referred to as the Good Friday Agreement). In *Framing the Troubles Online* (Reilly, 2011a), I argued that ICTs were unlikely to disrupt 'politics as usual' in Northern Ireland. My study of 55 websites, maintained by political parties, community groups and supporters of loyalist and republican paramilitaries, suggested that these were de facto 'islands of political communication' providing little opportunity for the informal learning about outgroups that might improve community relations in a society transitioning from a 30-year ethnonationalist conflict.[7] The online frames adopted by these actors were invariably informed by the zero-sum perceptions of space and politics synonymous with the conflict. These discourses of 'othering' were arguably a manifestation of the 'benign apartheid' entrenched since the Belfast Agreement.[8] After 30 years of violence, what has been achieved in Northern Ireland since the late 1990s might best be described as 'negative' peace, defined as the "absence of organised collective violence" (Galtung, 1967: 17). There has been an overall reduction in sectarian violence despite intermittent campaigns by 'spoiler' groups and, in particular, violent dissident republicans such as the Real IRA (see Edwards and McGrattan, 2010). However, societal cleavages and differences were institutionalised rather than confronted in a consociational framework of governance based on mandatory power-sharing between political elites drawn from the two main ethnic blocs. Group rights have typically been prioritised over those held by individuals who wish to move beyond such ethno-sectarianism (Aughey, 2007; Komarova, 2010; Shirlow and McEvoy, 2008). This is despite evidence that Catholics and Protestants are more amenable to the shared 'Northern Irish' identity than previously thought (Muldoon et al., 2008), with the 'two communities' thesis further challenged by the fact that nearly four in ten people in Northern Ireland define themselves as "Neither Unionist nor Nationalist" (Hayward and McManus, 2019: 140). Nevertheless, consociational assumptions about the inflexibility of social identities have continued to inform policy-making in the deeply divided society.

Many scholars have argued that a more inclusive approach towards peacebuilding, involving civil society and grass-roots political organisations from both ethnic blocs meeting in shared spaces, was needed in order to build positive relationships between members of antagonistic groups (Brewer, 2010; Dixon, 2012). Group affiliations in these spaces would not be minimised or hidden; the emphasis was on individuals treating each other as human beings rather than anonymous members of outgroups (Lederach, 1997). There is already some evidence that children educated in integrated schools are more likely to reject traditional unionist and nationalist identities, holding out the possibility that this form of contact with the 'other' community could help reduce prejudice against outgroups (Magill and Hamber, 2011; Paolini et al., 2004). However, only around 7 per cent of children in Northern Ireland are currently educated in integrated schools, with demand constantly exceeding the number of places available despite polls consistently showing public support for an expansion of the sector.[9] This was acknowledged in the Good Relations Strategy launched in May 2013, which aimed to provide more spaces and opportunities for intergroup contact through measures such as increased provision of shared educational facilities.[10]

In this context, residents' groups, such as the nationalist Garvaghy Road Residents' Coalition,[11] inevitably used their websites to engage in a competition of victimhood with members of the 'other' community (Reilly, 2011a). While these sites provided a platform for underrepresented groups that was not available to them in the mainstream news media, their respective audiences were still likely to consist of pre-existing supporters, professional journalists and even researchers. This homophily was due in part to the low visibility of these websites on the directories of commercial search engines such as Google, which directed users towards the pages of news media organisations and research institutions rather than the sites of political fronts and terrorist solidarity actors (Reilly, 2008). Overall, the relative obscurity of these websites, many of which were seemingly dedicated towards the airing of historic grievances, led me to conclude that there was little to no prospect of ICTs making a positive contribution to peacebuilding in Northern Ireland during this period. Websites, emails and other web-based applications were perhaps best viewed as an additional mode of communication that supplemented pre-existing relationships with mainstream news media. While cyber optimists characterised these online spaces as electronic 'agoras' in which people listened respectfully to each other and reflected upon their own views (Froomkin,

2003), my research provided further empirical evidence of the homophily associated with these online spaces (Cho and Lee, 2008). The early signs were that Web 2.0, the popular term for the section of the World Wide Web based on collaboration and the sharing of user-generated content (UGC), might further exacerbate existing sectarian tensions within Northern Ireland. Cyber enthusiasts welcomed this new era of 'mass-self-communication', in which the 'self-directed communication' of individuals could reach a potential global audience (Castells, 2009). Web 2.0 primarily revolved around two types of social media: 1) social networking sites (SNS) such as Facebook that facilitated interpersonal contact; and 2) sites like You-Tube that were specifically created to share both professional content and UGC (van Dijck, 2013: 8). While scholars such as Gauntlett (2011) suggested that the transition from 'Web 1.0' to 'Web 2.0' was akin to moving from private gardens to collective allotments, Northern Irish groups continued to fight over the same 'political turf' online. My first foray into social media research, in 2008, found that the symbols and language of the conflict dominated the Bebo profiles belonging to 10 individuals linked to the aforementioned residents' groups (Reilly, 2011a). Loyalist pages were decorated with the insignias of paramilitary organisations such as the Ulster Volunteer Force (UVF), while their republican counterparts shared images of the rioting that had taken place in nearby interface areas. Sectarian language permeated these profiles, as youths used the affordances of Web 2.0 to intimidate and threaten those from rival communities. This was congruent with the key findings of the few studies exploring how Northern Irish teenagers were using social media during the same period. Research carried out by the Centre for Young Men's Studies (2009) found that adolescents as young as 13 years old used Bebo and MSN Messenger to organise so-called 'recreational rioting', an oxymoron deployed by the Northern Irish print media to suggest that the violence between Catholic and Protestant youths at sectarian interfaces was non-political (Leonard, 2010). Towards the end of the 2000s, the Police Service of Northern Ireland (PSNI) began to publicly link SNS to the organisation of violence in locations such as the Rosemount area of Derry/Londonderry in 2008. It was notable how much of this media coverage conformed to the 'moral panic' discourses surrounding young people's 'risky' behaviours on social media (see Gabriel, 2014 for an overview). Online platforms were usually blamed for 'fuelling' antisocial behaviour in interface areas during this period. At the same time, young people criticised journalists for invading their privacy by using content from their social media profiles without permission, and expressed frustration at media coverage that portrayed them, and their use of digital media, as threats to the peace process (Gordon, 2018).

Social media, peacebuilding and the contact hypothesis

This book will explore whether citizen activity on social media during contentious parades and protests inflames or diffuses the sectarian tensions that surround these incidents, which often boil over into intercommunal violence. In this way, it will assess whether these affective publics, "activated and sustained by feelings of belonging and solidarity" (Papacharissi, 2014: 9), have the potential to contribute to peacebuilding in Northern Ireland. Peacebuilding is defined here as "any activity that fosters or supports sustainable structures and processes that strengthen the prospects for peaceful coexistence and decrease the likelihood of the outbreak, reoccurrence or continuation of violent conflict" (Bush and Duggan, 2014: 310). While liberal peace models typically create a 'poor quality peace' in which elite-level cooperation fails to address the root causes of intergroup mistrust (see MacGinty, 2009 for an overview), ICTs have been linked with more inclusive peacebuilding frameworks that engage populations directly affected by conflict and decentralise power from these political elites (Tellidis and Kappler, 2016). As far back as the late 1960s, Galtung (1967) predicted that the rapid growth of media technologies would favour associative peacebuilding approaches, which increased contact between antagonists, rather than dissociative ones that kept them apart. The agonistic pluralism theorised by Mouffe (2013) posited that a 'conflictual consensus' would emerge as former enemies were recast as 'adversaries' who respectfully disagreed about contentious issues.

There has also been some evidence to suggest that intergroup contact can reduce prejudice against outgroups. First articulated by Allport (1954) and elaborated more recently by scholars such as Hewstone et al. (2006) and Pettigrew et al. (2011), the contact hypothesis suggests that positive intergroup contact can reduce negative stereotyping of the 'other' community, especially in those circumstances when these groups enjoy equal status and are able to cooperate in areas of mutual interest. Subsequent research has built on Allport's work by identifying factors, such as the anonymity and accessibility provided by the Internet, that create an 'enabling psychological environment' for opposing groups to work together in pursuit of a superordinate goal (Amichai-Hamburger and Hayat, 2013). Research indicates that intergroup contact has both direct and indirect effects; although direct contact has been linked to the greatest reduction in prejudice against outgroups, the act of observing ingroup members interacting civilly with outgroup members also has a positive impact on such attitudes (Cao and Wan-Ying, 2017; Dovidio et al., 2017; Vezzali et al., 2014). However, it should be noted that negative contact with outgroup members, whether experienced directly or vicariously, can increase discrimination and prejudice towards such groups (Barlow et al., 2012; Dovidio et al., 2009). The effects of intergroup contact are more likely to improve the attitudes of the majority group towards the minority, rather than vice versa (Cao and Wan-Ying, 2017). Within divided societies such as Northern Ireland, the persistence of conflict between adversaries might also lead to the "reproduction of inequities and injustices" that fuelled the original conflict (McGrattan, 2014: 531). Furthermore, much of the aforementioned research was based on self-reported data gathered via questionnaires and as such may not be an accurate characterisation of how respondents perceive outgroups. Nevertheless, there does appear to be a consensus among researchers that positive intergroup contact in divided societies can generally "reduce anxiety and promote better inter-ethnic relations" (Hughes et al., 2011: 972).

Much of the early literature on 'cyberspatial' technologies suggested that the Internet had the potential to facilitate this intergroup contact within highly segregated societies, where neutral space might be difficult to access or not exist (Dahlgren, 2005). The lack of interpersonal cues present in computer-mediated communication was said to reduce the anxiety associated with intergroup contact (Wang et al., 2009). Mamadouh (2003) was among those to argue that websites could function as a platform for cross-cultural exchange; her study provided evidence that online interactions between Muslims and non-Muslims in the Netherlands could challenge the negative stereotypes of the former perpetuated in mainstream media after the 9/11 attacks. Probably the most well-known framework for using

ICTs to facilitate intergroup contact was the 'gradual model' articulated by Amichai-Hamburger and McKenna (2006). The authors posited that text-based interactions might help address the initial anxiety of participants and provide the basis for 'richer' forms of contact using audio and video, which would ultimately result in regular face-to-face interaction between members of different social groups. In this way, the Internet not only "created opportunities to alter perceptions", but also addressed the practical problem of facilitating intergroup contact in the real world (Amichai-Hamburger, 2008: 223). Subsequent research has explored the impact of *contact quality* on prejudices towards outgroups; video-based communication was found to be more effective than its text-based equivalent in improving attitudes towards individual outgroup members, with the opposite being true when it came to attitudes towards the outgroup as a whole (Cao and Wan-Ying, 2017).

This work has broadly focused on *structured* intergroup contact, which involves supervised online meetings, and *unstructured* contact which takes place in less regulated spaces such as websites and public Facebook groups (Amichai-Hamburger et al., 2015). In terms of the former, examples have included the Peace Project NGO that promoted peace in the Middle East, and the Dissolving Boundaries online educational platform which brought together school children from Northern Ireland and the Republic of Ireland (Amichai-Hamburger et al., 2015: 520). The Net Intergroup Contact platform (NIC) pledged to increase participants' knowledge about outgroups through a "jointly created wiki data bank" and an online chat facility supervised by a social psychologist (Amichai-Hamburger et al., 2015: 520). Yet, at the time of writing, the NIC platform is still unavailable to the public and there remains little empirical evidence to suggest that these projects have helped facilitate reconciliation in divided societies. In terms of the latter, Facebook pages such as Iran-Loves-Israel[12] were linked to more positive intergroup contact between Israelis and Iranians, albeit that it was highly likely that those contributing to these pages held positive views of the 'other' country (Schwab et al., 2019). This 'self-selection' problem has frequently been identified as a potential obstacle to using virtual spaces to host deliberative consultations in divided societies (see Fishkin, 2009 for example).

Social media peacebuilding initiatives have been accused of promoting 'technological solutionism', the term used by Morozov (2013) to critique the Silicon Valley inspired 'belief system' revolving around the Internet's supposed ability to 'fix' societal problems and bring citizens together. As I will discuss in the next chapter, Facebook and Twitter were widely acknowledged to have played a key role in the anti-government protests in the Middle East and North Africa labelled the 'Arab Spring', as well as the Occupy Movement against socio-economic inequality in the US and across the globe in 2011. Therefore, it was perhaps no surprise that such 'solutionism' was also applied to peacebuilding in divided societies such as Northern Ireland. Most notably, Peace on Facebook, a project created by Facebook in partnership with Stanford University's Peace Innovation Lab in October 2009, asserted that the online platform provided space for dialogue between social groups traditionally divided along ethnic or sectarian lines.[13] The project claimed to have facilitated 'friendships' between individuals drawn from a range of antagonistic groups, including Russians and Ukrainians during a recent armed conflict. However, there was little information available on the nature of these interactions and it appeared to be based on the information provided by users on their profiles. John (2019: 1) characterised the initiative as an example of "social media bullshit" designed to convince users that Facebook was a "force for world peace" while providing scant evidence to corroborate these claims of "cross-conflict friending". Moreover, the empirical evidence thus far has suggested that prospects for peace are unlikely to be enhanced via intergroup contact on social media, with platforms such as Twitter more likely to be used to spread hatred and violence than resolve sectarian conflicts as seen in Israel–Palestine and India–Pakistan (Kumar and Semetko, 2017; Wolfsfeld, 2018). It has even been argued that the architecture of these platforms "energises hatred and bigotry" and "turbocharges" the spread of misinformation and disinformation that undermines public trust in news media and democratic political institutions (Vaidhyanathan, 2018: 24). This book adds to this emergent literature by exploring whether the affective publics convened on social media escalate or de-escalate sectarian tensions in Northern Ireland around contentious public demonstrations.

Reconceptualising (digital) citizenship

Social media activity focusing on contentious parades and protests in Northern Ireland can be characterised as acts of digital citizenship.

Early work in this field suggesting that it revolved around the ability to locate and use political information (Mossberger et al., 2008) has gradually given way to a focus on how digital media are used to perform citizenship. Isin and Ruppert (2015: 69) define digital citizens as those who make digital rights claims online, such as "I, we, they have a right to". They enact themselves as subjects of power through acts such as communing, hacking and witnessing. The latter in particular has the potential to hold authority figures to account for their actions and may be conceptualised as a form of 'sousveillance' that counteracts surveillance cultures within contemporary societies (more on this in Chapter 4). Digital media has also been said to provide opportunities for the 'monitorial' form of citizenship first envisaged by Schudson (1998). Building on the seminal work of Lippmann (1922), he argued that citizens scan rather than read their informational environments and have their attention drawn to issues that require immediate action by mainstream news media. The 'presencing' of marginalised viewpoints, in conjunction with the large amounts of data made available online, theoretically make it much easier for citizens to scrutinise the behaviour of their respective governments (Harcup, 2016).

Silly citizenship and ritualised social media practices

The performance of citizenship for many citizens increasingly revolves around creating and sharing irreverent content during political debates on social media. Memes and parody accounts are examples of this 'silly citizenship', in which playfulness is increasingly integral to how citizens perform "political deliberation and participation" (Hartley, 2012: 151). Crucially, these discursive practices are not solely textual and include other types of media content such as videos. The 'spreadability' of such content has been found to be considerably higher if it has a visual component, provokes high-arousal emotions (particularly positive ones) and comes from a reputable and trusted source (Alhabash and McAlister, 2015; Shifman, 2015). In this way, a new model of digitally enabled citizenship has emerged based on self-representations "of, by, and for 'ordinary people'" (Hartley, 2012: 154). Young people in particular engage 'playfully' with public debates through these platforms. This is a potentially significant development given that this social group (many of whom were technically 'non-citizens', being under the age of 18) were traditionally less likely to engage in 'higher' forms of political participation such as joining protest marches or donating to NGOs (Hartley, 2010).

Highfield (2016a: 61) identifies several "ritualised social media practices" that are frequently adapted for political purposes. These will be explored throughout this book, so it is worth briefly defining their key characteristics.

First, there are *memes*, which are broadly defined as "pieces of cultural information that pass along from person to person but gradually scale into a shared social phenomenon" and have become a visual motif of digital culture (Shifman, 2015: 18). Unlike 'virals', which tend to consist of single cultural units, these are a 'collection of texts' based on the 'remixing' of an original image or video (Meikle, 2016; Shifman, 2015). Such has been their popularity among young people, memes have been described as the "fast food of the digital generation" due to their capacity to translate often complex issues into humorous content while making a meaningful contribution to public debates online (Denisova, 2016: 1).

Second, there is *wordplay*, which refers to the rituals of 'portmanteaugraphy' and 'hashtaggery' on Twitter. These textual responses to breaking news stories exemplify the 'concise flippancy' adopted by tweeters to convey topicality and humour in their posts while adhering to the site's character limit (Highfield, 2016a). For example, hashtags relating to the protracted negotiations over the UK's decision to leave the EU included #brexitshambles and #brexitchaos.

Third, there are *parody accounts* that typically make amusing contributions to popular hashtags on Twitter. Highfield (2016b) proposes a useful typology of these accounts, which include public figure-specific (poking fun at celebrities and public figures by subverting their public personas); character-specific (taking fictional characters from film or television and placing them in contemporary settings for comic relief); stereotypes of people or groups (appropriating the language stereotyping certain groups in order to challenge these representations); organisations (mocking institutional and corporate Twitter accounts); and non-human entities (in character as animals, buildings and other objects). Recent examples of such accounts include Elizabeth Windsor (@Queen_UK) and Lord Voldemort (@Lord_Voldemort7).

Finally, there are *intertexts* which reappropriate pre-existing media items and apply them in different contexts in order to convey specific emotions and opinions. Probably the most widely known examples of these are reaction GIFs (graphics interchange format), which 'screen-cap' moments from popular films and television shows and use these as a response to a previous post (Highfield and Leaver, 2016: 53). Crucially, the recipient does not necessarily need to be familiar with the pop culture icons in order to understand the emotion or senti-ment expressed therein. Recent examples include captioned GIFs from US sitcoms such as *Parks and Recreation*.

There has already been some evidence of these practices being deployed to frame contentious episodes. In the run-up to the 2016 US presidential election internet-based political memes were distrib-uted by far-right groups on Reddit subforums and online platforms to promote white supremacy, Islamophobia and misogyny (Nagle, 2017). While it would be reductive to attribute Donald Trump's victory to these digital exploits, they helped these groups 'hack the attention' of key demographics including young white men who "disliked political correctness" (Marwick and Lewis, 2017: 1).

There has also been some evidence to suggest that memes are being used by activists to hold authority figures to account for their actions. Probably the most well-known example in recent years was the 'pepper-spray cop' meme, which saw remixed images of UC Davis campus police officer John Pike pepper-spraying protesting students in November 2011 spark a national debate about policing and social justice in the US (Bayeri and Stoynov, 2016). Therefore, one of the key objectives of this book is to explore the ritualised social media practices of the publics mobilised on social media during contentious public demonstrations in Northern Ireland.

Digital citizenship and surveillance realism

The key role of corporate social media such as Facebook and Twitter in these acts of digital citizenship may serve to undermine rather than bolster democratic institutions. These are sociotechnical assemblages which shape public discourse and whose connective affordances can be leveraged by political entrepreneurs to magnify the differences between different political 'tribes' (Bartlett, 2018). Vaidhyanathan (2018: 9) argues that Facebook contributes to political polarisation through its key design feature, namely that the "most inflammatory material will travel the farthest and the fastest". This is perhaps best illustrated by the rise of 'clickbait', those images, videos and headlines that "trigger an affective response from a user that leads them to click on the item" and, in doing so, generate revenue for its creator or distributor (Benkler et al., 2018: 9). There is also the ongoing controversy over how companies such as Twitter deal with abuse and threats on their platforms. Gillespie (2018: 56) asserts that they are "too hospitable" towards these forms of "banal cruelty", and that harassment has become a "condition of social media". Systems of self-regulation have been heavily criticised by users who believe these companies should be more proactive in tackling hate speech and abuse hosted on their sites. In December 2018, for instance, Amnesty International labelled Twitter a "toxic place for women" in light of research findings showing how female journalists and politicians in the UK and US were frequently abused on the microblogging site, with black women being disproportionately targeted.[14] Hence, it is perhaps no surprise that the 'platform' metaphor has been frequently deployed by social media companies in order to convince users that they are 'champions of free speech' and play down their responsibilities as online intermediaries (Gillespie, 2018).

Corporate social media may also entrap citizens who use their services to express rights claims. The likes of Facebook and Twitter financially benefit from the activity of 'prosumers' who create and share user-generated content on their respective platforms (Andrejevic, 2012; Fuchs, 2014). The Marxist critique of social media argues that these corporations accumulate capital through targeted advertising, which is based on the data generated by individual users every time they interact with their platforms (Fuchs, 2014). This can be characterised as a form of 'communicative' or 'surveillance' capitalism that treats users as commodities themselves (Dean, 2009; Fuchs, 2014). Seemingly innocuous social practices such as 'liking' and 'following' provide the attention and popularity that are integral to these business models. In effect, platforms such as Facebook engage in the mass surveillance of their users by collecting, analysing and selling their personal data to advertisers and other commercial interests (van Dijck, 2013). There is a distinct lack of transparency about these processes in their terms of service, which euphemistically refer to 'sharing' information with third parties in order to obfuscate this monetisation of user data (Fuchs, 2014). Indeed, researchers have argued that these privacy policies deliberately contain vague language in order to limit public understanding of how these data are used (Draper and Turow, 2019).

A series of 'data scandals' have made citizens increasingly aware that social media are surveillance assemblages that routinely harvest their personal data. These included the leaks by whistleblower Edward Snowden in June 2013 that revealed the US National Security Agency had direct access to data held by Facebook, and the revelations in March 2018 that Cambridge Analytica had acquired without consent personal data from millions of Facebook profiles to micro-target key demographics during Donald Trump's 2016 US presidential campaign (Hintz et al., 2018). Yet, research suggests that members of the public feel unable to do anything about this surveillance and thus continue to use these platforms on a regular basis (Draper and Turow, 2019; Hintz et al., 2018). That is not to say that citizens are unconcerned by how these companies use their data and monitor their behaviour; rather, many perceive this shift in agency from citizens to corporate social media as an inevitable trade-off for the convenience of using their services (Hintz et al., 2018). This book will add to the emergent literature by exploring how citizens use corporate social media to perform citizenship in 'post-conflict' Northern Ireland.

Research approach

Before providing an overview of each chapter, I wish to briefly explain the research approach adopted in this book. In *Framing the Troubles Online* (Reilly, 2011a), I utilised thematic analysis (TA) in order to identify and evaluate the online frames of civil and 'uncivil' actors in 'post-conflict' Northern Ireland. This flexible, thematic approach was again used in this book project to analyse data gathered from 14 semi-structured interviews conducted with relevant stakeholders, including bloggers, community workers, and representatives of the communication teams from the main political parties, between October 2009 and September 2013. TA was also applied to the study of online comments collected from Facebook (N = 56,260), Twitter (N = 20,185) and YouTube (N = 1,586) between December 2012 and July 2015. Specific details on the hashtags, YouTube videos (N = 54), and public Facebook pages from which data were collected are provided in each chapter. The results of a content and framing analysis of local and national newspaper coverage of the flag protests (N = 425) and Ardoyne parade disputes (N = 44) are also elaborated in order to contextualise online comments about these events.

Social media data were collected and sample characteristics identified using the text-mining software tool Discovertext (www.discovertext. com). Time frequency graphs were created to identify the peak periods during which content about these contentious parades and protests was shared online. In the case of the YouTube videos analysed in Chapter 4, video content was scrutinised and field notes taken in order to capture the events caught on camera by these eyewitnesses. For Twitter, a coding scheme building on the work of Lotan et al. (2011) was devised to analyse the user profiles identified in the corpora. A total of 10 categories were created to fully capture the range of actors contributing to these Twitter streams, including professional journalists, bloggers, political actors, and citizens who expressed no political preferences on their profiles.

The six phases of TA proposed by Braun and Clarke (2013) were then implemented, beginning with the initial reading of each Facebook post, tweet, and YouTube comment, and ending with the definition of themes that emerged from the entire corpus. Two coders read each comment initially to explore emergent themes from the data and to then decide whether this content met the requirements of the study. Field notes were used to capture relevant information, such as heavily retweeted content and angry back-and-forth exchanges between supporters and opponents of the Orange Order. The inductive construction of codes was completed through manual data analysis that focused on how tweeters interpreted key events and issues. The forcefulness of online comments, as well as the use of derogatory and sectarian language, was noted in order to assess the nature of the debate surrounding these issues, in a similar vein to previous work involving the study of YouTube comments (Reilly, 2014). Congruent with previous research using TA (Braun and Clarke, 2013; Buetow, 2010), numbers are not typically deployed to quantify the presence of themes in these data. However, they are used to explore the actors contributing to key hashtags during the flag protests, as well as the dominant themes of comment threads on public Facebook pages such as the Loyalist Peaceful Protest Updater (LPPU).

A key challenge was how to illustrate key themes that emerged from these data, and whether it would be ethical for those responsible for these posts to be identified.[15] Certainly, a literal interpretation of its Terms of Service would suggest that users should have no expectation of privacy when posting content on platforms such as Twitter, thereby permitting researchers to disclose the identity of tweeters and use their words without needing to ask permission.[16] However, there remains no consensus among social scientists in relation to participants' perceptions of privacy, with some arguing that such studies require greater scrutiny (Zimmer, 2010). At the time of writing, the most recently published ethical guidelines for online research produced by the Association of Internet Researchers encourages researchers to "do no harm" to "unaware participants", but acknowledges that 'grey areas' remain in terms of ethical decision-making (Markham et al., 2012). In this case, there did not appear to be a compelling reason for identifying those unaware participants who had unwittingly spread rumours or used intemperate language that might have been (mis)construed as inciting violence.

A 'medium-cloaked' strategy towards data anonymisation was adopted, primarily because it was neither feasible nor appropriate to obtain informed consent from those responsible for these online comments. An in-depth discussion of how this ethical stance was constructed can be found in an article I co-authored with Filippo Trevisan (Reilly and Trevisan, 2016), but the key points were as follows: first, direct quotes from public figures such as bloggers, politicians and professional journalists were used to illustrate key themes as they were considered to be public figures; second, while there was certainly no obligation to 'please' participants, I was wary of inadvertently contributing to the online shaming of loyalists that had caused such controversy during this period (which will be discussed in more detail in Chapter 5). The identification of these unaware participants might have exposed them to potential reputational or even physical harm. Therefore, a number of measures were taken to protect the anonymity of those participants who typically lacked the resources to control information about themselves in the public domain (Kozinets, 2010). These included the removal of personally identifiable information, such as username and location, and paraphrasing their tweets in order to avoid them being located using a search engine. While acknowledging that it may not be possible to fully guarantee their anonymity, the focus here was very much on what was being said rather than on who said it (Trevisan and Reilly, 2014). Finally, it was acknowledged that for some researchers this might appear to be an overly strict and cautious ethical stance. However, this reflected my own interpretation of the socio-political context in which these data were collected, as well as the potential implications of identifying participants in these circumstances.

Limitations

There were three main limitations that should be acknowledged. First, the dearth of geotagged tweets makes it difficult to say for certain whether many of these online commenters were in a position to influence or report on events on the ground. Therefore, this study assessed the extent to which geographically dispersed affective publics appeared to be helping reduce sectarian tensions around these contentious public demonstrations. Second, despite Discovertext allowing researchers access to the complete public data stream of platforms such as Twitter (the 'firehose'), it is difficult for the individual researcher to verify the representativeness of these data. It was not possible to access the more difficult to reach 'hard data' identified by Burgess and Bruns (2015), such as longitudinal datasets and social media posts that didn't mention certain keywords. Furthermore, discussions about these contentious parades and protests conducted on private Facebook pages were, by definition, off-limits due to the ethical stance described above. Third, the social media data analysed in this book should be viewed as the "traces of behaviour" of a small but vocal minority that lacked the robustness of traditional opinion polls (Mahrt and Scharkow, 2013: 24). The preferences revealed by clicks, likes and retweets reveal very little about the motivations and emotions of those responsible for such actions online (Karpf, 2016). A study of viral behavioural intentions on social media found that participants were most likely to carry out the least cognitively demanding behaviour; while regular tweeters were more selective about what they shared online, most chose to retweet rather than reply to such content (Alhabash and McAlister, 2015: 15). Therefore, in the absence of corroborative evidence, it would be misleading to automatically infer the attitudes of those responsible for the social media posts analysed in this book. The same might be said for those who did not express their opinion in online spaces. Previous research has indicated that the majority of individuals who access online spaces are unlikely to make public contributions (Papacharissi, 2014) and the views of these 'watchers' are impossible to detect using text-mining tools. Nevertheless, the purpose of this study was to analyse how (rather than why) Northern Irish citizens used social media to make digital rights claims in relation to contentious issues such as the re-routing of the Ardoyne parade and the flag protests. Therefore, it was appropriate to focus on the themes that emerged from the data despite these inherent limitations.

Outline

The book is organised into seven chapters. In Chapter 1, the evolving relationship between social media, contentious politics and social movements is explored. The role of digital media in social movements since 2011 is analysed, using exemplars such as Occupy Wall Street and the popular uprisings in the Middle East and North Africa later labelled the 'Arab Spring'. The chapter moves on to explore the evolving role of digital media in contentious politics in Northern Ireland. Data from organisations such as Ofcom are used to empirically investigate the news consumption practices of citizens and the levels of public trust in professional news media and political institutions in the social media era. Finally, the results of interviews conducted with key stakeholders (N = 14) between October 2009 and September 2013 are elaborated, in order to critically evaluate the impact of Web 2.0 on political participation in this deeply divided society prior to the flag protests.

Chapter 2 focuses specifically on the role of social media in the flag protests between December 2012 and March 2013. Speaking at an event on social media and Northern Irish politics held at the University of Ulster in December 2013, loyalist activist Jamie Bryson would claim that social media "hadn't helped us [the flag protesters] in the slightest".[17] This chapter empirically investigates this claim by providing the first qualitative study of LPPU; this public Facebook page was used by loyalists to coordinate the protests and was suspended in January 2013 after an emergency injunction filed on behalf of an unidentified Catholic man who had been threatened on the page. The results of a thematic analysis of 24,244 comments posted on LPPU and its backup page during January 2013 are presented in order to assess the type of mobilising information provided on the page, and whether there was much evidence of 'trolling' by critics of the protests. The chapter contextualises these results through a content analysis of coverage of the flag protests in the three most widely read newspapers in the region, the *Belfast Telegraph*, the *Irish News*, and the *News Letter*, between 3 December 2012 and 28 February 2013 (N = 347).

The polysemic nature of Twitter hashtags and their capacity to mobilise 'affective publics' connected via affectively charged expression (Papacharissi, 2014) is examined in Chapter 3. The loyalist action dubbed 'Operation Standstill', announced in the first week of January 2013, was a 'lightning rod' for Northern Irish tweeters, who were angered by the economic and reputational harm being caused by the flag protests. Hashtags such as #backinbelfast and #takebackthecity served as conversation markers for those who wished to express opposition to the demonstrations and encourage people to support those bars, restaurants and businesses negatively impacted. Twitter also provided communicative spaces for citizens to criticise protest provocateurs such as Jamie Bryson and Willie Frazer, with some shaming loyalists for hate speech posted on pages such as LPPU and mocking their poor spelling and grammar. This chapter empirically explores the discursive affordances of Twitter during hybrid media events through a thematic analysis of 4,479 tweets hashtagged with #flegs, a supposedly comical reference to how 'flag' is pronounced in a working-class Belfast accent. The key influencers, type of information shared and characterisation of loyalist flag protesters in this hashtag will be analysed. Finally, it will examine the extent to which public expression on the hashtag was irreverent and innocuous, or whether such activity perpetuated negative stereotypes of loyalists as 'uneducated bigots'.

In Chapter 4, the focus switches to citizens' use of social media to document the actions of the PSNI during these demonstrations. The ubiquity of smartphones has provided unprecedented opportunities for citizens to engage in 'sousveillance', defined broadly as the "use of technology to access and collect data about their surveillance" (Mann et al., 2003: 333). During the flag protests, loyalists accused the PSNI of engaging in 'political policing' and used social media to share evidence corroborating their claims that they had been 'heavy-handed' towards the protesters. This chapter presents the first in-depth qualitative analysis of this footage, much of which was uploaded by witnesses to YouTube, presumably with the intention of highlighting the alleged police brutality. It does so by presenting the results of a thematic analysis of 1,586 comments posted in response to 36 videos uploaded to the video-sharing site loyalists between December 2012 and March 2013. It will explore the extent to which such 'sousveillance' footage elicited sympathy for loyalist claims that the PSNI had been heavy-handed, and how the views expressed in these comments sections compared with mainstream media representations of both the protesters and the policing operation.

Memes and parody accounts are examples of the 'silly citizenship' theorised by Hartley (2010) to capture citizens' 'playful' engagement with political issues online. In terms of the latter, these are often deployed to satirise and hold politicians and authority figures to account for their public statements and actions. In the case of Northern Ireland, self-styled non-sectarian 'parody group' Loyalists Against Democracy (LAD) emerged as one of the most vocal critics of the flag protests in December 2012. Its supporters argued that the group articulated the views of the 'silent majority' by highlighting the bigotry and sectarianism of loyalists on pages such as LPPU. Conversely, critics accused the group of peddling negative stereotypes of working-class loyalists by shaming them for their poor spelling and grammar in their social media comments. Chapter 5 explores the role of LAD in contentious politics in Northern Ireland between December 2012 and November 2013. It presents the results of the first empirical study of content posted on the group's Facebook and Twitter profiles, with a view to exploring whether such content could persuasively be framed as satire. It will also examine the extent to which loyalists were represented as 'social abjects' akin to the 'chav' stereotype used to demonise white working-class communities in England (Tyler, 2013). The role of the group in campaigns such as #givepootstheboot will be explored to assess their evolving role within the Northern Irish information ecosystem as a focal point for the contestation of contentious political issues.

The Ardoyne parade dispute provided further evidence of how social media activity could both inflame and diffuse sectarian tensions around contentious parades and protests in Northern Ireland. The culture war narrative was invoked by unionists and loyalists in their condemnation of the decision by the Northern Ireland Parades Commission in July 2013 to re-route the return leg of an annual Orange Order parade away from the nationalist Ardoyne district in North Belfast. It sparked four consecutive nights of violent clashes between loyalist rioters and the PSNI in areas such as North Belfast. Fears of a repeat of this violence were not realised in July 2014, despite the failure of representatives from both sides to broker a solution to the impasse. July 2015 saw a return to violence as loyalist protesters attacked PSNI officers enforcing the Parades Commission's determination to prevent the return leg from travelling home via its traditional route. Chapter 6 explores what role, if any, tweeters played in escalating and de-escalating tensions surrounding the contentious parade in 2014 and 2015. The lifespan of misinformation and disinformation about the dispute shared on the microblogging site will be examined to assess the reach of content that had the potential to generate violence between loyalists and the Ardoyne residents. It will also explore the ways in which tweeters framed the dispute from a rights perspective and whether there was any evidence of Mouffe's 'conflictual consensus' emerging on the platform during this period. A critical thematic analysis of 7,388 #Ardoyne tweets, collected in July 2014 and July 2015, was conducted in order to investigate these issues. The results are contextualised through a content analysis of 44 articles published in Northern Irish and Irish newspapers during the Twelfth week across both years.

The last chapter summarises the main contributions of the book to contemporary debates about the role of social media in contentious politics within divided societies such as Northern Ireland. It considers whether the use of online platforms to spread misinformation and disinformation during contentious public demonstrations is evidence of the information crisis seen in other nation states, or a symptom of the democratic dysfunction in Northern Ireland's power-sharing institutions. Finally, it explores the implications of citizens' use of social media during such incidents for promoting peace and reconciliation in this divided society.

Notes

1 Although it was rebranded X in July 2023, the microblogging site is referred to as Twitter throughout this book to reflect the time frame in which data were collected and analysed.
2 The term Northern Ireland is used throughout this book in recognition of its current constitutional status.
3 'Irisgate' refers to the revelations in January 2010 that DUP MP Iris Robinson broke parliamentary rules to arrange a £50,000 loan for her teenage lover. The renewable heating incentive scandal revolved around a botched scheme to encourage businesses and farms to move from fossil

fuel heating to wood-burning boilers. For more, see: www.irishtimes.
com/news/environment/q-a-what-is-the-northern-ireland-cash-for-
ash-scheme-1.2907866 (accessed 10 October 2018).

4 Nationalists and republicans call it 'Derry', while their unionist and
loyalist counterparts call it Londonderry. In this book I use Derry/
Londonderry to recognise the lack of consensus over this name.

6 A full breakdown of the UK EU referendum can be found here:
www.bbc.co.uk/news/politics/eu_referendum/results (accessed 10 January 2020).

7 For more on Vote Leave's campaign, see: https://blog.ted.com/social-
media-is-a-threat-to-our-democracy-carole-cadwalladr-speaks-at-
ted2019/ (accessed 10 February 2020).

7 See the Malcom Sutton Index of Deaths from the conflict in Ireland,
available at: https://cain.ulster.ac.uk/sutton/tables/Status_Summary.html
(accessed 10 February 2019).

8 The Belfast (or Good Friday) Agreement was signed by the main political parties in Northern Ireland on 10 April 1998. It was ratified in refer-
enda held in Northern Ireland and in the Republic of Ireland, with power
devolved to the newly formed Stormont Assembly a year later. For more
on this, see: https://cain.ulster.ac.uk/issues/politics/election/ref1998.
htm (accessed 10 January 2020).

9 The Integrated Education Fund lobbied the Stormont Assembly to set a
target of 10 per cent of Northern Irish children to be educated in integrated schools by 2021. For more on this, see: www.belfasttelegraph.
co.uk/news/northern-ireland/integrated-schools-roadmap-to-end-division-
in-northern-ireland-36813844.html (accessed 10 February 2019).

10 The *Building a United Community* report can be accessed at: www.executi-
veoffice-ni.gov.uk/sites/default/files/publications/ofmdfm_dev/together-
building-a-united-community-strategy.pdf (accessed 10 May 2019).

11 The Garvaghy Road Residents' Coalition, led by former PIRA prisoner
Breandán Mac Cionnaith, came to prominence during the Drumcree
dispute in Portadown in the mid-1990s, when the nationalist residents
group and loyalists were engaged in a stand-off over the route of an
annual Twelfth parade. For more on this, see: https://cain.ulster.ac.uk/
issues/parade/develop.htm (accessed 10 January 2020).

12 See www.facebook.com/IranlovesIsrael.OfficialPage/

13 For more on Peace on Facebook see: www.facebook.com/peace?_rdr
(accessed 10 January 2019).

14 The Toxic Twitter study involved 778 women journalists and politicians.
The report can be accessed here: https://decoders.amnesty.org/projects/
troll-patrol/findings (accessed 10 March 2019).

15 Ethics approval for this book project was granted by the universities of Leicester and Sheffield respectively.

16 For more, see: https://twitter.com/tos (accessed 10 October 2014).

17 Jamie Bryson spoke at 'Transformative Networks – Social Media, Politics and Protests' at the University of Ulster's Belfast campus on 10 December 2013. A full transcript of his comments was provided by blogger Alan Meban at: https://sluggerotoole.com/2014/01/04/if-you-ask-me-one-thing-i-could-have-done-without-in-the-last-twelve-months-its-social-media-jamie-bryson/ (accessed 10 April 2017).

1

Social media, contentious politics and social movements

This book examines the ways in which contentious parades and protests in 'post-conflict' Northern Ireland are contested by affective publics mobilised on social media. In this way, it will contribute to the extant interdisciplinary scholarship on digital citizenship and the role of digital media in contemporary social movements. This chapter contextualises the research findings presented throughout this book by exploring three key issues. First, it introduces the contentious politics framework and applies it to the Northern Irish conflict. Second, it explores the evolving relationship between ICTs and contentious politics in the contemporary era. The role of digital media in social movements since 2011 is analysed, using exemplars such as Occupy Wall Street and the popular uprisings in the Middle East and North Africa later labelled the 'Arab Spring'. Third, the chapter explores the evolving role of digital media in contentious politics in Northern Ireland. Data from organisations such as Ofcom are used to empirically investigate the news consumption practices of citizens and levels of public trust in professional news media and political institutions in the social media era. Finally, the results of interviews conducted with key stakeholders (N = 14) between October 2009 and September 2013 are elaborated, in order to examine the impact of 'Web 2.0' on political participation in the deeply divided society prior to the flag protests.

Contentious politics and the Northern Irish conflict

In order to explore the role of social media in contentious parades and protests in Northern Ireland, one must first understand the terrain of contentious politics. Contentious politics describe those "interactions in which actors make claims bearing on other actors' interests, leading to coordinated efforts on behalf of shared interests or programs, in which governments are involved as targets, initiators of claims, or third parties" (Tilly and Tarrow, 2015: 7). These are moments in which existing levels of polarisation within a society are 'inflamed' by "takeoff issues" (Bode et al., 2018: 217). It is a theoretical framework that has frequently been used to study the Northern Irish conflict in the late twentieth century. Northern Ireland was defined as a hybrid regime due to its combination of "authoritarian and representative mechanisms of rule" and "composite forms of contention" (Tilly and Tarrow, 2015: 75). This was congruent with the Irish republican framing of the Troubles as an ethnic conflict in which 'settler' Protestants suppressed 'native' Catholics to ensure their hegemony in the "illegitimate statelet" (Guelke, 2014). Further evidence to support this 'hybrid regime' thesis came in the form of elections held against the backdrop of the cycle of protests and violent confrontations between what could crudely be defined as 'pro and anti-state forces'. Tilly (2008: 172) went so far as to identify a "repertoire of contention", involving public rallies and protests, that were frequently deployed by various political factions during the conflict.

Flag protests: birth of a social movement?

Many of these tactics were adopted during the union flag protests and the Ardoyne parade disputes in pursuit of political objectives. These were what Tilly and Tarrow (2015) referred to as *familiar contentious performances and episodes,* deployed as part of a broader *contentious campaign* to protect unionist and loyalist culture from attack by Sinn Féin and the republican movement. The flag protesters could be defined as a social movement insofar as they were a "networked group of claims-making actors" capable of making a sustained challenge to the authority of political elites on behalf of marginalised groups. Social movements are a "principal social form" through which collectivities both articulate grievances and engage in collective action, such as public demonstrations, in pursuit of common objectives (Snow et al., 2004: 3). This conflict with political elites is what differentiates social movements from 'legitimate' political actors such as political parties and interest groups (Vromen, 2017: 29). While it is beyond the scope of this book to fully explore the history of social movement theory, it is worth noting that such movements are often defined as 'identity fields' due to their use of shared symbols, identities and practices to establish the boundaries of discursive communities (Della Porta, 2015). It would be reasonable to surmise that the union flag was a symbol of unity for loyalists who engaged in the public demonstrations analysed in this book.

The Flag Dispute (Nolan et al., 2014: 88) questioned whether the flag protests were a 'unifying movement' due to the high levels of internal fragmentation among its supporters. Six broad drivers of mobilisation were identified including the desire to defend unionist and loyalist identity, ideological opposition to the Belfast Agreement, dissatisfaction with the political institutions, and socio-economic disadvantage. Although the nominal rallying cry for working-class loyalists was based on the change to the flag protocol at Belfast City Hall, it was the combination of these drivers, rather than one specific factor, that convinced the protesters of the need to take urgent action in December 2012. In this respect, the flag protests were comparable to other social movements, whose success often rest upon how much brokerage is required to accommodate the different preferences of their constituent organisations (Gamson, 1990; Tilly and Tarrow, 2015). Indeed, it could be argued that the failure of the flag protest movement to reverse the decision of Belfast City Council was due in no small part to its internal divisions and the lack of a "workable strategy" to secure its core objective (Nolan et al., 2014: 54). A new political party, the Protestant Coalition (PC), eventually emerged after a split in the flag protest movement over the decision by the Ulster People's Forum to move from blocking roads to 'white line' protests in February 2013. The self-styled 'anti-politics' party, led by protest spokesperson Willie Frazer, made minimal electoral impact and was only in the media headlines due to its campaign against Facebook's decision to remove its page in August 2013.[1]

Political opportunity structures and the flag protests

The factors contributing to contentious episodes such as the flag protests can be elaborated through the lens of political opportunity structures, a key element of social movement theory. Its proponents argue that it is too reductive to attribute mass mobilisation to changes in socio-economic structures alone; rather, collective action is inextricably linked to the "presence of mobilization resources, as well as the opening of political opportunities" (Della Porta, 2015: 4). Specifically, social movements are more likely to act in those circumstances where there is more than one independent power centre, growing instability within political institutions, restrictions placed on collective claim-making, and, crucially, the availability of influential allies or supporters for those wishing to make such a challenge (Tilly and Tarrow, 2015: 59). Although social movement theories have been criticised for focusing too much on these structures at the expense of the agency of protesters (Della Porta, 2015), there was some evidence to suggest that a combination of these factors provided a 'political opportunity' for the flag protest movement. I wish to draw particular attention to two of these factors, namely the growth in unionist and loyalist disillusionment with the Stormont Executive and the socio-economic deprivation within working-class loyalist communities.

First, there were a number of political crises that beset the Stormont power-sharing institutions. For the purposes of brevity I will not go into these in detail, but the Democratic Unionist Party (DUP) were embroiled in a series of high-profile scandals between January 2010 and September 2012. This began in January 2010 with 'Irisgate', when DUP member of the legislative assembly (MLA) and MP Iris Robinson (the wife of the First Minister) was alleged to have broken parliamentary rules in procuring £50,000 to help start up a restaurant on behalf of a 19-year-old with whom she was having an affair.[2] The largest party in the Executive was also rocked by the Red Sky scandal in October 2010, after whistleblower Jenny Palmer told the BBC Northern Ireland current affairs programme *Spotlight* that party officials had forced her to vote in favour of extending a maintenance contract to a company accused of producing substandard work on properties owned by the Northern Ireland Housing Executive.[3] These controversies occurred in the context of increasing unionist and loyalist disillusionment with both the Stormont Executive and the peace process in general. A relatively low percentage of unionists (39 per cent) felt the Assembly was doing a good job of representing their interests in the period leading up to the flag protests (Fealty, 2013). Furthermore, data from the 2012 Northern Ireland Life and Times Survey showed that only 44 per cent of Protestants believed that community relations would improve within five years, the lowest figure reported since 2003 (Morrow, 2014).

There was a strong sense of indignation within working-class loyalist communities at what they saw as the failure of unionist politicians to protect unionist and loyalist culture from a peace process that had benefited republicans at their expense (INTERCOMM and Byrne, 2013). The loyalist protests during this period constituted a "claim to validity" (Hands, 2011), that urged political elites to pay attention to their grievances and stop this perceived 'culture war'. The contentious nature of these parades and protests was a manifestation of the failure of the Northern Ireland Executive to address conflict–legacy issues nearly 15 years after the Belfast Agreement. Since the late 1990s unionist and loyalist political representatives had repeatedly called for the abolition of the Parades Commission, arguing that it should be replaced with an alternative system for dealing with parades (details of which were not fully disclosed). There was also a recognition by some unionist leaders that a way forward on contentious parades could not be achieved without the agreement of the DUP and Sinn Féin, the two largest parties in the Executive.

Certainly, the failure to address these issues helped create a context in which sectarian violence was more likely to be sparked by contentious parades. During the 2012 marching season there was widespread condemnation of the Young Conway Volunteers (YCV) flute band, who were filmed playing the sectarian 'Famine Song' and marching in a circle outside St Patrick's Church in Belfast during the annual Twelfth demonstrations. Tensions were raised during subsequent loyalist and republican parades in the area, which boiled over into violence in the neighbouring districts of North Belfast. The YCV were at the centre of yet more controversy during a Royal Black Institution parade on 25 August, after they and several other bands defied a Commission ruling banning the playing of music during a parade as it passed by St Patrick's Church. A riot by nationalist youths afterwards resulted in seven PSNI officers and one member of the public being injured. A parade by a republican flute band a week later (2 September) led to several nights of loyalist rioting in the vicinity of Carlisle Circus, a major junction of the Antrim Road which runs from Belfast city centre to the village of Dunadry in County Antrim. It was in this context that working-class loyalist communities viewed the decision to alter the flag protocol at Belfast City Hall as yet further evidence that they were losing the culture war being waged against them by Sinn Féin.

Second, there was some evidence to suggest that the perceived high levels of socio-economic deprivation within working-class loyalist communities played a role in the mobilisation of flag protesters in December 2012. The social basis for these protests appeared to be different from those of the mass mobilisations in Europe and North America the year before, although all could be viewed through the lens of neo-liberal globalisation, with its 'winners' and 'losers' brought into sharp focus by the 2008 global economic recession. Youth unemployment in particular was identified as a key driver of protest movements such as Occupy Wall Street in the United States and Los Indignados in Spain. The precariat, defined loosely as "young, unemployed, or only part-time employed, with no protection, and often well-educated" (Della Porta, 2015: 4), were part of a broad anti-austerity coalition, which included cultural workers and the lower middle classes, that spearheaded the protests. There was, however, little evidence that a similar coalition was mobilised during the flag protests. The 2013 and 2014 Northern Ireland Life and Times Surveys revealed that a narrow majority of Protestants (51 per cent in 2014) favoured the designated days protocol, compared with 43 per cent who agreed with the protesters that the flag should be flown throughout the year (Morrow, 2014). Although some middle-class and more affluent unionists tacitly supported the protests, they would not physically participate due to, among other factors, the fear that they might lose their jobs if they were identified in news reports (Nolan et al., 2014: 65). Hence, this was not a mass mobilisation of unionists and loyalists on the scale of the protests against the Anglo–Irish Agreement in November 1985, during which a crowd of approximately 70,000 people gathered at a rally in Belfast City Hall to hear speeches by unionist leaders such as the then DUP leader Dr Ian Paisley. [4]

What little information we have about the background of the protesters has come from interview and focus group-based studies that have concentrated more on their motivations and experiences than their socio-economic status. Focus group participants in one study stated that identity politics, rather than socio-economic factors, was the key driver of the protests (INTERCOMM and Byrne, 2013). A more nuanced narrative linking socio-economic deprivation and loyalist collective action emerged from Nolan et al.'s *The Flag Dispute*. The authors cited evidence from the 2012 Northern Ireland Poverty and Social Exclusion Survey to show how the most deprived areas in the region were predominantly Catholic rather than Protestant. [5] As with white working-class males in parts of England, it was the perceived economic loss and dislocation from political elites that inspired the flag protest movement (Nolan et al., 2014: 106). This fed into the zero-sum perceptions of many working-class loyalists, who felt that they had yet to see the economic benefits of a peace process that worked to the advantage of Catholics, nationalists and republicans (Novosel, 2013; Smithey, 2013). The DUP in particular were held responsible for failing to protect the cultural, economic and political interests of these communities in 'post-conflict' Northern Ireland.

Clearly it was not inevitable that these political opportunities would lead to the wave of public demonstrations seen across the region between December 2012 and March 2013. Koopman (2004) was among those to argue that awareness of divisions within political elites, as well as other 'regime weaknesses', may be key determinants of these 'waves of contention'. Certainly, most citizens in this divided society were fully aware of the aforementioned schism between the DUP and Sinn Féin over conflict-legacy issues, especially in light of their extensive coverage in local news media. Moreover, characterising political opportunities as structures that lie beyond the scope of social movements overlooks the key role of political entrepreneurs in creating collective action frames that galvanise support for these protests (Morris and Staggenborg, 2004; Snow et al., 2004). The 40,000 anti-Alliance (the political party who proposed the new flag protocol) leaflets distributed on behalf of the DUP and Ulster Unionist Party (UUP) may have provided the initial impetus for the flag 'protest waves' in December 2012. However, the protest movement would prove unsustainable when protest provocateurs such as Jamie Bryson and Willie Frazer began to exert greater influence over its future direction. They arguably failed to complete the intellectual tasks associated with successful social movements, such as formulating ideologies, interacting with news media and building a coalition of supporters (Morris and Staggenborg, 2004). Furthermore, the affective ties activated by social media that bound the flag protesters together in December 2012 may also have served to undermine this 'movement' in the long run, as people grew tired of the disruption caused by the protests.

Social media, connective action and contentious politics

It was the role of social media in the flag protests that differentiated this contentious episode from its antecedents in Northern Ireland. Tilly and Tarrow (2015) assert that ICTs fulfil three key functions in

contentious campaigns, namely assembling people in one specific protest site, coordinating multi-site demonstrations, and facilitating connective action. In effect, social media allows citizens to self-organise
more easily and therefore reduce the cost of collective action (Vromen,
2017). Facebook, in particular, was identified as playing a key role in
mobilising early participants in the mass public demonstrations in
Egypt and across the Middle East in 2011 (Gerbaudo, 2012; Tufekci
and Wilson, 2012). Online platforms provided 'social information',
real time information about "what other people were doing politically", that encouraged others to participate in these collective actions
(Margetts et al., 2016: 12). Case studies such as the Copenhagen Climate Change conference and the anti-G20 protests in London (both
2009) also challenged long-held assumptions about the central role of
organisations in brokering and coordinating large-scale public demonstrations (Bennett and Segerberg, 2013). Social movements were
increasingly viewed as essentially a series of communicative acts rather
than the outcome of shifting political opportunity structures and the
mobilisation of resources by organisations. In contrast to traditional
modes of collective action, formal organisations were not necessarily
integral to this new generation of protest campaigns that revolved
around the individualised 'logic of connective action' (Vromen, 2017).

#OWS (Occupy Wall Street) illustrated how activists could use
Twitter to 'stitch together' large-scale connective action networks
based on the sharing of easily personalised action frames, such as "We
are the 99 per cent", across online and offline networks (Bennett and
Segerberg, 2013). As will be discussed in Chapter 3, hashtags such as
these functioned as framing devices that helped transform crowds
into publics (Papacharissi, 2014; 2016). The 'polysemic' nature of these
hashtags gave these publics their own "distinct mediality", enabling
citizens, both online and offline, to identify with its broad campaign
objectives of ending social and economic inequality (Papacharissi,
2014: 2). Jackson and Foucault Welles (2016) characterised protest
hashtags as "networked counterpublics", broadcast networks that help
focus attention on the views of minority groups that are typically
absent from the mainstream media coverage. There are also some
signs that non-elite individual actors are increasingly likely to curate
these broadcast networks, rather than NGOs and advocacy groups
that have been so integral to collective actions in the past (Vicari,
2017: 12). This illustrates how social media activism engages those

who have previously not participated in formal politics (Zuckerman, 2015). Indeed, research conducted over the past decade has indicated that the effects of social media use are particularly strong when it comes to political expression, especially among young citizens who are increasingly sceptical about political institutions (Boulianne, 2015; 2019; Boulianne and Theocharis, 2018; Loader et al., 2016). Accidental exposure to political information on platforms such as Facebook and Twitter has also been linked to a reduction in the "online engagement gap between citizens" with varying interests in news and politics (Valeriani and Vaccari, 2016).

Critics have nevertheless dismissed such online activism as 'clicktivism' or 'slacktivism' that is inferior to 'higher' forms of participation, such as joining protest marches; it creates ineffectual, incoherent social movements due to its reliance on 'civically promiscuous' citizens, whose activism consists merely of 'liking' and 'sharing' activist content (Morozov, 2011). A broader critique of such connective actions has emerged in the intervening period questioning the 'horizontalism' of these movements. The crowd-enabled conceptualisation of connective action, for instance, neglects the role played by 'networked micro-celebrity activists', those "politically motivated non-institutional actors" with large followings who engage in advocacy online (Tufekci, 2013: 850), and that of other 'soft' leaders in relaying collective messages on Twitter (Gerbaudo, 2015; Poell et al., 2016). Activists responsible for updating the social media accounts of Occupy protest camps, for instance, became de facto authority figures within these movements (Kavada, 2015). A new category of so-called 'serial transnational activists', those with a professional background in the information technology sector who appear agnostic at best about liberal democracy, were also credited with using the microblogging site to amplify multiple protest hashtags, irrespective of their knowledge of each specific campaign (Mercea and Bastos, 2016).

Gerbaudo (2017: 187) argues that the techno-libertarian narrative proclaiming these movements as 'leaderless' is "ethically and politically dangerous" as it absolves these broadcasters and influencers of responsibility for their actions. A related concern is how connective action fails to capture the contextual factors, such as the specific characteristics of media ecologies and the political economy of social media platforms, that help explain the rise and fall of social movements (Hoskins and Tulloch, 2016; Mattoni, 2019). Drawing on nearly a decade of research into social movements in Italy, Mexico, and Spain, Treré (2019) critiques the 'communicative reductionism' within the literature that 'fetishises' social media as 'neutral' tools that inevitably deliver movement outcomes. He asserts that much of this research overlooked the vital 'backstage' work conducted by activists, both online and offline, to sustain their collective identities as well as the symbolic and emotional dynamics that power these movements. In a similar vein, it has been argued that scholars such as Bennett and Segerberg (2013) focused too much on how beliefs shared via social media motivate participation at the expense of other factors, such as the role of social connections in convincing 'non-believers' to participate (Earl and Garrett, 2019). The prevalence of 'spatial dualism' in popular discourses about the Internet, differentiating 'the digital' from 'the real world', has been blamed for creating a vision of digital protest as "inherently emancipatory and separated from the materiality of physical spaces" (Treré, 2019: 8). Conversely, the materialities of platforms such as Facebook may actually work to the detriment of these movements, especially in light of algorithms that determine the visibility of activist content (Neumayer et al., 2019: 2). This has led some activists to be more cautious about the type of information they share on these platforms. For example, the Italian Student Movement Anomalous Wave used "Web 2.0 technologies in a 1.0 way" between 2008 and 2009, choosing not to disclose sensitive information on these corporate platforms in recognition of their data collection practices (Treré, 2019: 75).

The dismissal of online activism as inferior to 'higher' forms of participation overlooks the fact that they are increasingly deployed in tandem during contentious campaigns. Scholars such as Tufekci (2013) contest the clicktivist critique, arguing that protest hashtags are important interventions in the 'attention economy' for activists and social movements. Social media also provide these actors with unprecedented opportunities to influence 'political information cycles', which diminish the traditional agenda-setting power of professional journalists and political elites while also providing "fluid opportunity structures with greater scope for timely intervention by online citizen activists" (Chadwick, 2013: 64). During the 'Arab Spring' for instance, social media were used to share stories, such as the self-immolation of Tunisian street trader Mohamed Bouazizi, that put a 'human face' on political oppression and inspired dissidents to organise demonstrations against their respective governments (Howard and Hussein,

2013). Crucially though it appeared that much of this online activism followed rather than preceded protest activity on the ground, with its primary audience being tweeters situated overseas who were unable to participate in these protests (Wolfsfeld et al., 2013). As I will discuss in more detail in Chapter 4, similar storytelling techniques were used in the Black Lives Matter campaign to highlight police brutality towards black communities in the US since July 2013. Research indicated that Twitter facilitated large-scale informal learning about this issue, as demonstrated by the Twitter onlookers bewildered at the ferocity of the police response and the recognition among some conservatives that these men may have been killed unjustly (Freelon et al., 2016a: 79). This resonates with the key findings of research conducted into how Twitter was used to share information about the ideologies underpinning the Occupy movement and the UK People's Assembly Against Austerity (Gleason, 2013; Mercea and Yilmaz, 2018). Nevertheless, the most important contribution of social media to these 'networked' social movements may be the 'signalling' of their capacities to frame issues on their own terms and disrupt the 'business' of political elites who refuse to listen to their demands (Tufekci, 2017). While online platforms are typically one part of a larger repertoire of protest deployed by activists, its connective affordances remain invaluable for groups historically neglected by mainstream news media. This book will add to the literature by exploring how social media was used to signal the capacities of loyalists who felt left behind by the peace process, as well as their critics who accused them of dragging Northern Ireland back towards its recent violent past.

Web 2.0 and contentious politics in Northern Ireland before the 2012 flag protests

A key argument in this book is that the flag protests marked a watershed moment in terms of citizens using digital media to make rights claims in Northern Ireland. In order to contextualise this research, it is first necessary to examine the relationship between Web 2.0 and contentious politics prior to December 2012. As discussed in the previous chapter, my initial research into the role of social media in 'recreational rioting' suggested that sites such as Bebo exacerbated sectarian tensions in contested urban interface areas (Reilly, 2011b). Much of the evidence cited by community workers was anecdotal in nature and conformed to moral panic discourses emphasising the risky behaviours of young people online (Reilly, 2012). Hence, in *Framing the Troubles Online*, I debated whether blogs and social media might usher in a new era of political mobilisation that threatened the peace process, especially in light of the rise of online social networking among citizens in this deeply divided society. These platforms have certainly risen in popularity in the intervening period, with the percentage of adults using these services rising from 47 per cent in 2009 to 60 per cent in 2017 (Ofcom, 2017a). The 2015 Communications Market Report found that three-fifths of Internet users believed that new communication methods in general had made their lives easier, with one in five describing themselves as being 'hooked' on social media (Ofcom, 2015). However, the most recently available data suggests that the importance of social media in the everyday lives of these citizens should not be overstated. Twitter, for instance, remains something of a minority interest with only an estimated 18 per cent of Northern Irish adults using the microblogging site in 2017 (Ofcom, 2017a: 10). Moreover, citizens in the 'post-violence' society appear sceptical about information they encounter online and prefer to get their news from verified, traditional sources. While 26 per cent of citizens were said to use Facebook or YouTube to keep up with the news (Ofcom, 2017b: 28), only 21.1 per cent trusted online platforms as a source of information (McGookin, 2018). Despite declining public trust in professional journalism due to their perceived role in promoting an adversarial politics that reinforces ethnic divisions, television remains the predominant news source for most adults, with social media the least trusted source. For example, research suggests that 72 per cent of adults aged over 16 in Northern Ireland use television as their main source of news (Ofcom, 2017a). This book will add to the research on the information ecosystem in Northern Ireland by exploring the influence of professional journalists on social media information flows surrounding contentious parades and protests.

Blogs as subaltern counterpublics in 'post-conflict' Northern Ireland

The Northern Irish political blogosphere, which first emerged in the 2000s, appeared to have great potential as a shared space in which contentious political issues could be contested by Catholics and

Protestants. *Slugger O'Toole* (*Slugger*), in particular, was heralded as a 'secular' space for political discussions due to the "multiplicity of voices" on its platform and the code of conduct created by its founder Mick Fealty, which could be aptly summed up as "play the ball, not the man" (Hoey, 2017: 157). Slugger has remained one of the most well-known political blogs on the island of Ireland since it was founded in June 2002, with politicians from both nationalist and unionist parties said to be among its readership.[6] However, it should be acknowledged that this blogosphere consisted of a relatively small number of sites and had a predominantly Northern Irish audience. Analysis of the top 25 Northern Irish blogs identified by the British political magazine *Total Politics* in 2011 revealed that Slugger received the most traffic, being ranked 216,538 on the global list and 22,937 within the UK.[7] The next highest ranked blog in the list was *Open Unionism* (ranked 3,079,559 globally) with three (*New Unionism*, *The Dissenter* and *East Belfast Diary*) unranked, presumably due to there being insufficient data available.[8] The three interviewees who namechecked Slugger characterised it as a positive development in the blogosphere. Paul Smyth, Public Achievement CEO and founder of Where is my Public Servant (WIMPS), did acknowledge that it could be a "bit of a bear pit" that discouraged some citizens from contributing:

> It's not a space for civil discourse, it's cynical hacks you know – people try to show how clever they are and outdo each other you know it's – I think it's failed to be what it could be in terms of engaging citizenry in constructive debate around important issues. Because I think people are terrified to comment on there. I mean I used to comment on it and you'd just get totally unwarranted attacks coming from people you've never seen.
>
> (Paul Smyth, Public Achievement)

This echoed the sentiments of blogger and occasional Slugger contributor John Mooney (aka 'FitzJamesHorse'), who criticised the 'group-think' within the site and its censuring of commenters who didn't conform to its 'letsgetalongerist' editorial stance.[9] The assertion that these blogs were inhabited by 'cynical hacks' also provided a timely reminder of how sparsely populated this blogosphere was. Evidence of its small digital footprint was found in the linking patterns of these blogs during this period. The software package Issue Crawler was used to perform a co-link analysis of these 25 blogs in October

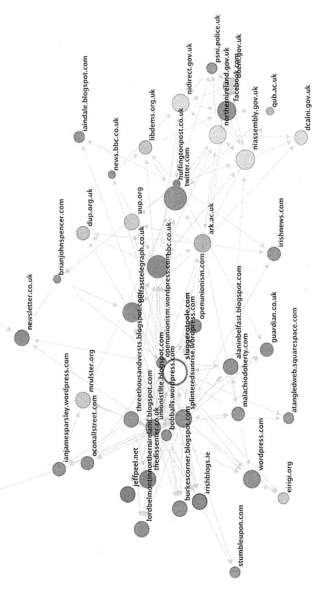

Figure 1.1 IssueCrawler network for Northern Irish political blogs, 2014.

2013. It revealed that there were only 50 nodes in the network in total, with *Slugger* linking to news media websites such as the *Irish News* (irishnews.com) and *News Letter* (newsletter.co.uk), and other blogs such as *Alan in Belfast* (alaninbelfast.blogpost.com) and *Splintered Sunrise* (splintered.sunrise.wordpress.com) (see Figure 1.1).

The rise of social media as a vehicle for public expression might explain why the Northern Irish blogosphere failed to expand beyond this collection of sites. Alan Meban (aka 'Alan in Belfast') asserted that the late 2000s were the "heyday for blogs and activist media" with many bloggers turning to Facebook and Twitter instead to "publish ideas very quickly, to squirt them out and broadcast them and be done" (Hoey, 2017: 155). This resonated with the commentary provided by *Open Unionism*'s Paul Watterson in an interview I conducted with him in June 2012. He argued that 2009–2010 denoted the high-water mark for the unionist blogosphere, with social media largely to blame for its demise:

> I have the feeling that not so many people are interested in sitting down and reading an 800 or 1,000 word diatribe anymore. With Twitter it's limited obviously in its functionality, where it, where it works well being able to get a message out that you've read somewhere that hasn't gone mainstream yet.
>
> (Paul Watterson, Blogger)

He pointed to the 'tribal' nature of the blogosphere, with the notable exception of *Slugger* which was "more constructive". The polemical stance taken by bloggers often generated angry responses and Watterson noted that asking open questions might lead to more dialogue with those who disagreed with his posts:

> If you put up a polemic basically as I say people who agree with you won't say anything, but people that disagree will say you're wrong but they will do it in the same polemic tone, so you're wrong without giving you a reason why you're wrong but if it's more of an open question, then you're getting more dialogue I guess, more comment on it.
>
> (Paul Watterson, Blogger)

This characterisation of the blogosphere was shared by Owen Polley, the blogger behind *Three Thousand Versts of Loneliness* (http://threethousandversts.blogspot.com) and campaign manager for the Northern Ireland Conservatives. Referring specifically to comments he had received on his personal blog, he noted:

It can go one of two ways really [...] well three ways, to be a sort of echo chamber for the point of view that you're putting across and you get these people coming along and saying, you know, great, we agree, whatever. You can get, you can get it going the other way, where it just becomes a sort of forum for pretty mindless abuse and what you want to happen is the third route where people take on the ideas and engage with them.

(Owen Polley, Blogger and NI Conservatives campaign manager)

He also identified the late 2000s as the peak of the unionist blogosphere and attributed the high attrition rate of pro-union bloggers to them "putting their energies into Facebook and Twitter" instead.

Further evidence that this political blogosphere was 'withering on the vine' was demonstrated by the fact that only nine of the blogs from the 2011 *Total Politics* list (including *Open Unionism*) had been updated within six months of the time of writing (January 2019).

Blogging republican media activism

Blogs have nevertheless been instrumental to the development of Irish republican media activism over the past decade. The most authoritative study of this online dissident counterculture to date was conducted by Paddy Hoey, who argued in his book *Shinners, Dissos and Dissenters* that online magazines such as the *Blanket* and *Fourthwrite* facilitated the emergence of subaltern counterpublics that discursively challenged the political status quo. Both dissident loyalists and republicans have had few opportunities in the news media to express their opposition to the Agreement since 1998. McLaughlin and Baker (2010) assert that this was due to the pervasiveness of the 'propaganda of peace', which mobilised public support for a neo-liberal agenda that conflated prosperity with peace and framed the Agreement as a 'self-evident good' beyond critique. Both loyalist and republican dissidents were characterised as "dangerous and transgressive threats to the peace process", irrespective of whether they were engaged in campaigns of political violence (Hoey, 2018: 8). Although republican sites were arguably even more of a minority interest than the 'secular' political blogs discussed above, they provided a platform for commentary on a variety of political issues from a diverse set of actors. The *Blanket*, started by former Provisional IRA prisoner Anthony McIntyre and his wife Carrie in 2001, provided a focal point for criticism of Sinn Féin's participation in the Stormont Executive and decision to support the PSNI. Hoey (2018: 26) noted that the site "sought to escape the narrow corridor of identity politics" by providing a platform for those wishing to satirise pro-Agreement republicans, and publishing editorials from loyalist representatives, such as former UDA member David Adams. Yet, there was also a recognition that these blogs were more likely to facilitate the online contestation of offline events rather than directly challenge the sectarian divisions that persisted in the post-violence society (Hoey, 2017).

The Obama effect: Northern Irish political parties and social media

Similar trends emerged from my study of how the main political parties in the region used social media for political campaigning. Interviews with representatives from the communication teams of these parties (with the exception of the Traditional Unionist Voice) indicated that they saw greater value in using social media than their static, text-based websites of the mid-2000s. Facebook and Twitter were the two most favoured platforms, although the DUP interviewee mentioned that they had used YouTube to post videos of party election broadcasts and conference speeches. The 2008 Barack Obama presidential campaign was frequently cited as an influence on the social media communication strategies developed by these parties. The Progressive Unionist Party (PUP) interviewee had first-hand experience of working on the Obama campaign and the UUP communication officer asserted that 'everyone' had borrowed elements from it. There was a sense among both unionist and nationalist parties that they had to raise their game on social media and that these platforms had the potential to energise their respective electoral bases:

> The experience of Obama has ensured that all parties must raise their game in engaging the online community. Ramping up Twitter followers, Facebook friends is becoming increasingly important.
>
> (Social Democratic and Labour Party (SDLP)
> Communication Officer)

> I think that most people would say that this, the great strength of the Obama campaign it wasn't so much the fact that he was, uh, broadcasting the propaganda as it were through the, the Twitter and Facebook it was just a great way of getting people involved and getting the message not necessarily even party members or activists but getting everybody

to do a little bit who, you know, were feeling supportive or enthusiastic for his campaign at the time. I mean if we could obviously recreate that in a very small sense I would see that as a big achievement.

(Owen Polley, Blogger and NI Conservatives campaign manager)

While by no means a dissenting voice when it came to extolling the virtues of digital media, the DUP interviewee acknowledged that the digital divide was a barrier towards parties prioritising social media over traditional modes of campaigning:

At this stage Northern Irish election campaigning [is about] knocking doors in this election and the next one, for a couple after that, is still going to be the primary method of getting out there, getting, you know, your message to the largest number of people is still going to be knocking doors giving them a leaflet.

(DUP communication officer)

Nevertheless, all parties engaged in some form of monitoring of social media to get feedback on how their representatives fared during media appearances. For instance, the Alliance communication officer monitored hashtags devoted to two leaders' debates on BBC and UTV during the 2010 Westminster elections for feedback on the performance of its then leader David Ford:

We were looking at it [Twitter] and a lot of people were saying we liked that or we didn't like that. We would say to David, and he was able to improve his responses to a question or something like that.

(Alliance communication officer)

As per my study of party websites (Reilly, 2011a), Sinn Féin had the most sophisticated social media strategy (Reilly, 2013). They were the first to 'dip their toe' into the field of paid-for advertising on social media, as seen during Martin McGuinness' unsuccessful bid to become President of Ireland in 2011. The Northern Ireland Conservatives, which had a limited budget, availed of the support provided by its UK-wide sister party in order to get its website developed by a private company. However, most parties were not engaged in the sophisti-cated data collection and micro-targeting techniques employed by Obama, that have become synonymous with US presidential cam-paigns. These were small, poorly resourced communication teams that wanted to develop their social media portfolio but could not, due to organisational constraints. A recurring theme in this interview-based study was that representatives were not forced to use social media and that there was little in the way of training for those who wished to do so. Younger politicians such as Sinn Féin's Eoin Ó'Broin were said to demonstrate higher levels of digital literacy than their older colleagues, with Martin McGuinness relying on an aide to update his Twitter account during this period. The Sinn Féin interviewee suggested that experiences during the Troubles, coupled with low levels of trust in online information, might have explained why older representatives were reluctant to engage with social media:

> There would be a certain, I suppose a certain degree of security consciousness amongst us, amongst a certain generation I suppose, in terms of the data they put out there and make available.
>
> (Sinn Féin Communication Officer)

Political parties perceive 'echo chamber' effect on social media

Interviewees provided little evidence to suggest that political parties were reaching across the sectarian divide on social media. All confirmed that they were most likely to be contacted by supporters on these platforms, rather than, in the words of the Alliance representative, "those who slagged them off". The SDLP were said to be receiving only positive feedback for their use of online platforms, with the 'Find your representative' section increasingly popular among visitors to its website. In the case of Facebook, the Sinn Féin interviewee attributed this to the fact that people needed to 'like' their party page on the site in order to comment on it. This was a sentiment shared by the DUP member, who noted that it was predominantly younger supporters of the party who sent them messages on social media:

> Younger people would tend to come across something on Facebook group or people using Twitter, the space is growing but it started, at the start it was, you know, primarily, mostly people under the age of 40, still very young you know, it's that sort of younger people I think that. I think, it's not terribly scientific but I think you get people who are, people who are sort of very supportive of the party don't tend to have a reason to maybe ask or you know send messages.
>
> (DUP Communication Officer)

Lagan Valley MP Jeffrey Donaldson was identified as being one of the most active DUP representatives on Facebook. Yet, the majority of people 'friending' Donaldson were from a unionist background and it was acknowledged that it was mainly a forum for 'unionist discussion'. The few interactions with critics of the region's largest pro-union party on the site were antagonistic in nature and linked to high-profile controversies such as then DUP leader Peter Robinson's decision to temporarily stand down as First Minister in January 2010. Although supporters actively defended Robinson on the official party page, the interviewee had to moderate comments on its various social media platforms in order to limit any abuse of its members:

> Most of the comments are moderated before they go online, you know, I'd say it would be me who would do most of that [...] They do range from the very amusing sometimes you feel, it might be abusive but it can still be funny.

Perhaps unsurprisingly given their prominent role in the Northern Ireland Executive, the DUP and Sinn Féin were the two parties that bore the brunt of such online abuse. The latter also moderated comments on their social media pages, despite having a policy of being as 'open as possible' in order to encourage people to engage with the party online. This was justified as a necessary response to the small minority who 'trolled' Sinn Féin online and used sectarian remarks to abuse party members:

> Well I took the decision, um, probably going back a couple of months now, that, that I would limit it [ability to comment freely on page] and the, just sort of say, the, just sort of tell you, the policy that we had was that if we be as open as possible more people make their comments whether they agree or disagree to it, just to try to encourage that, but the danger in doing that they could open up all sorts of stuff [...] That sectarian element unfortunately, so we again made a, a united decision and that was that everything would have to be approved before leaving it in the open platform. Now that doesn't mean to say if you trawled through all 500 videos on the website that you wouldn't see as very nasty or wrong comments on it, that haven't been taken down at this stage.
>
> (Sinn Féin communication officer)

The quote above illustrates the challenges these two parties faced trying to filter out sectarian comments received via their social media accounts. The anonymity associated with these sites was said to be emboldening people to say abusive and hurtful comments that they wouldn't be prepared to say in face-to-face conversations. Nevertheless, both believed that platforms such as Facebook and Twitter would become increasingly important campaigning tools in future election campaigns in the divided society. The DUP interviewee suggested that the duties of the party press officer would inevitably become more focused on social media as more and more people 'were getting their news online'. Sinn Féin were in the unique position of being able to compare how social media was being used for political campaigns north and south of the border, and noted these platforms had facilitated higher levels of public engagement with their policies during recent Irish parliamentary elections. However, the party representative suggested that sectarian exchanges between the party and its opponents in the north were perhaps inevitable in a society transitioning out of conflict. It was anticipated that social media might provide the spaces for more 'policy-focused conversations' as the Executive and Assembly 'matured'. In other words, the 'normalisation' of politics in the 'post-violence' society was viewed as a prerequisite for moving towards a more civil discourse online.

Conclusion

Contentious episodes are inevitable in deeply divided societies such as Northern Ireland that remain highly polarised and segregated. The rallies and street demonstrations between December 2012 and March 2013, triggered by the change in the Belfast City Hall flag protocol, were familiar contentious performances situated within a broader campaign by anti-Agreement loyalists against the alleged 'culture war' of the republican movement. It was a social movement in the sense that it represented a challenge to the authority of the political elites within the Stormont Assembly, and emerged in response to a growing sense of indignation within working-class loyalism at being 'left behind' and poorly represented by these institutions. This perception that they were being overlooked in favour of their nationalist counterparts was compounded by the failure of the Executive, the DUP and Sinn Féin in particular, to create shared spaces for the resolution of conflict legacy issues. It was therefore no surprise that contentious parades such as Ardoyne sparked violence in contested urban interface areas during this period. However, this was a very fragmented movement that was ultimately fatally undermined by its internal divisions and the failed leadership of political entrepreneurs such as Bryson and Frazer.

While there were some continuities between the flag protests and previous contentious episodes, this marked the first mass mobilisation within Northern Ireland that was contested on social media. Platforms such as Facebook and Twitter had helped 'stitch together' connective actions, based on personalised action frames, during the Occupy movement and the 'Arab Spring' in the 18 months prior to the flag protests. Despite the reductive analyses of critics who dismissed this as merely 'clicktivism', these online platforms were a vital component of the repertoire of protest deployed by social movements to mobilise support for their causes. In the case of Northern Ireland, there was little evidence prior to 2012 that social media would greatly enhance the capacity of citizens to make rights claims and seek greater involvement in the practice of contentious politics. Early SNS, such as Bebo, were linked to the organisation of so-called 'recreational rioting' by a small minority of youths who lived near sectarian interfaces in Belfast in the late 2000s. A sparsely populated blogosphere tended to be divided along tribal lines, with dissident republicans in particular benefiting from the communicative space to articulate their opposition to the peace process. While platforms such as *Slugger* offered opportunities for a multiplicity of voices to be heard, there was a sense that people were often reluctant to contribute to political discussions online due to a fear of being shouted down. Yet, the experience of political parties in the region between 2009 and 2012 was instructive in relation to the importance of contextual factors in shaping the nature of political debate on Web 2.0. All of the parties were speaking almost exclusively to their supporters via their array of social media accounts, with interactions with critics from the 'other' community often antagonistic. It was acknowledged that the 'trolling' of party profiles increased during controversial episodes such as 'Irisgate'. Nevertheless, there was a degree of cautious optimism that there would be greater civility in online interactions with political opponents in the future, especially if there was to be further 'normalisation' of politics in the post-violence society. This book will now turn to explore the extent to which such contextual factors shaped the social media activity surrounding the flag protests.

Notes

1 More information on the PC can be found here: http://powerbase.info/index.php/Protestant_Coalition (accessed 10 March 2019).

2 A BBC Northern Ireland investigation revealed not only details of Iris Robinson's affair with Kirk McCambley, but also how she had failed to declare her stake in his business. She resigned from the DUP shortly afterwards and received psychiatric treatment in a London clinic. For more on this, see: www.independent.co.uk/news/uk/politics/stormonts-first-minister-peter-robinson-unseated-after-year-of-scandal-1965819.html (accessed 10 May 2019).

3 Lagan Valley Councillor Palmer revealed that DUP special advisor, Stephen Brimstone, had pressured her to extend the Red Sky contract. The company fell into administration in April 2011. For more on this, see: www.bbc.co.uk/news/uk-northern-ireland-14045046 (accessed 10 June 2019).

4 A full chronology of the protests against the Anglo–Irish Agreement can be found here: https://cain.ulster.ac.uk/othelem/chron/ch85.htm (accessed 10 May 2019).

5 The majority of these areas were in North Belfast. For more on the report, see: Tomlinson et al. (2013).

6 Research commissioned in 2008 by ComRes in conjunction with Stratagem found that 96 per cent of members of the Northern Ireland Assembly read *Slugger* either regularly or occasionally. Unfortunately, there are no links to the original survey, please see here for details on *Slugger*: https://en.wikipedia.org/wiki/Slugger_O%27Toole (accessed 10 January 2019).

7 The *Total Politics* Top 25 Northern Irish Blogs 2011 can be viewed here: www.totalpolitics.com/articles/news/top-25-northern-irish-blogs-2011 (accessed 1 April 2019). Please note this was the only year in which these awards ran.

8 These data were generated using Alexa Pro on 3 August 2014. The service can be accessed here: www.alexa.com/siteinfo (accessed 1 February 2019).

9 Mooney criticised the lack of transparency in *Slugger*'s moderation policy and raised questions about its link to local PR company Stratagem. The blogpost can be accessed here: https://fitzjameshorselooksattheworld.wordpress.com/2012/08/09/slugger-otoole-redux/ (accessed 10 May 2019).

2

Too many cyberwarriors? The case of Loyalist Peaceful Protest Updater

In December 2012, Belfast City Council voted in favour of a new protocol on the flying of the union flag above City Hall, which would see it flown on 18 designated days rather than every day, as had previously been the case. This provoked a loyalist 'flag protest' campaign disrupting rush-hour traffic in towns and cities across Northern Ireland, culminating in rioting in east and north Belfast in January 2013. Much of the initial media coverage focused on how far-right groups such as Britain First collaborated with the Ulster People's Forum (UPF) and loyalist paramilitaries to organise these protests through social media.[1] Public Facebook pages enabled loyalists to not only share information on upcoming protests with their supporters, but also discuss related issues such as their growing antipathy towards the PSNI and unionist political parties for their alleged complicity in Sinn Féin's 'war' against unionist and loyalist culture. These pages were subject to increased scrutiny by the PSNI in January 2013 as a result of a high court injunction lodged by an unidentified Catholic man from North Belfast, who had been the subject of a death threat on one of these pages. At the same time, critics of the protests such as 'parody group' Loyalists Against Democracy (LAD) used social media to highlight the sectarianism of loyalists posting content on these pages. Their mocking of loyalist tropes, which often focused on the poor spelling and grammar of 'cyber loyalists', was criticised by some commenters for reinforcing negative stereotypes of working-class loyalist communities (which will be examined in more detail in Chapter 5).

This chapter sets out to add to the limited empirical data available on how the flag protests were organised using digital media, through the analysis of comments posted on Loyalist Peaceful Protest Updater

(LPPU) and its successor Loyalist Peaceful Protest Updater Backup (LPPUB) during January 2013. It will focus on the ways in which these public Facebook pages provided a platform for loyalists to articulate the perceived grievances that underpinned the flag protests. The chapter will also provide further insight into the 'dialogic' potential of social media by analysing how critics and supporters of the flag protests engaged with these issues, and one another, during this period. It does so by exploring the background to the flag protests, analysing the newspaper coverage of the role of social media in these demonstrations (N = 347), and presenting the key findings of an analysis of 24,244 comments posted on these pages during January 2013.

The origins of the union flag protests

On 3 December 2012, Belfast City Council voted in favour of a new protocol that would see the union flag fly over City Hall on 18 designated days rather than all year round, as had been the previous arrangement. The Alliance Party, who proposed the motion, argued that this was a 'sensible compromise' compatible with the findings of the Equality Impact Assessment on the flag protocol carried out a few months earlier.[2] The moderate, centrist party inevitably bore the brunt of loyalist anger at the decision, with its Carrickfergus office destroyed in a suspected arson attack and several others picketed on a daily basis in the weeks after the vote. Both the DUP and UUP were quick to condemn the death threat made against its East Belfast MP Naomi Long and a petrol bomb attack on a police vehicle outside her constituency office (Melaugh, 2013; Nolan et al., 2014). Yet, the two main unionist parties were accused of 'whipping up hatred' towards the party by distributing 40,000 'anti-Alliance' leaflets to households across Belfast in the weeks running up to the vote. These depicted Alliance as a threat to unionist and loyalist identity and urged citizens to inform their elected representatives about their opposition to the proposed changes (Kane, 2012). First Minister and DUP leader Peter Robinson defended the controversial leaflet, claiming that it "did not call on people to come on to the streets, but asked people to engage in the democratic process."[3] Nevertheless, none of the main political parties could have anticipated the scale of the street protests across Northern Ireland. For instance, in the week before Christmas (17–23 December) 10,000 people were said to have participated in the flag protests (Nolan et al., 2014: 4).

Four modes of protest were utilised by loyalists between December 2012 and March 2013. First, rallies were held every Saturday outside Belfast City Hall; second, marches were organised to and from the city's most famous landmark building; third, pickets were held outside a number of public buildings; and, finally, and perhaps most controversially, roadblocks were erected across arterial routes in towns and cities to disrupt rush-hour traffic (Nolan et al., 2014: 9). The disruption was on a scale not seen in Northern Ireland since the Drumcree crises in the mid-1990s, which saw several weeks of protests and rioting within both loyalist and republican neighbourhoods in response to the re-routing of a contentious Orange Order parade away from the nationalist Garvaghy Road area in Portadown.[4] The Northern Ireland Confederation of British Industry (CBI) estimated the loss of revenue to Belfast traders at between £10–£15 million, as customers stayed away from the city centre due to the number of marches and rallies held during the festive period.[5] Dubbed 'Operation Standstill', the second week of January saw loyalists create roadblocks across the region between 6 p.m. and 8 p.m., causing significant disruption to commuters. In March 2013, PSNI Chief Constable Matt Baggott informed the Northern Ireland Policing Board that the cost of policing these protests had been over £20 million.[6]

Although most of the flag protests passed off peacefully and without incident, a minority ended in violent clashes between loyalists and the PSNI. Throughout January 2013, in towns such as Carrickfergus and Newtownabbey, baton rounds were used to disperse rioters who were throwing petrol bombs at police officers. The police were also attacked by loyalist mobs for six consecutive nights near the sectarian interface that separated the predominantly nationalist Short Strand district from the surrounding loyalist community of the Lower Newtownards Road in East Belfast (Melaugh, 2013). Petrol bombs, bricks and other missiles were thrown at the PSNI as they tried to disperse the crowds who had gathered to block roads in support of the flag protests. Although elements of the UDA and UVF had tried to 'soften' flag protest-related violence (Nolan et al., 2014: 81), senior members of the latter were blamed for orchestrating this violence and a gun attack on PSNI officers in East Belfast on 5 January.[7]

Such violence marked a turning point in the protests, both in terms of public opinion and the police operation to arrest those responsible for protest-related criminality. Whereas a poll conducted in December

2012 found that 51 per cent of respondents agreed with loyalists exercising their right to protest against the change to the flag protocol, the majority of respondents (77 per cent) wanted the protests to stop immediately when surveyed a month later. Closer inspection of the January 2013 poll data revealed that not everybody supported the immediate cessation of the protests, with 45 per cent of unionist participants feeling that they should continue.[8] Nevertheless, attendance at 'seats of protest' began to dwindle once it became clear that the PSNI would arrest protesters who engaged in violence or illegally blocked roads. Data obtained by Nolan et al. (2014: 123) revealed that a total of 362 cases were brought before the courts, with men aged between 16 and 24 years old accounting for the highest proportion (57.5 per cent) of indictable prosecutions, such as attempted murder. Operation Dulcet also targeted so-called 'flag provocateurs', including ex-BNP fundraiser Jim Dowson, North Down political activist Jamie Bryson and South Armagh victims' campaigner Willie Frazer. They were identified as key influencers within an 'anarchic' and 'rudderless' movement that lacked organisational coherence (Nolan et al., 2014: 80). These arrests not only deterred others from engaging in street protests, but also prompted the UPF tactical move from blocking roads to white line protests in late January 2013.

Flag protests: conflict by cultural means?

The vote to alter the flag protocol was viewed by working-class loyalists as yet another republican attack on unionist and loyalist culture. The flag was seen as a symbol of their 'Britishness' that was being "airbrushed from the 'new' Northern Ireland" (INTERCOMM and Byrne, 2013: 7). Unionist politicians were heavily criticised for failing to protect loyalists from this 'culture war'. First Minister Peter Robinson, in particular, was condemned for having 'sold out' these communities through his participation in the power-sharing Executive with Sinn Féin. This was symptomatic of an ever increasing disconnect between the power-sharing institutions and working-class loyalist communities (Novosel, 2013). Loyalists believed they had not seen the economic and political benefits of peace experienced by their republican counterparts (Smithey, 2013). 'Truth recovery' investigations were characterised as republican conspiracies designed to discredit the British state due to the fact that they almost exclusively focused on atrocities committed by the police and army (McGrattan, 2013). Moreover, there was evidence to suggest that working-class Protestants were being 'left behind' in terms of educational achievement, with boys from such backgrounds receiving the lowest grades at GCSE level in Northern Ireland and considered likely to struggle to gain employment in the future (Nolan, 2014; Purvis and Working Group, 2011). Hence, many observers felt that the flag dispute was a "lightning rod" for loyalist dissatisfaction not only with the performance of the Stormont Executive, but also the peace process in general (McDonald, 2013).

The 'culture war' narrative was disputed in the 2014 Northern Ireland Peace Monitoring Report, which showed that the number of loyalist bands and parades in Northern Ireland had reached record levels by 2013 and that they continued to receive generous subsidies from the EU Peace III Programme (Nolan, 2014: 162). An alternative interpretation might be that these cultural expressions of loyalism were increasing in frequency due to fears about the erosion of unionist and loyalist culture. The perceived failure to address such victimhood, whether real or imagined, was arguably a defining characteristic of the 'post-violence' society created by the Belfast Agreement (Brewer, 2010). The Agreement might have transformed the nature of the Troubles but it had not addressed the zero-sum perceptions of politics and space held by members of rival communities (Shirlow and McEvoy, 2008). The consociational approach towards conflict management institutionalised ethnic divisions through manufacturing consensus between unionist and nationalist political parties in the power-sharing Stormont Executive, with societal cleavages entrenched rather than confronted. The rationale was that the leaders of the main political parties, many of whom had already proven adept at using discourses of 'imagined hurts' to mobilise their constituents during the conflict, would legitimise the Agreement by extolling its virtues to their respective ethnic blocs (McGarry and O'Leary, 1995; Murtagh et al., 2008). The increasing alienation of working-class loyalists from the main unionist parties appears to militate against such a scenario. Declining unionist and loyalist support for the Agreement has been a notable trend since 1998. One poll in May 2013 showed that as few as 40 per cent of unionists expressed support for the Agreement, with only 39 per cent believing that the Stormont Assembly was doing a good job in representing the interests of all citizens in Northern

Ireland (Fealty, 2013). In this context, the flag protests and the related 'culture war' narrative could be seen as further evidence of working-class loyalists no longer supporting the Agreement and feeling increasingly alienated from unionist parties such as the DUP. This chapter will now move on to consider the extent to which Facebook functioned as a communicative space in which 'cyber loyalists' could not only organise protests, but also express their dissatisfaction with the peace process.

Social media and the flag protests

From the very outset, social media was used to mobilise publics on both sides of the flag dispute. A message posted on the Save the Union Flag Facebook page was the 'rallying call' for the protests that followed the controversial flag vote on 3 December 2012. Loyalists also used social media to express their anger at a video of the flag being lowered at City Hall, which was posted online by the republican media outlet *An Phoblacht* (Nolan et al., 2014: 40). As will be discussed in this and the next two chapters, social media appeared to reinforce sectarian divisions during this period, particularly among young people, who reported an increase in threats of violence and online sectarian abuse (Young, 2014). Statistics obtained from the PSNI showed that 2,111 social media related incidents were reported to the police between January and May 2013, compared with 2,887 reported incidents during the whole of 2012. A deeper dive into these data revealed that 229 of these related to content posted on social media during the peak of the flag protest movement in January and February 2013.[9] One such incident resulted in two loyalist Facebook pages, Loyalists Against Short Strand and LPPU, being shut down for carrying threats against an unidentified Catholic man.[10] This prompted Justice Minister David Ford to call on the PSNI to monitor sites such as Facebook in order to identify and prosecute those who posted hate speech or incited others to commit criminal acts.[11]

Social media as an information source in newspaper coverage of protests

While social media appeared to be mobilising affective publics in relation to the protests (more on this in Chapter 3), it is perhaps less clear how integral these platforms were in the coordination of the protests. Nolan and colleagues (2014: 70) characterised social media as "a central nervous system for the communication of feeling and the construction of solidarity" between the protesters. They went on to argue that, apart from amplifying sectarian abuse online, social media had very little impact upon events on the ground. Yet, as previously discussed in relation to the 'social media revolutions' of 2011, there was a thinly veiled technological determinism in the media coverage of the flag protests in December 2012. Reporting by both BBC Northern Ireland and Ulster Television (UTV) emphasised the central role of social media in organising the protests and focused on flag protest-related violence rather than the broader issues underpinning the demonstrations.[12]

A content analysis of newspaper coverage of the flag protests (N = 347) provided some empirical data to support this assertion. Articles were analysed from the three most widely read newspapers, the *Belfast Telegraph* (including its sister publication *Sunday Life*), the *Irish News*, and the *News Letter* between 3 December 2012 and 28 February 2013 (see Appendix 1). The first 'spike' in coverage of the flag protests was on 8 December 2012, as a crowd of approximately 2,000 loyalists held a rally outside Belfast City Hall to protest against the controversial vote to alter the flag protocol (see Figure 2.1). There were other noticeable spikes in coverage when the Council met for the first time since the flag vote (7 January) and in the final week of February when 'flag provocateurs' such as Bryson and Frazer were arrested.

The episodic nature of this coverage was reflected by its seemingly constant focus on criminal justice proceedings, warnings from local businesses about losses incurred as a result of the disruption, and political responses to the flag crisis, such as the formation of the Unionist Forum in January 2013. For example, 34.8 per cent of articles in the *Belfast Telegraph* in December 2012 focused on the consequences of the protests (see Appendix 1, Figure A1.1). There were occasional references to social media, as demonstrated by reports that loyalists were using Facebook to share details of where Parachute Regiment flags could be purchased in advance of a protest held on the same day as the annual Bloody Sunday commemoration march.[13] Elsewhere, rumours spread on social media occasionally surfaced in the media coverage of the protests. Probably the most controversial

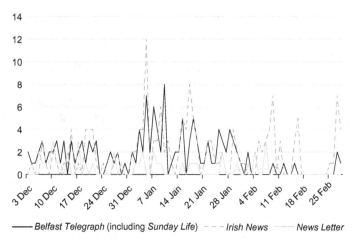

Figure 2.1 Number of flag protest articles in main Northern Irish newspapers, December 2012–February 2013.

instance related to false reports that An Garda Síochána officers were policing the flag protests, which was denied by both Justice Minister David Ford and a PSNI spokesperson in an article published on 8 January.[14] In contrast, there were relatively few articles providing specific detail on how social media was being used to coordinate the protests. *Irish News* security correspondent Allison Morris was one of the few journalists to probe the role of social media in a movement that appeared to 'lack structure and organisation'. Her article featured a quote from protest provocateur Jim Dowson criticising the 'cyber-warriors' for bringing loyalists onto the streets without considering issues such as "event management, crowd control, safety measures and stewarding".[15]

Facebook and PSNI urged to remove hate speech and abuse on social media

Overall, the *Irish News* provided the most extensive coverage of how affective publics used social media during the protests, albeit that this only peaked at 6.9 per cent of articles published in January 2013 (see Appendix 1, Figure A1.2). Much of this revolved around the afore-mentioned legal case that led Facebook to suspend two loyalist pages for hosting death threats against an unidentified Catholic man (referred to as J18 in the legal proceedings). Both the *Belfast Telegraph* and *Irish News* reported on Facebook's closure of the two pages, LPPU and Loyalists Against Short Strand, as well as the legal challenge to force Facebook to reveal the identity of the poster responsible for the threat. While these articles typically included statements from politicians calling for the platform to take stronger action to tackle hate speech, the *Irish News* acknowledged the right of protest provocateurs such as Willie Frazer to use social media to articulate their viewpoints. An editorial published on 2 January argued that "there should be little need for Facebook to silence him" unless his comments were unacceptable on grounds of "libel or taste".[16]

The largest nationalist paper in the region did not neglect the sectarianism and threats of violence on platforms such as Facebook. A few days later, the paper's editorial was highly critical of the PSNI's failure to arrest anybody in connection with messages posted online inciting violence, asserting that "people who use social media need to realise that threats made online can result in a criminal conviction".[17] Indeed, all three of these newspapers carried the statement from Chief Constable Matt Baggott to the Northern Ireland Select Affairs Committee on 24 January, in which he confirmed that he was seeking clarification from the Attorney General after 40 files sent to the Public Prosecution Service in relation to "communications sent via social media" were rejected.[18] Operation Dulcet featured prominently in the final week of February 2013; newspapers such as the *Belfast Telegraph* reported on a video posted on Facebook by Jamie Bryson in which the loyalist activist mocked the PSNI for not being able to find him.[19]

Flag protest leaders conspicuously absent in early coverage of protests

These newspapers gave little credence to loyalist claims that the police were brutalising loyalist flag protesters, typically featuring statements from senior PSNI personnel praising the actions of their officers and directly refuting such allegations. This was arguably a manifestation of what was widely regarded as an incoherent movement that lacked both a clear organisational structure and media strategy. While Bryson, Dowson and Frazer extolled the virtues of the 'people's protests', significant differences emerged between them in relation to the decision to move to white line protests on 31 January 2013. Frazer was removed from his position as UPF spokesperson a week later due to his opposition to the change. Moreover, the lack of a centralised communication strategy was illustrated by the sources cited by these newspapers in their coverage of the protests. Billy Hutchinson and Jim Allister, two of the politicians who articulated loyalist anger at the flag decision, were among the most quoted in *Belfast Telegraph* coverage of the protests in December 2012 (see Appendix 1, Table A1.2). However, it was noticeable how few of the protest provocateurs were quoted in these articles. Johnny Harvey, the United Protestant Voice leader who was widely credited with having organised the first wave of protests, was only quoted in two articles in the same paper. Indeed, in December 2012 there was only one article profiling 'flag provocateurs' such as Frazer. Even then, its specific focus was on the allegations that loyalist paramilitaries were coordinating the protests, rather than providing a platform for them to articulate their positions (Black, 2012).

Bryson, Frazer, and the newly formed UPF were more prominent in these papers' coverage in the following two months, particularly in the *Irish News* where Frazer was the most quoted actor in January 2013 (see Appendix 1, Table A1.6). This was also the case for Frazer in the *News Letter*'s coverage of the protests in February 2013 (see Appendix 1, Table A1.10). However, many of these articles probed controversial remarks and gaffes made by the victims' campaigner, such as his allegations that the Provisional IRA had put horsemeat in beefburgers.[20] Bryson was also the subject of coverage scrutinising his background, including one article in the *Irish News* which revealed he had been a mascot at a Northern Ireland international football match a few weeks before the protests began.[21] Whether intentional or not, this coverage undermined the credibility of these protest leaders and left them open to much ridicule among members of the public. It was in this context that public Facebook pages functioned as communicative spaces in which flag protesters challenged such 'partisan' media coverage of the demonstrations.

Facebook, prefigurative digital participation and the flag protests

Thus far, there has been no empirical investigation of the content posted on loyalist Facebook pages active during the flag protests.

There were more people discussing the flag dispute on these pages than participating in the street protests. Statistics from the Office of National Statistics suggested that the average attendance at the weekly Saturday demonstrations at City Hall between January and March 2013 was just 124 people.[22] In contrast, there were 16,203 comments collected from LPPU between 2 and 22 January 2013 for the purpose of this study. One interpretation of this finding might be that it showed the limitations of using Facebook to encourage 'unaffiliated participants' to take part in high-risk protest events (Mercea, 2012). Empirical work has indicated that the ICTs reinforce rather than increase high-risk participation within advocacy groups; face-to-face interaction with other members has been positively linked to participation in physical acts of protest (Diani, 2000; Pickerill, 2003). Conversely, scholars such as Karpf (2012; 2016) and Tufekci (2017) have argued that social media campaigns are important components of the 'repertoire of protest' adopted by social movements in order to attract as much attention as possible for their agendas. Political expression on platforms such as Facebook might be considered a form of digital prefigurative participation that either precedes or supplements high-risk activism (Mercea, 2012). Such participation allows 'unaffiliates' to help construct and articulate the identity of the social movement or advocacy group, while also giving them access to logistical information about the planned protest events (Valenzuela, 2013).

This study explores how critics, supporters and 'unaffiliated' participants used LPPU and LPPUB to share information and engage with the perceived grievances that underpinned the flag protests. Although no specific information pertaining to its origins was publicly available, LPPU emerged as one of the critical information hubs during Operation Standstill in January 2013. As discussed above, it was one of two pages shut down due to the emergency injunction filed on behalf of an unidentified Catholic man ('J18') in a Belfast court on 28 January 2013. It re-emerged a few days later as LPPUB.

Lemert (1981) has identified three types of mobilising information (locational, tactical and identificational) that are used to promote collective action on behalf of social movements and advocacy groups. In approaching this research, it was anticipated that the page administrators might be reluctant to publish information pertaining to their identities due to the threat of police prosecution, as well as the LAD campaign to expose those behind the protests (more on this in Chapter 5). However, they were expected to use the page to provide locational information about upcoming protests to supporters, and to articulate any changes in the overall strategy of the movement. Jamie Bryson claimed that the use of social media to convey the decision to move from blocking roads to white line protests, in which protesters position themselves in the centre of the road but do not obstruct traffic flow, caused much consternation among its online supporters. He claimed that the 'instant opinions' and 'emotional reactions' on pages such as LPPU made it difficult for him and others to control the movement, going so far as to suggest that social media "didn't help us in the slightest" (Alan in Belfast, 2014). This was congruent with the views of 'rank and file' protesters, who suggested that "social media was distrusted as a means of communicating any significant messages" (Nolan et al., 2014: 79). This study will empirically examine the extent to which this change in strategy divided opinion among these commenters, as well as the nature of the debate between supporters, 'unaffiliates' and critics on the page.

Specifically, there were three main research questions that emerged regarding the role of LPPU and LPPUB in the union flag protests:

1. What type of mobilising information was shared on these pages during this period? How did commenters respond to this information?
2. What were the key themes in relation to the protests discussed on these pages?
3. How did critics and supporters of the protest engage with one another on LPPU and LPPUB?

These were explored through a thematic analysis of comments posted on LPPU and LPPUB. Discovertext (www.discovertext.com) was used to collect and archive posts from the public Facebook pages between 3 January and 17 February 2013, a period covering the violence in East Belfast, the J18 case, and the internal debate over the change to white line protests. A total of 24,244 comments were analysed; 16,203 were extracted from the original iteration of the page between 2–22 January, with 8,041 taken from its backup page between 22–30 January. There were several noticeable 'spikes' in comments on LPPU and LPPUB, such as on 12 January following violent clashes

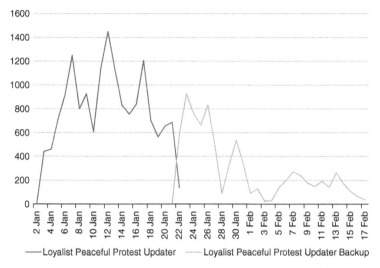

Figure 2.2 Number of comments posted on LPPU and LPPUB page, 3 January–17 February 2013.

between flag protesters and nationalists near the Short Strand (N = 1,448) and on 30 January on the eve of the UPF decision to move to white line protests (N = 537) (see Figure 2.2).

There were 3,991 commenters within the LPPU sample, compared with 1,713 in LPPUB. A long tail distribution of user activity was evident across both; approximately half of those who posted on these pages during this period did so only once (52.51 per cent of LPPU users, compared with 48.89 per cent of LPPUB commenters). The page administrators were the most frequent contributors to these discussions, accounting for 10.65 per cent and 14.29 per cent of the comments in these datasets respectively. Congruent with previous research into online political talk in 'third spaces' (Graham and Wright, 2014), these pages were dominated by a small group of highly active users. The 50 most prolific tweeters were responsible for 24.91 per cent of the LPPU comments, with the equivalent group accounting for 38.89 per cent of the content on LPPUB. Analysis of these accounts revealed that 12 Facebookers were among the top 50 commenters in both datasets. Furthermore, a total of 761 users were active on both pages during this period, meaning that 44.4 per cent of those posting on LPPUB in February 2013 had done so on LPPU before its closure. However, as a direct consequence of the J18 case, it was highly likely that some comments posted on these pages had been removed for breaching community guidelines in relation to the posting of hate speech and threats against individuals. It was also impossible to ascertain what watchers (disparagingly referred to as 'lurkers') thought of the content posted on these pages, nor how such content was shared on private Facebook pages.

A purposive sample was used to identify three subsamples for analysis. Each of these represented one of the 'spikes' in activity on the two pages shown in the time-series graph above. Content posted on LPPU on 7 January (N = 1,254) was selected for analysis due to the fact that this was the date of the first Belfast City Council meeting since the flag vote. It was anticipated that mobilising information about Operation Shutdown, which began a few days later, would be shared during this period. The other two subsamples were taken from LPPUB; comments posted on 26 January (N = 830) and 30 January (N = 549) were included in order to capture any debate between 'cyber loyalists' about the UPF decision to move to white line protests. While this chapter will primarily adopt a qualitative approach towards the analysis of these data, the characteristics of the subsamples provided further evidence of the long tail distribution of commenting on these pages. The average number of comments per thread ranged from 17 to 21 across these datasets, albeit that the Standard Deviation for LPPUB1 and LPPUB2 suggested there was some variation in these commenting patterns (see Table 2.1). A total of 552 users were responsible for the 1,254 comments on LPPU. These sample

Table 2.1 Characteristics of three subsamples taken from LPPU and LPPUB.

Sample	Number of comments	Number of unique commenters (excluding page administrator)	Number of threads	Average number of comments per thread (excluding original post)	Standard deviation (SE)
LPPU	1254	552	75	16.27	2.11
LPPUB 1	830	347	40	20.35	4.51
LPPUB 2	549	195	34	15.76	4.19

characteristics included 'orphan' posts eliciting no responses, which accounted for a relatively small percentage of the total number of comments analysed from LPPU (2.63 per cent), LPPUB1 (1.93 per cent) and LPPUB2 (2.37 per cent) respectively. However, responses to these posts may have been unavailable due to their deletion by the Facebookers responsible, or the page administrators.

Comment threads were coded and quantified in order to illustrate key themes within these datasets. These were broad categories, such as 'criticism of media', which were then qualitatively explored in the results section. Page administrators played a key role in both instigating and structuring these threads. Although it was not possible to fully establish how these data were influenced by their moderation, administrators such as 'Dan' and 'SR' were the most frequent contributors across all three periods of data collection. However, it should be noted that the highest percentage of comments attributed to these users was still only 11.89 per cent in the relatively small LPPUB2 sample, where the majority of commenters (60.5 per cent) posted only once. While page admins were responsible for starting 59.3 per cent and 55.36 per cent of the threads during the first two sampling periods (not to mention 91.5 per cent in LPPUB2), the remainder were attributed to citizens who were not part of the protest leadership. In this sense, the study provided some evidence to support Dowson's characterisation of an incoherent movement in which social media gave 'cyberwarriors' free rein to directly intervene in discussions about its strategy.

Results and discussion

LPPU used primarily for sharing locational mobilisation information (unlike backup page)

There were no significant differences in terms of the dominant themes that emerged from the study of the threads and 'orphan' posts on these two pages. Of the LPPU threads, 32 (42.67 per cent) revolved around the provision of mobilisation information to supporters (see Figure 2.3). A similar trend emerged from the study of LPPU 'orphan' posts, with 15 of these (45.45 per cent) focusing on the protests planned to coincide with the first council meeting since the controversial flag vote. Nevertheless, it was clear that the discussions on LPPU focused

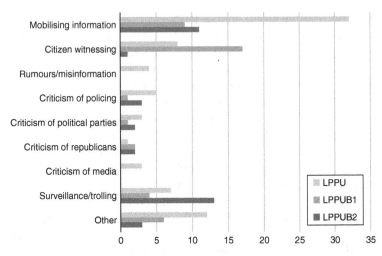

Figure 2.3 Main themes in threads on LPPU and LPPUB, January 2013.

more on mobilising information than those in LPPUB1 and LPPUB2. For example, threads revolving around how loyalist Facebook pages were being 'trolled' by republicans and 'spied upon' by professional journalists accounted for the largest proportion (38.24 per cent) of LPPUB2 (see Figure 2.3). As expected, there were no threads in which explicit identificational mobilisation information was shared. While the content analysis above showed an increase in media scrutiny of protest spokespersons such as Bryson and Frazer in January 2013, there were surprisingly few threads focusing explicitly on these provocateurs. The few that did often degenerated into antagonistic exchanges between their critics and supporters. For example, the two LPPU threads highlighting their role concentrated exclusively on Frazer, with one of the admins arguing that he was one of the "few who spoke for PUL interests" after several commenters mocked him for gaffes such as the aforementioned 'horsemeat conspiracy'. The other LPPU thread in which he was discussed saw a commenter condemn Frazer for telling the widow of UDA leader John McMichael that she wouldn't receive any financial compensation for her loss due to the fact that her husband was a terrorist. Again, a page administrator and several other commenters defended his actions, with some even questioning the veracity of the allegation. Although the majority of commenters were broadly supportive of Frazer, this illustrated how provocateurs did not enjoy the widespread support from the 'people's protest' that they often claimed publicly.

Overall, more of these threads revolved around the sharing of information about planned demonstrations than discussions about the tactics deployed by the protesters. This was particularly evident in LPPU, where 16 out of 26 threads (61.54 per cent) contained mobilising information such as the time and location of protests. Reflecting the overall lack of organisational coherence, members of the admin team often had to ask for this information themselves. For example, one asked "is there meant to be a protest outside the City Hall tonight are [sic] is it a rumour?", leading to a discussion about other rumoured protest sites in Belfast. There were also threads in which LPPU administrators sought to mobilise 'cyber loyalists' to 'troll' parody and republican social media accounts; they were encouraged to visit public Facebook pages such as Short Strand Gold Ball Throwers Take No Nonsense from Protesters to 'stand up' against those disparaging the protesters. It should be noted that, in one of these threads, one commenter urged loyalists not to respond to such online abuse as "that's exactly what they want you to do". However, this lone voice was drowned out by LPPU contributors intent on seeking (online) retribution. A similar pattern of eliciting and providing information was evident in 'orphan' posts across all three datasets. For example, 10 of the 47 orphan posts in LPPUB2 saw page administrators or supporters share mobilising information, including one post inviting loyalists to join the eponymous social media campaign to secure the release of Jamie Reilly, one of the loyalists arrested as part of Operation Dulcet.

Page administrators frequently urged participants to 'keep it peaceful' and provided information on how acts such as the covering of faces and blocking roads might transgress the right to peaceful assembly. In light of the UPF's decision to move to white line protests on 30 January, it was perhaps no surprise that such tactical mobilising information was more prominent in the data collected from LPPUB. Two thirds of the LPPUB1 threads focused on the actions and behaviour of protesters during the demonstrations. Commenters questioned the efficacy and safety of white line protests, as well as the UPF's right to speak on behalf of the protest movement. While the page administrators expressed support for the change in tactics, they acknowledged that the announcement "had taken some protesters by surprise".

However, the LPPUB1 thread that generated the most responses (N = 105) revolved around a suggestion by page administrator 'AA' that nightly street protests should be abandoned in favour of larger, weekly mass demonstrations, to be held at a number of different locations including Belfast City Hall and Stormont. Keen to stress this was a personal opinion and not reflective of the views of other page administrators, they argued this would maximise publicity for the protests. While the majority of commenters agreed that the time of the nightly protests should move to 7 p.m. in order to maximise the number of participants, a small minority of the commenters characterised these tactics as counter-productive. One proposed that the protests be moved off the streets altogether and held on footpaths, but this was dismissed by 'AA' and most of the other commenters on this thread. This was one of several LPPUB1 threads in which new tactics for the protest movement were proposed, contested and eventually dismissed by other contributors. For example, one debated a proposal for images of the union flag to be projected onto buildings across the city, which was dismissed as 'unnecessarily antagonistic' due to what appeared to be a tongue-in-cheek suggestion that it might include prominent housing developments in the staunchly republican Divis district in West Belfast.

While it would be misleading to characterise discussions about tactics as agonistic, the analysis suggested that Facebook afforded Dowson's 'cyberwarriors' opportunities to express their views about the decisions taken by both the UPF and protest provocateurs such as Bryson and Frazer. What is perhaps less clear is the extent to which the behaviour of protesters was influenced by these online commentaries.

Polarised responses to citizen witnessing on LPPU and LPPUB

The most common theme in the LPPUB1 threads was the sharing of eyewitness perspectives on flag protest events. Whether intended as a form of citizen journalism or not, such content illustrated the strength of support for the nightly protests and weekly demonstrations at Belfast City Hall. For example, one LPPU thread revolved around an image taken by an eyewitness showing the turnout at one of the rallies held at City Hall, which they claimed had approximately one thousand protesters in attendance. This led some commenters to accuse the BBC and UTV of 'shit-stirring' in their claims that "no more than a few hundred" had been in attendance. The thread was 'trolled' by 'Gerard', a self-identified republican who mocked the low turnout at flag protests. While his posts had been deleted by one of the page administrators, many of the remaining comments in the thread used sectarian language to criticise the 'troll'. Indeed, republicans opposing the protests were characterised as "inbred cunts", "rebel scumbag" and "fenian scum" in this thread. This was illustrative of how critics were able to hijack these acts of citizen witnessing to dismiss claims about the 'unfair' treatment of loyalists. Yet, as per the above discussion about tactics, supporters of the protests also challenged the claims made by those who posted such content. In LPPUB1, for instance, one seemingly innocuous picture of the City Hall protest would lead to a row between two loyalists about whether the weekly demonstrations were attracting large numbers or not. Several of the other commenters in the thread asked why there was such apparent disunity among those who claimed to support the protests.

Most of the threads in the study categorised as 'citizen witnessing' might be better defined as 'unsubstantiated' citizen journalism. Very often these began with posts providing no visual evidence to corroborate the claims made therein. For example, in one LPPU thread a loyalist wrote that her friend had been 'grabbed' by the police while on the phone and minding her own business, but provided nothing to substantiate the allegation. The most commented upon LPPUB1 thread (N = 101) was generated by an update from one of the page administrators about their meeting with Peter Robinson. Refuting media reports that UPF representatives had been invited to a meeting with the First Minister, they confirmed that they had 'stormed' one of his meetings; 'O'Robinson' was heavily criticised for his silence when challenged about why he was "not on the streets with his electorate". No evidence was provided to support this version of events, and one commenter contradicted this story by claiming that Frazer did in fact have a 'behind closed doors' meeting with Robinson. Two commenters questioned the representativeness of the UPF and argued that only a 'loyalist military command' could act in the interests of the working-class loyalists at the centre of the protests. It was not clear whether they were advocating paramilitary violence, or for the leaders of groups such as the UDA to broker a peaceful solution to the dispute.

The most polarised responses to UGC posted on these pages were generated by sousveillance footage purporting to show the alleged brutality of the PSNI towards protesters. A total of 14 LPPUB1 threads discussed footage showing several police officers restraining a 42-year-old man, who was later charged with two counts of disorderly behaviour and resisting arrest. While I will discuss this particular video in Chapter 4, it is fair to say that it provided limited evidence of PSNI brutality. Nevertheless, there were 'orphan' posts urging protesters to report the incident to Amnesty International. Links to the BBC complaints system were shared to encourage loyalists to report the 'biased' media for their failure to cover the incident.

Page administrators were responsible for instigating 10 of the 13 threads focusing on the footage, providing multiple links to the video in posts claiming that the PSNI had treated the man like a "bloody animal". This was symptomatic of their distrust towards the 'PSNIRA'. For example, rumours and misinformation about the alleged role of An Garda Síochána officers in policing the flag protests were present in LPPU. Both the page administrators and supporters of the flag protests asked for confirmation of whether this was true; responses referred to corroborative evidence on Twitter and an article in the *Belfast Daily* which suggested that the Chief Constable had asked for Garda officers to be drafted in to help with policing the protests. Responses to this rumour were inevitably hostile, with one loyalist characterising it as an 'act of war'.

The sharing of this 'sousveillance' footage on LPPUB led to much condemnation of the 'PSNIRA' for this allegedly unprovoked attack on an innocent bystander. One commenter claimed that they too had been assaulted by the police for attempting to record the incident. The police were characterised as "English stormtroopers" who had "too many Catholics" in their ranks and were controlled by "haters of Ulster". It was suggested that the solution to these issues was to bring back the Royal Ulster Constabulary (RUC) and the Ulster Defence Regiment, key components of the security services during the Troubles. This illustrated the 'whataboutery' invoked in relation to 'political policing', with a few commenters comparing the treatment of loyalists to the internment of republicans in the early 1970s. Such intemperate language was commonplace in responses that were critical of the PSNI. However, there were conspicuously few comments directly threatening police officers or inciting violence, with the exception of one calling for the officers in the sousveillance footage to be shot. One interpretation of this finding was that the page administrators had removed content that might be viewed as threatening police officers due to the J18 case.

There was far from unanimous support on these public Facebook pages for the proposition that this footage constituted sousveillance. As I will discuss further in Chapter 4, the decontextualised events caught on camera led critics to challenge the notion that this was de facto evidence of PSNI brutality against loyalists. These included 'fact-checking' claims that the man was a 'defenceless pensioner' by providing links to media reports confirming he was 42 years old. Others argued that he was clearly being aggressive towards the police officers and resisting arrest. In one case, it was claimed that the policing captured on camera represented the "typical experience for Catholics in the north", as demonstrated by the treatment of the Ardoyne residents during the annual Twelfth demonstrations. This was challenged by one commenter who blamed Ardoyne parade-related violence on the nationalist residents. However, not all comments disputing the sousveillant properties of this video were civil and there were many examples of republican 'trolling'. For example, the two most commented on 'sousveillance' threads (with 56 and 41 comments respectively) saw 'trolls' assert that the man 'hadn't been hit hard enough' as well as dismissing allegations that the PSNI had 'brutalised' the flag protesters. Supporters of the flag protests levelled sectarian abuse at these Facebookers, calling them 'taigs' whose 'papish views' were not welcome. It was perhaps no surprise to find many calls for page administrators to ban these users from the page.

Supporters of 'people's protest' turn away from mainstream unionist parties

While the Alliance Party were blamed for the change to the flag protocol, loyalist anger was primarily directed towards the DUP and First Minister Peter Robinson. Political unionism was frequently accused of not doing enough to push back on the 'Sinn Féin/IRA' 'war' on unionist and loyalist culture. Robinson's call for the protests to end was dismissed by the page administrators with several commenters referring to him as a 'traitor' for sharing power with Sinn Féin. The consensus among loyalist commenters on these pages was that the DUP had abandoned them and that they were only interested in the opinions of working-class loyalists when they 'needed a vote'. This was illustrated by the widespread antipathy towards the Unionist Forum. As per the aforementioned vignette about the UPF 'meeting' with Robinson, the page administrators dismissed its claims to represent the interests of the protesters. Indeed, this sense of being 'forgotten' by unionist political parties was illustrated by one thread discussing a speech by DUP MLA Sammy Wilson in the Assembly. One of the page administrators referred to his disclosure that the Orange Order had received significant funding from the European Union as evidence that the institution, like the DUP, had 'sold out' working-class loyalists.

Although critical of the Unionist Forum, the page administrators led conversations about PUP and TUV proposals to resolve the flag dispute. There was limited support for TUV leader Jim Allister's proposal that the union flag fly over council offices all year round while only being displayed on civic buildings on designated days. Critics argued that the flag should be flown over all buildings 365 days per year and some accused Allister of being as bad as other unionist politicians in not attending the protests. In another LPPU thread, 'Dan' confirmed his support for the TUV and urged all Protestants to do the same in order to ensure their voices were heard. There was very limited support for this proposition for a variety of reasons, including fears that voting TUV would split the unionist vote and lead to a Sinn Féin First Minister. Curiously, 'Dan' appeared to express support for the PUP too later that day, suggesting that the party was 'heading into a good light' courtesy of its public statements about the protests. Like the thread discussing the TUV, there was a mixed response among commenters, with some praising leader Billy Hutchinson and others criticising its 'lefty politics' and UVF links. There were also concerns raised about whether voting for the PUP and TUV would make any difference given that unionist parties had let down loyalists in the past. This illustrated how supporters of the flag protests on these pages were turning their backs on political institutions that they felt were actively working against their interests.

Trolling becomes more pervasive on backup page

There were signs of 'trolling' throughout each of these datasets, peaking in LPPUB2 when over a third (37.14 per cent) of its threads were dominated by hostile exchanges between critics and supporters of the protests. One interpretation of this finding was that the media coverage of the J18 case led to more Facebookers searching for and commenting on its backup page. An alternative explanation was that, by the end of January, citizens were using social media on a regular basis to find out information about the locations of street protests, which increased the likelihood of them accessing LPPUB.

Sectarian abuse was frequently directed towards republican 'trolls', with many of their posts deleted by the page administrators. Those that were available for analysis fell broadly into two categories. First, there were critics who dismissed claims that the PSNI were brutalising loyalists and ridiculed flag protesters for their apparent 'obsession' with the union flag. Ironically, they often invoked a form of 'whataboutery' themselves in contributions arguing that the PSNI treatment of nationalist residents in Ardoyne was much more 'brutal' than that experienced by loyalists. Second, there were comments that appeared to mock the flag protesters. In LPPUB2, for instance, two 'trolls' taunted 'cyber loyalists' by stating that they would face prison sentences for posting hate speech on LPPUB. Others disparaged the intelligence and even the appearance of protesters. Bryson was ridiculed for his speech impediment and for only receiving 157 votes in a local election. Frazer was characterised as a 'joke' for a number of gaffes including his erroneous claim that an Armagh school was an IRA training camp after he mistook an Italian flag flown on its premises for an Irish tricolour. These commenters also highlighted the poor spelling and grammar of loyalists on the page, as demonstrated by one post that called one of the page administrators an "illiterate wee ball bag" for spelling George Square incorrectly in a post discussing the location of an upcoming Glasgow protest.

There was one LPPUB1 thread in which a female critic of the protests was praised for her 'good input' and encouraged by one of the page administrators to comment on the page. Loyalists who mocked her Irish name and made sectarian remarks about her background were instructed to desist and let her 'have her say'. She condemned police brutality towards the protesters and argued in favour of a more balanced and neutral PSNI when dealing with protests, irrespective of their cause. However, it should be noted that this was the only instance in which critics of the flag protests appeared to be actively encouraged to post on either page. Furthermore, the deletion of many trolling comments made it difficult to fully assess the extent to which critics were mocking the intelligence, spelling and grammar of the flag protesters.

Page administrators resisted calls by commenters to make the page private in order to restrict what critics ('the great unwashed') and the media could see about upcoming protests. Instead, they deleted antagonistic comments and engaged in the online shaming of 'republican trolls'; this was a somewhat elastic term that appeared to be applied to all Facebookers who challenged loyalist narratives on the page, irrespective of their stated political affiliations. Page administrators directed loyalists towards the social media accounts of tweeters who had participated in a coordinated campaign to report LPPUB to Facebook for violating its terms of service, leading to angry responses from many commenters.

This online shaming was extended to journalists who were said to be surveilling the page for potential stories. For example, one LPPUB2 thread began with a link to the Facebook profile of an occasional contributor to the *Andersonstown News*, who was accused of re-publishing comments from the page. This Facebooker was one of several to be named, shamed and blocked from posting on LPPUB. The shutdown of LPPU was also referred to in multiple threads in LPPUB1 and LPPUB2. Links were shared to the BBC coverage of J18, alongside warnings that the solicitor for the unidentified Catholic man was looking at content posted on the page in relation to the case. Administrators also warned loyalists about the possible legal sanctions they might face if they used language that the PSNI deemed incitement to violence. While they didn't specifically address hate speech, they did appear to have deleted comments posted by loyalists for this reason.

Conclusion

The analysis of LPPU and LPPUB in January 2013 certainly provided some evidence to support Jamie Bryson's statement that social media hadn't helped the protesters in the slightest. The 'instant opinions' proffered by 'cyberwarriors' on these Facebook pages exposed the divisions within the 'people's protest', especially in relation to the decision to move to white line protests and over which political party best represented the protesters. The incoherence of the protest movement was laid bare on these public Facebook pages, with there even being visible disagreements between the page administrators in terms of these issues. There was also much criticism of protest provocateurs such as Bryson and Frazer, suggesting that they enjoyed far from universal support among the protest movement. That is not to say that these pages didn't play a key role in mobilising support for the protests. Rather, the study found evidence that both LPPU and LPPUB were used to share locational, mobilising and tactical information. They also provided communicative spaces in which loyalist grievances, conspicuously absent from the media coverage of the protests, could be aired. These included allegations of PSNI brutality towards working-class loyalists and anger at the complicity of the DUP and UUP in Sinn Féin's alleged 'war' on unionist and loyalist culture. However, this often resulted in the contestation of key issues, as demonstrated by the debate over whether protesters should place their faith in the PUP or TUV to best represent their interests. Although the page administrators attempted to shape the nature of the debates that took place on these pages, they appeared unable to foster consensus about the future plans for the protests.

It was noticeable how the number of posts encouraging loyalists to participate in the protests decreased as the focus switched to republican trolling and increased media scrutiny of LPPUB. The J18 case marked a watershed moment in the role of public Facebook pages in the flag protest movement; from then onwards page administrators repeatedly warned posters not to post sensitive information online and took a proactive approach towards not only the online shaming of these 'trolls', but also the deletion of posts that might be deemed to incite violence. In terms of the former, journalists and alleged republican 'trolls' were subjected to vitriolic and sectarian abuse by loyalist commenters, usually prior to them being banned from the page. The concurrent increase in comments challenging the narratives of the flag protesters led many loyalists to call for the page to be made private in order to prevent such 'trolling'. Criticism of the flag protests on LPPU and LPPUB fell into several categories, including *ad hominem* attacks on Bryson and Frazer and fact-checking loyalist claims of police brutality. Whataboutery was invoked by both critics and supporters of the flag protesters, as both sides argued that the PSNI was biased against their respective communities. The combative and sectarian nature of these exchanges at least partially explained why there were fewer threads in which logistical and tactical mobilising information about the protests was shared towards the end of January 2013. Although access to LPPUB remained unrestricted through February 2013, the sharing of logistical information appeared to have migrated to more private spaces, such as individual Facebook pages and Instant Messaging apps. This finding was congruent with previous research suggesting that loyalists distrusted social media as a means of sharing significant messages (Nolan et al., 2014). Indeed, the study suggested that the antagonistic exchanges between critics and supporters on public Facebook pages reinforced the victim mentality of loyalist flag protesters, while simultaneously focusing attention on their lack of organisational coherence.

Notes

1 Dowson was a founding member of the far-right group Britain First. For more, see: www.dailyrecord.co.uk/news/politics/scots-ex-bnp-chief-seen-fuelling-1525117 (accessed 10 August 2014).

2 The Alliance Party issued a document of Frequently Asked Questions in relation to the dispute, providing a rationale for designated days.

3 Robinson defended the leaflet and called for an end to the violence. For more, see: www.bbc.co.uk/news/uk-northern-ireland-21003296 (accessed 10 August 2014).

4 Further information on Drumcree can be found here: https://cain.ulster. ac.uk/issues/parade/savaric98.htm (accessed 10 March 2018).

5 The NI CBI called for the Council to provide financial assistance to affected traders. For more, see: www.bbc.co.uk/news/uk-northern-ireland-20972438 (accessed 10 August 2014).

6 For more, see: www.theguardian.com/uk/2013/apr/03/union-flag-protests-arrested-northern-ireland (accessed 10 August 2014). According to Nolan et al. (2014), the final cost of the operation was £21.9 million.

7 Matt Baggott criticised senior UVF members for coordinating the violence in East Belfast in January 2013. For more see: www.theguardian.com/uk/2013/jan/07/senior-uvf-figures-belfast-violence.

8 This poll was conducted by IPSOS MORI on behalf of the BBC current affairs programme *Spotlight*. For more, see: www.bbc.co.uk/news/uk-northern-ireland-21331212.

9 These statistics were obtained by blogger Brian Spencer. They can be accessed here: http://eamonnmallie.com/2013/03/think-before-you-tweet/ (accessed 10 August 2014).

10 The man was not identified by the media for legal reasons. For more, see: www.belfasttelegraph.co.uk/news/northern-ireland/facebook-loyalist-flag-pages-shut-down-29039564.html (accessed 10 August 2014).

11 "Flag protests: Loyalty no excuse for violence, says police chief". BBC, 12 December 2012, available at: www.bbc.co.uk/news/uk-northern-ireland-20622185 (accessed 10 August 2014).

12 For an example of BBC coverage, see here: www.bbc.co.uk/news/uk-northern-ireland-20589957 (accessed 10 March 2018).

13 B. McDaid, "Para flags insult: massacre victim's sister urges calm", *Belfast Telegraph*, 19 January 2013, p. 13.

14 A. McKernon, "Flags Crisis – 'No substance' to claims about drafting gardai in", *Irish News*, 8 January 2013, p. 5.

15 A. Morris, "Flags Crisis – Analysis – Rallies run by 'movement' without structure or voice", *Irish News*, 21 December 2012, p. 12.

16 "Editorial – Little cause to silence Frazer", *Irish News*, 2 January 2013, p. 20.

17 "Editorial – Serious threats on social media", *Irish News*, 4 January 2013, p. 20.

18 D. McAleese, "I need more officers … what 'nervous' Baggott told MPs", *Belfast Telegraph*, 25 January 2013, p. 9.

19 D. McAleese, "Cocky Bryson taunts the Chief Constable as he dodges arrest over city flag protest marches", *Belfast Telegraph*, 28 February 2013, available at: www.belfasttelegraph.co.uk/news/northern-ireland/cocky-jamie-bryson-taunts-psni-chief-constable-as-he-dodges-arrest-over-city-flag-protest-marches-29099958.html (accessed 10 July 2018).

20 "Flags Crisis – Frazer: IRA put horse meat in beef burgers", *Irish News*, 26 January 2013, p. 2.

21 C. Young and M. Connolly, "Bryson Unmasked – Leading loyalist was mascot for Northern Ireland side just weeks before flag protests," *Irish News*, 26 February 2013.

22 For more analysis, see: http://belfastmediagroup.com/flag-protests-your-super-a-to-z-guide/ (accessed 10 August 2014).

3

"You can't eat a flag": Northern Ireland Twitter responds to the flag protests

Protest provocateurs such as Jamie Bryson and Willie Frazer were lambasted for attempting to take Northern Ireland back to the dark days of the Troubles. Fears of a return to such disorder were exacerbated by reports claiming that loyalists planned to disrupt electricity supplies in East Belfast.[1] Although this was nothing more than an unsubstantiated rumour, it was undeniable that the protests were damaging the local economy. Pubs of Ulster, the professional body for the Retail Licensed Trade in Northern Ireland, estimated that the dispute had caused a 30 per cent drop off in trade between December 2012 and February 2013.[2] The violent clashes between loyalist rioters and the police in areas such as East Belfast were also projected to have a very negative impact on the number of international tourists due to visit in 2013.

Twitter played a key role in mobilising affective publics who were angry and frustrated at the financial losses experienced by local businesses and traders, especially in Belfast City Centre. The loyalist action dubbed 'Operation Standstill' was a lightning rod for Northern Ireland Twitter, the small but highly active group of tweeters who dominate the discussion of contentious politics on the microblogging site. In addition to #backinbelfast, hashtags such as #positiveni, #takebackthecity and #Operationsitin emerged as conversation markers for tweeters wishing to criticise the protest provocateurs and express their opposition to the demonstrations. Cyber loyalists were named and shamed for posting hate speech online, with some tweeters mocking them for their poor spelling and grammar.[3]

Like the LPPU Facebook page analysed in the previous chapter, to date there has been no research exploring how Northern Ireland

Twitter responded to the flag protests. This chapter sets out to address this gap by empirically investigating these 'protest-response' hashtags. It does so by providing an overview of the literature on Twitter and hybrid media events, and presenting the results of a qualitative analysis of #flegs, one of the most popular hashtags used by critics of the protests. It explores the key influencers, the type of information shared and the characterisation of flag protesters within this hashtag.

Twitter as an ambient news environment

Twitter has the potential to disrupt hegemonic elites by turning ordinary citizens into opinion leaders (or 'influencers') and giving them a platform to make their voices heard (Murthy, 2013: 31). It differs from Facebook in the short length of each post, with each tweet initially restricted to just 140 characters before this limit was increased to 280 in November 2017.[4] Hence it is perhaps best defined as a microblogging platform, designed to "broadcast short but regular bursts of content" to audiences beyond a user's social network (Murthy, 2013: 12). Twitter's key functions include: the verbatim reposting of a tweet (Retweets); favourites (Favs) which allow tweeters to either endorse or bookmark tweets without specifying why; modified tweets (MTs) that alter the original post and usually provide additional commentary on its subject; and @replies that respond directly to a post from another tweeter (Bruns and Burgess, 2015: 25). Recent additions to the Twitter interface have raised the visibility of such content, as demonstrated by 'mentions' which allows tweeters to keep track of how other people are engaging with their posts (Tufekci, 2017: 55). As discussed in the Introduction, the social media company benefits financially each time citizens engage with content hosted on its platform.

Twitter has been characterised as an 'always-on, ambient news environment' ideally suited for breaking news stories (Murthy, 2013; Papacharissi, 2014). The hashtag, defined as the "prefixing of a keyword or phrase with the # symbol" (O'Reilly and Milstein, 2012: 43), typically shapes how people engage with these stories. First proposed by technologist Chris Messina in 2007 as a way of categorising groups on Twitter, hashtags emerged as key conversation markers around disasters. They have been utilised by both elite and non-elite actors to engage in a form of networked gatekeeping, the process whereby they co-create and co-curate flows of information during such incidents (Meraz and Papacharissi, 2013). For example, #qldfloods functioned as a news stream for those affected by the 2011 South East Queensland floods, enabling them to share their eyewitness testimonies with mainstream media and provide advice to other flood-affected residents (Bruns et al., 2012: 7). These communicative spaces also enable citizens to aid those caught up in disasters. Belgian citizens, for instance, used #hasselthelpt to connect stranded festival-goers with residents of a nearby town in the aftermath of the 2011 Pukkelpop disaster (Reilly and Atanasova, 2016). This illustrates how the microblogging platform facilitates the emergence of 'ad hoc publics' temporarily united by shared interests during crisis events (Bruns and Burgess, 2015).

Twitter, affective publics and hybrid media events

This chapter focuses on how citizens availed of the discursive affordances of Twitter to articulate their opposition to the flag protests. In this way, it provides further insight into how the storytelling structures of Twitter facilitate the emergence of affective publics. These formations leave distinctive digital footprints and are mobilised through "affective statements of both opinion and fact", making them ideal vehicles for connective actions (Papacharissi, 2016: 317). A popular hashtag is a form of 'presencing' for marginalised groups who lack agency and voice, allowing them not only to establish a public presence but also choose their own frames free from the ideological refraction of the news media (Couldry, 2012: 50). While these publics have the potential to disrupt dominant political narratives, they do not yet appear to have the capacity to sustain collective actions; indeed, their most significant contribution to digital activism may be symbolic insofar as they create an "online home" for social movements where "there is little happening on the ground" (Papacharissi, 2016: 317).

The polysemic nature of hashtags enables tweeters to express a range of different emotions during hybrid media events, defined as incidents "whose significance for media professionals, politicians, and non-elites is being reconfigured by the growth of social media" (Vaccari et al., 2015: 1044). While the classic definition of a media event proposed by Dayan and Katz (1992) emphasises its integrative function, its hybrid equivalent includes both 'ceremonial' and 'disruptive' incidents in which competing narratives emerge and shift as circumstances unfold (Sumiala et al., 2018: 12). Citizens now have much greater influence on the processes of 'making meaning' from such incidents (Vaccari et al., 2015: 1042). Indeed, platforms such as Twitter intensify communication about these events and enable both elite and non-elite actors to contribute to these news streams, demonstrate solidarity with others, and critique the broader socio-political context in which they occur (Sumiala et al., 2018). Chadwick (2013: 64) suggests that these processes are emblematic of a hybrid media system which weaves together older and newer media logics and provides "fluid opportunity structures" in which online citizens can intervene in these "political information cycles".

These public formations were perhaps best illustrated by the 'hashtagged solidarity' that emerged in the immediate aftermath of the November 2015 Paris terror attacks, which saw ISIS gunmen and suicide bombers kill 130 people in a series of coordinated atrocities in the city centre. Hashtags such as #parisattacks and #jesuisparis trended on Twitter as events unfolded on 13 November (Petersen et al., 2018). The former, like #qldfloods, was used to share both citizen and professional journalist accounts of incidents such as the siege at the Bataclan theatre. The connective affordances of Twitter were leveraged to provide material assistance to the thousands of citizens seeking shelter in the aftermath of the atrocities. Journalist Sylvain Lapoix urged citizens to tag their tweets with #PorteOuverte (or 'Open Door' in English) if they were looking for somewhere to stay or were able to offer refuge to others. #PorteOuverte had both affective and informational affordances, providing material assistance to those stranded as a result of the atrocities while allowing tweeters across the globe to express their solidarity with the victims. Universalism was also much in evidence in both #PrayforParis and #PrayforSyria, which trended on Twitter in the days following the attacks. There were few antagonistic tweets in both corpora, but those that conflated media, migration and terrorism in #PrayforSyria were heavily retweeted (O'Loughlin et al., 2017: 197). Despite non-elites having more opportunities to shape information flows during such incidents, pre-existing solidarities and antagonisms were inevitably reproduced in these hashtags. This chapter will explore whether the same trends emerged during the flag protests.

Northern Ireland Twitter responds to the flag protests

In early January 2013, there appeared to be little respite for Belfast city traders who had experienced significant financial losses during the first five weeks of disruption caused by the protests. Media headlines reminiscent of the Troubles referred to the 'mass exodus' of people from the city centre as they sought to avoid being caught up in the protests.[5] There were also signs that tourism in Northern Ireland was being harmed by the protest-related disorder. On travel website TripAdvisor, tourists reported that some of the protests had "gotten a bit hairy" during their visit to Belfast, while others contemplated cancelling their trip due to the "risk of bombs or other unrest".[6] Protest provocateurs, such as United Protestant Voice (UPV) leader Johnny Harvey, were undeterred by these negative headlines and announced plans for dozens of further protests over several consecutive days in early January. Further details of 'Operation Standstill' emerged in newspaper reports suggesting that rush-hour demonstrations were due to be held across Northern Ireland and "as far afield as Liverpool" on 11 January.[7] Specific information on these protest sites was not disclosed to the news media, with one anonymous loyalist source asserting they wanted to "catch the police on the hop and stretch them as thinly as possible".[8]

There was a swift response to Operation Standstill from Northern Irish tweeters who wished to express their support for city centre traders. Adam Turkington, programme director for the annual Culture Night Belfast, created #Operationsitin, a social media inspired campaign to encourage people to come out and support Belfast's bars and restaurants. People were invited to tag their tweets with this hashtag in order to "stand up against the protesters".[9] On the first night of the loyalist action, Turkington tweeted that "People of Belfast" should not let the protests put them off visiting the city centre, reminding them that "our eateries are well stocked & the kegs are full".[10] A similar sentiment was evident in #positiveni, which was used by tweeters to share positive images that countered the negative media headlines about the flag protests. The Northern Ireland Bureau, the diplomatic mission of the Executive in North America, was among several public bodies who encouraged tweeters to share photos of their favourite locations in the region.[11] Overall, these hashtags propagated affectively charged expression that was both critical of the protests and positive about the progress made since the 1998 Agreement.

#Backin' Belfast

These hashtags were overshadowed by a series of professional social media marketing campaigns promoting the 'brands' of Belfast and Northern Ireland. The award-winning #Backin'Belfast (BB), launched by the Belfast Visitor and Convention Bureau (BVCB) in January 2013, set out to "drive footfall in the city and restore confidence among citizens and businesses".[12] BB purchased advertising slots on print media and radio courtesy of the extensive financial support it received from the Department of Enterprise, Trade and Investment and Belfast City Council. The eponymous hashtag was used to share YouTube endorsements from local celebrities such as Snow Patrol frontman Gary Lightbody, who also gave permission for the band's song 'Take Back the City' to be used in its promotional videos. BB was lauded as one of the most successful campaigns of this nature in Ireland. Data provided by the BVCB showed that it had made 31.5 million Twitter 'impressions', with 88 per cent of consumers in the region seeing or hearing about the campaign.[13] This was one of several 'pro-business' social media hashtags that emerged during the flag protests, which included #takebackthecity, inspired by the song, and #LoveBelfast, which was used interchangeably with #backinbelfast to promote Belfast's hospitality sector. These 'brands' were attributed to blogger Inga Novilyte, who was alleged to have run a number of social media accounts promoting local businesses with her partner Andrew Donaldson, a Public Relations expert and former police officer. Like BB, they sought celebrity endorsements from the likes of Gary Lightbody and promoted #takebackthecity by giving away t-shirts to staff working in local hostelries. They extolled the virtues of a campaign that had not "cost the tax payer a penny" compared with the extensive funding received by BB.[14] Yet, they were subject to further scrutiny in light of media reports in March 2014 alleging that Love Belfast was not a registered company and that Donaldson had a previous criminal conviction for fraud.[15]

#Flegs

The publics affectively rendered by Twitter were also connected via black humour and irreverence. #Flegs was an example of 'wordplay' presumably created in order to mock the way working-class loyalists

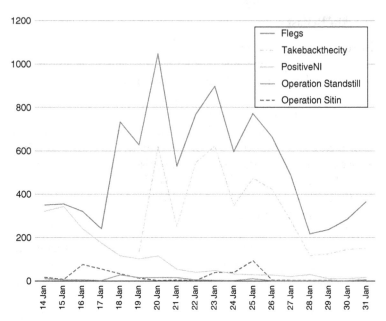

Figure 3.1 Tweets with flag protest response hashtags, 14–31 January 2013.

pronounced the word 'flag'. A time-series graph shows how there were more tweets tagged with #flegs (N = 4,479) than other hashtags such as #Operationstandstill (N = 105) during this period (see Figure 3.1).

While it was not possible to fully establish the origins of #flegs, it was already being used on the night of the controversial Belfast City Council vote to alter the flag protocol. Not all #flegs tweets gleefully mocked the protesters, nor engaged in the online shaming synonymous with 'parody group' Loyalists Against Democracy (LAD) (discussed in more detail in Chapter 5). The first iteration of #flegs contained many inoffensive tweets from public figures, including one from author and theatre producer Hugh Odling-Smee joking he was showing respect for everyone's identity by "wearing a celtic shirt and Union Jack pants".[16] The analysis presented below empirically explores the discursive affordances of #flegs, with a specific focus on whether this hashtag perpetuated negative stereotypes of the flag protesters.

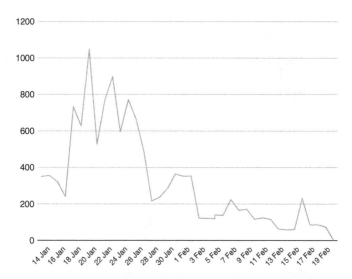

Figure 3.2 Number of tweets tagged #flegs, January–February 2013.

One research question was investigated in this study:

1. How did #flegs tweeters characterise the flag protesters?

This was explored through a thematic analysis of 4,479 tweets hashtagged with #flegs collected using Discovertext between 14 and 31 January 2013 (see Figure 3.2). The 'peak' on 20 January coincided with the loyalist protest outside a concert marking the beginning of Derry/Londonderry's term as UK City of Culture. There were further peaks in the final week of January 2013, following loyalist rioting in Newtownabbey and media coverage of Willie Frazer's allegation that the Provisional IRA had put horsemeat in beefburgers. As discussed in the Introduction, the limitations of the sampling technique meant that replies to these tweets were not available to the researcher.

The majority of the corpus consisted of retweets/modified tweets (56.3 per cent), followed by original tweets (25.1 per cent) and @ replies (18.6 per cent) (see Figure 3.3).

Geotagged tweets

There were few geotagged tweets in the corpus, with only 91 (2.03 per cent) tagged to a specific location by their respective authors. The

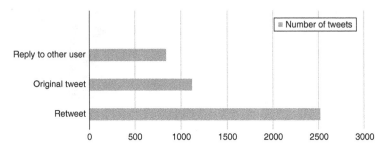

Figure 3.3 Classification of #flegs tweets.

overwhelming majority were within Northern Ireland (75), with most of these situated in the Greater Belfast area (33). One tweeter based in Carryduff, County Down tweeted eight times in the corpus, while another based in Carrickmore, County Tyrone was responsible for ten of these geotagged tweets. Other notable locations in the corpus included Vietnam, Sydney (Australia) and Tirana (Albania). All were deemed relevant to the study due to their use of the hashtag to engage with the flag protest issue. This dearth of geotagged tweets was congruent with previous research suggesting that geotagging is not a common practice among tweeters due to privacy concerns (Malik et al., 2015).

Profile of #flegs tweeters

A long tail distribution of user activity was evident in #flegs. Of 2,321 unique tweeters identified in the study, 1,702 (73.33 per cent) contributed only once to the hashtag. The top 50 most prolific tweeters were responsible for 44.1 per cent of the tweets in the dataset. These findings were congruent with previous research which suggests that small groups of highly engaged Twitter users dominate online conversations about political events (Anstead and O'Loughlin, 2011; Lotan et al., 2011).

Most (46 per cent) of the top 50 tweeters appeared to be citizens whose bios contained no information pertaining to their socio-political identity (see Figure 3.4). Bloggers and political commenters, such as Orangeman and unionist activist Alan Day (@Kilsally), accounted for 20 per cent of these 'super participants'. Five of the eight political tweeters self-identified themselves as republican, whereas there were

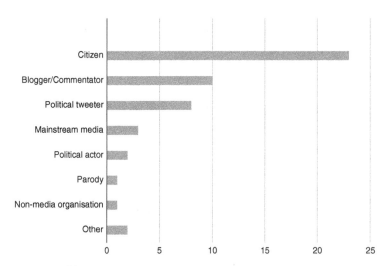

Figure 3.4 Top 50 #flegs tweeters by actor type.

no unionist or loyalist tweeters represented in this group. Elsewhere, it was perhaps surprising that there were more mainstream media organisations and professional journalists (three) than parody accounts, given the supposedly irreverent nature of this hashtag. Newspapers such as the *News Letter* (the third most active account, posting 58 tweets to the hashtag) used #flegs to draw attention to their coverage of the protests.

The actor analysis revealed that the majority (72.03 per cent) of #flegs tweeters were citizens who disclosed no political affiliation on their bios (see Figure 3.5). There were comparatively fewer political tweeters (6.55 per cent), professional journalists (2.5 per cent) and political actors (2.2 per cent). There were nearly twice as many republican political tweeters as loyalists, with one-fifth of the political tweeters in the dataset not disclosing their position on the constitutional status of Northern Ireland on their bios. Sinn Féin representatives accounted for nearly one-third of the political actors in the corpus, followed by the Alliance Party, Social Democratic and Liberal Party (SDLP), Northern Ireland Conservatives and Progressive Unionist Party (PUP). Representatives from the Democratic Unionist Party (DUP) (3) and Ulster Unionist Party (UUP) (1) made noticeably fewer contributions to #flegs during this period. It should

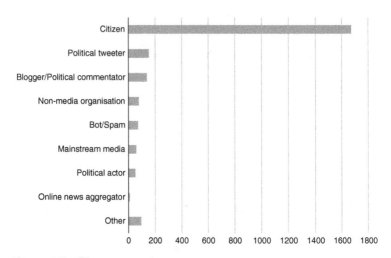

Figure 3.5 #Flegs tweeters by actor type.

be noted that the category of 'Other' included a number of parody accounts poking fun at public figures, such as Loyalists Against Democracy.

The study found four instances of what appeared to be bot activity in the hashtag. Probably the most significant one showed the negative impact of the protests: "So far there's reports of a GP being refused access to a patient by protesters and a man refused passage to visit his wife in hospital #flegs" was tweeted 22 times by 22 different tweeters between 19 January and 17 February 2013. Closer inspection of these Twitter accounts revealed that they had all been suspended by March 2014. Subsequent searches revealed that an identical tweet had been posted from Wishaw Cairde (@WMCairde), a republican account, a week earlier, on 12 January. A similar pattern emerged in relation to three other tweets condemning the protesters. For example, "Watching the Nolan show and slowly losing hope for humanity #arseholes #flegs" was tweeted eight times between 19 January and 26 February via eight different Twitter handles. While these accounts had also been suspended by the time of data analysis, an identical tweet authored by Brandy (@Hairemovalcalgc) was discovered. According to its score (4.5 out of 5) on Botometer (https://botometer.iuni.iu.edu/#!/) this account was highly likely to be a bot. Clearly it is difficult to say for certain whether these were bots or an orchestrated campaign by critics to shape conversations about the flag dispute on the hashtag. It should also be acknowledged that none of the tweets posted by these suspect accounts had been retweeted in the corpus, suggesting that if it had indeed been a coordinated effort to manipulate #flegs it had been unsuccessful.

Authors of retweeted content

A total of 379 unique tweeters were responsible for the 606 #flegs tweets retweeted during the period of data collection. The actor analysis again found that the majority (58.05 per cent) were citizens who expressed no political preferences in their profile information (see Figure 3.6). The next most prominent actor types were political tweeters (9.76 per cent), followed by non-media organisations, such as Hudson Bar (@HudsonBar) (4.49 per cent), and bloggers/political commenters, such as Mick Fealty (@mickfealty) (4.22 per cent). As per the actor analysis for the entire dataset, a clear majority of political actors and tweeters in this cohort were supportive of Sinn Féin and the republican movement. Finally, the category of Other included parody accounts such as Union Fleg (@UnionFleg) and sports personalities such as Ulster Rugby player Darren Cave (@darrencave13). Although there were fewer professional journalists

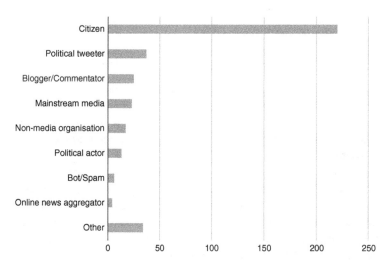

Figure 3.6 Authors of retweeted content in #flegs.

and media organisations than citizens in this group, their tweets were among the most shared in the corpus. For instance, the *Irish News* security correspondent Allison Morris 'authored' the most retweeted tweet, which was shared 75 times; she refuted loyalist claims that the media were "not covering flag protests fairly", alleged that she had been threatened six times during the protests and warned "if we [journalists] can't work safely we can't cover [the protests]".[17]

A total of 214 tweets were deemed non-relevant to the study. These included tweets referring to supporters of Glasgow Celtic and Rangers Football Clubs bringing flags to their matches. One tweet from Belfast Giants ice hockey player Stephen Murphy, tagged with #flegs and shared 19 times, showed a picture of his teammate Andrew Dickson with the number 35 written on his back and appeared to have no reference to the flag issue.[18] Tweets posted by a far-right blogger on a range of topics including an alleged Zionist conspiracy behind the 9/11 attacks were also removed as part of this process. While acknowledging that this might have been evidence of how such groups were trying to hijack #flegs, it was not considered relevant to the study's focus on representations of the flag protesters. In addition, 58 tweets were no longer available for analysis and were therefore excluded. A critical thematic analysis of the remaining tweets (N = 4,207) was conducted between January and June 2014.

Results and discussion

Northern Ireland Twitter versus the 'Loyalist Spring'

There was unsurprisingly little support for the flag protests among the #flegs tweeters. With the exception of a couple of loyalists who mistook the hashtag for one articulating the grievances of the protesters, the overwhelming majority expressed their anger at the impact of the protests on the local economy, the peace process, and the reputation of Northern Ireland overseas. In the last two weeks of January 2013 in particular, there were many tweets from citizens clearly frustrated at being stuck in traffic jams caused by the nightly protests. Images of police Land Rovers and deserted streets in Belfast City Centre were shared under the hashtag in order to illustrate the impact of this disruption on Belfast's retail sector. The consensus was that this was an unnecessary distraction from more important issues, such as the austerity cuts to public services and high levels of youth unemployment since 2010. This sentiment was perhaps best articulated in several tweets citing a soundbite attributed to former SDLP leader John Hume: "You can't eat a Flag". Many also tagged their tweets #backinbelfast and #takebackthecity in support of the eponymous campaigns, and explicitly expressed their support for independent businesses and shops said to be on the verge of closure due to the reduced footfall in the city centre. This narrative was challenged by a couple of tweeters who argued that areas such as the Woodstock Road in East Belfast had been 'dead' several months before the protests began. Such claims were dismissed by tweeters such as Matt Johnston (@cimota), who reported that shop owners who had been coping with the recession had been "finished off" by the protests.[19] There were also numerous vignettes about how people's lives were being negatively impacted by the 'Loyalist Spring', a sarcastic reference to the uprisings in the Middle East and North Africa a year earlier. For example, Faith and Pride, a group of gay Christians based in Belfast, used the hashtag to announce that they were cancelling planned social events due to the "expected civil disobedience".[20]

Professional journalists influential but heavily criticised for fixation with protests

#Flegs was used to break news about the protests, such as the UPF decision to move to white line protests and the PSNI's decision to release images of suspected rioters caught on CCTV to the news media. Both citizens and professional journalists co-curated these information flows within the hashtag, the former often providing links to articles on the websites of media organisations such as the *Belfast Telegraph*. As demonstrated by the aforementioned tweet by Allison Morris, informational tweets from professional journalists were much more heavily retweeted than those of citizens. These often provided no visual corroborative evidence, as demonstrated by a text-only tweet by BBC NI journalist Kevin Sharkey on 18 January confirming that protests were "blocking Woodstock link, Donegall Road at Broadway, Shore road Mt.Vernon".[21] The *News Letter* official account used the hashtag to share links to its online coverage of the protests, which included one tweet (retweeted eight times) that linked to a page on its website carrying an official statement by the UPF accusing the PSNI of "political policing".[22] That is not to say that citizens themselves were not collecting information about the protests and sharing it via the hashtag. Indeed, many posted links to a website (nicrowdmap.com) containing information on the location and times of Operation Standstill protests. There were also many tweets in the corpus warning commuters about traffic delays on key arterial roads in the Greater Belfast area. However, for the most part, the informational dimension of the hashtag appeared to revolve around the coverage provided by mainstream media and professional journalists, many of whom had been deployed to cover the nightly street protests and weekly rallies at Belfast City Hall.

Although mainstream media and professional journalists were clearly influential in the information flows in the hashtag, they were not held in high esteem by many of the #flegs contributors. The news media were frequently criticised for giving airtime to loyalist activists such as Bryson, with republican tweeters accusing journalists from organisations such as RTE (Ireland's national public service broadcaster) of overlooking their 'racist agenda' and erroneously depicting the protests as peaceful. Citizens also engaged in 'dual screening', the process of switching between broadcast media and social media to provide commentary during media events (Anstead and O'Loughlin, 2011; Vaccari et al., 2015). Tweets in the corpus were hashtagged #nolan, #spotlightni and #utvinsight in response to debates about the flag dispute on the eponymous shows. More than two-thirds of these referred to the radio and television programmes hosted by BBC Northern Ireland presenter Stephen Nolan. He was criticised for fixating on the protests at the expense of bigger issues such as the rise in youth unemployment or the plight of Oscar Knox, a child diagnosed with cancer who had been interviewed on one of his shows in January 2013. Statements made by Bryson and DUP representatives on these programmes claiming the protests had been peaceful were strongly rejected on the hashtag. Nolan was maligned by a few tweeters for not challenging Bryson about a YouTube video in which he appeared to cheer as loyalists attacked houses in Short Strand during one of the weekly Saturday marches past the nationalist enclave. Tweeters also criticised a 'loyalist mob' in the audience for Nolan's television show, which was considered unrepresentative of the views of the wider population on the flag dispute. Many derogatory and offensive remarks were made about individual audience members, including several tweets fat-shaming a loyalist woman who spoke during the show. These citizens, the majority of whom did not self-identify as either loyalist or republican on their bios, felt that Nolan's 'platforming' of speakers such as Bryson legitimised what was widely perceived as a campaign of unlawful street protests.

This 'dual screening' also illustrated the level of political partisanship on social media during this period of political volatility. Results from a poll commissioned for the BBC *Spotlight* programme, which aired on 6 February, were contested by republicans in a flurry of tweets accusing the programme makers of ignoring Irish identity needs in the survey. Its representativeness was also challenged by some tweeters, one of whom crudely suggested that pollsters must have only knocked the doors of the 'retired, ill and unemployed'. Elsewhere, several tweeters characterised a debate on *UTV Insight* about the flag dispute as 'depressing' due to the lack of common ground between unionist and nationalist politicians debating the issue. There was also a handful of tweets in the corpus, both critical and supportive, focusing on a Channel 4 mini-documentary in which the owner of the restaurant 'Made in Belfast' intimated that she would be relocating due to the protests. Overall, mainstream media appeared to be very influential in the information flows on the hashtag, courtesy of the heavy retweeting of content produced by professional journalists and the ways in which citizens linked to articles posted on their websites and social media. However, the news media were often accused of failing to accurately capture the views of the 'embarrassed majority'.

Loyalist culture war narrative dismissed by #flegs tweeters

The rationale for the flag protests was heavily criticised by the overwhelming majority of #flegs tweeters. They frequently reminded loyalists that the controversial decision by the Belfast City Council merely brought Belfast in line with flag protocols elsewhere in the United Kingdom. Several tweets provided visual evidence of how the flag had only flown over Belfast City Hall on designated days between 1910 and the 1950s. The loyalist 'culture war' narrative, so frequently invoked on LPPU and LPPUB (see Chapter 2), was unsurprisingly given little credence here. A meme, shared 11 times during the period of data collection, articulated the frustration of many tweeters at the erroneous claims by Bryson and others that the 'equality agenda' had removed cultural and political rights from loyalists. It stated "You're not being 'oppressed' when another group gains rights that you've always had".[23] A couple of tweets also accused loyalists of hypocrisy for demanding respect for the Union Flag whilst burning the Irish tricolour during a protest outside Belfast City Hall. Republican community worker and visual artist Breandán Clarke went as far as to suggest that it was the "unionist/loyalist psyche" that couldn't adjust to the issue of equality.[24] Elsewhere, the talking points deployed by protest spokespersons such as Bryson and Frazer were brutally dismantled by tweeters contributing to the hashtag. Most notably, loyalist claims that the dispute had been caused by the Alliance Party were challenged by tweeters, who referred to the controversial anti-Alliance leaflet distributed in the run-up to the divisive vote.

Many of the #flegs tweeters felt loyalists were the beneficiaries rather than the victims of 'political' policing. Unsubstantiated anecdotal evidence was often provided to illustrate how the PSNI were caving in to loyalist 'bigots' who were bringing the region to a standstill. For example, one tweeter claimed to have witnessed a police officer asking a bus driver whether they should ask the protesters to move aside to allow the vehicle to pass. Loyalist claims of 'PSNIRA' brutality towards the protesters were dismissed in the corpus. Most notably, there were a small number of tweets focusing on the 'sousveillance' footage of the man arrested in East Belfast on 26 January, which had been shared and contested on LPPU (see Chapter 2). While one tweeter did acknowledge that his legs had been tied together, its sousveillant properties were dismissed in a number of tweets querying why he hadn't been treated for any injuries given the allegedly 'brutal' attack captured on camera. As per the LPPU debate over the footage, one tweeter provided a link to a BBC news report to debunk claims he was a pensioner and show that he had been charged with resisting arrest. An element of 'whataboutery' also existed in many of these responses, amid claims that there was one law for flag protesters and another for the nationalist residents of Ardoyne, who the PSNI had prevented from obstructing a contentious Orange Order Twelfth parade in the area a few months earlier (to be discussed in Chapter 6). The flag protesters were also told that they didn't know the meaning of the term 'police brutality' in a tweet sharing footage of nationalist Garvaghy Road residents being physically removed from the road in order to facilitate a contentious Orange Order parade in Portadown in 1997. Blogger and activist Dara Gallagher (@dargall) perhaps best captured this sentiment, asserting that "battering" nationalist and republicans was defined as 'sensible policing' while the same approach applied to flag protesters was considered 'heavy-handed'.[25] Nevertheless, the PSNI's decision to take a firmer line on the protests at the end of January 2013 was broadly welcomed by these tweeters.

Loyalist assertions that their protests were both lawful and peaceful were heavily contested. One tweeter quoted Karen Quinlivan QC's statement that those participating on the weekly march past Short Strand were engaging in an "illegal activity".[26] The failure of the protesters to apply for permission from the Parades Commission for the weekly marches from East Belfast to the City Hall was frequently referred to in these tweets. Others shared links to official legal sources defining the right to peaceful assembly and protest, presumably with the intention of highlighting the illegality of the street demonstrations. For example, Professor Aoife Nolan, an expert in International Human Rights Law, directed "flegs fans" to the UN Special Rapporteur on the parameters of peaceful assembly.[27] There were many references to the fact that loyalists were breaking the law by covering their faces and blocking the 'Queen's Highway'. Indeed, one of the most heavily shared images in the corpus (retweeted 26 times after being posted on 16 February) was a picture of a sign erected by the PSNI saying "No face coverings beyond this point", which was captioned "only in Belfast Lol".[28] If anything, the decision to move to white line protests after 31 January coincided with an increase in criticism of the tactics used by the protesters. Concerns were raised about cars being attacked if their drivers didn't 'beep their horns' in support as they passed protesters positioned on the white lines down the middle of the road. However, there were many more warning that the recent snowfall had made many of the roads 'treacherous' and that positioning protesters so close to oncoming traffic would lead to someone getting killed. The white lines decision was one of several announcements by UPF spokespersons that were condemned and mocked by tweeters in equal measure. For example, Bryson's statement urging loyalists to refuse to pay bail charges and accept jail sentences was met with much derision. Political commentator Chris Ryder was among those to tweet his hopes that the courts would "lavishly reward the jail-wish of Bryson and his #flegs ilk" by giving them long sentences.[29] The prominent role of teenagers (labelled 'feral' by a few tweeters) and ex-BNP fundraiser Jim Dowson in the protests were also condemned, as was the involvement of loyalist paramilitaries in the violence seen in East Belfast in January 2013.

Playing the man, not the ball?

#Flegs functioned as a communicative space in which Northern Irish tweeters directed their anger towards flag protest spokespersons such as Willie Frazer and Jamie Bryson. The latter in particular was the subject of many memes, one of which was an advert for a fictional breakfast cereal ridiculing his speech impediment. Pictures of the North Down activist holding a hurling stick and an 'Erin Go Bragh' flag were also circulated during this period, with tweeters jokingly describing him as a republican secret agent.[30] Loyalist suggestions that Bryson was 'Ulster's Mandela' were ridiculed, with a screenshot of a Facebook post that likened him to the South African anti-apartheid revolutionary shared under the hashtag for the amusement of others. It was a surprise then that so few of these tweets tagged the Twitter accounts of the two most prominent protest provocateurs (only 8 for Bryson and 10 for Frazer). Those that did so challenged them on the veracity of their public statements. One cited census data from 2011 showing that there were 17,000 more Catholics than Protestants in Belfast, presumably to remind Bryson that the city no longer had a majority of residents identifying as either unionists or loyalists.[31] Frazer was reminded that protesters were breaking the law when they obstructed roads, as well as being tagged in abusive tweets calling him a 'pumpkin pie hair cutted freak' and a 'wee weasel'. It is fair to say that such tweets failed to conform to the 'play the ball, not the man' etiquette promoted by *Slugger O'Toole*.

The vast majority of abusive comments about the two most prominent UPF spokespersons were not specifically targeted at their official accounts. This might have been due to the fact that many tweeters didn't know what their handles were. An alternative interpretation was that they were sharing these comments under #flegs for the amusement of others rather than to get into a row with Bryson and Frazer. For the purposes of brevity, it is not possible to list all the offensive terms used to describe them here, but they included references to Frazer being a 'pervert', and 'losing his marbles' in light of his Provisional IRA horsemeat conspiracy theory. His withdrawal from a protest in Castlederg due to ill health on 25 January was also mocked by these tweeters, with one suggesting that he must have eaten a 'dodgy burger' in a tweet that appeared to reference this story. Frazer subsequently revealed in an interview for the *Belfast Telegraph* that he was being treated for cancer during the protests.[32] Bryson bore the brunt of the abuse from #flegs tweeters, who referred to him using a series of crude nicknames such as "loyalist skeletor" and "Orville the duck" (a reference to his alleged similarity to the puppet used by ventriloquist Keith Harris on UK children's television shows in the 1980s). Tweets mentioning him by name were frequently written in such a way as to make fun of his speech impediment. For example, one tweet mocked his announcement that he would stand in the Mid-Ulster by-election by claiming that "Jim Bwyson" was a "gweat candidate" and 'rwising star'. He was also compared to gay icon and 1980s popstar Jimmy Somerville and urged to 'come out of the closet' in a couple of tweets alluding to his opposition to equal marriage but paradoxically conveying homophobic sentiments. Similar undertones were evident in tweets mocking Frazer's removal as an official UPF spokesperson, with references to him and Bryson having had a 'lovers' tiff'.

There were no such ad hominem attacks upon unionist political representatives, despite the fact that they were heavily criticised for the controversial anti-Alliance leaflet issued in the run-up to the Council vote on the flag protocol. The DUP were accused of adopting a contradictory stance on the flag dispute which saw some party representatives participate in street protests despite its leadership calling for their cessation. Its leader, and First Minister, Peter Robinson was lambasted for claiming that the arrest of Shankill Road bomber Sean Kelly in connection with a paramilitary-style assault in North Belfast posed a greater challenge to the peace process than the protests. His UUP counterpart Mike Nesbitt was accused of being [Ian] Paisley's 'lapdog' and turning the second largest pro-union party in Northern Ireland into the DUP of the 1980s. The TUV were called out for cynically exploiting the flag dispute to gain votes, with their leader Jim Allister branded a hypocrite for sharing a platform with Jim Dowson while proclaiming his support for law and order. It was not just unionist politicians who were subject to criticism on the hashtag. Sinn Féin's call for a border poll was characterised by several tweeters as 'unhelpful' and 'pouring petrol on the flames' of the protests. Such tweets were nevertheless few in number and greatly overshadowed by the negative remarks about unionist politicians. That said, there were some positive observations about political actors in the corpus. With the exception of a couple of critical comments about its proposal for a 'quango' to address the flag issue, there was much support for the besieged Alliance Party, with one tweeter suggesting they might see an increase in their vote due to people voting in protest at the '#flegs idiocy'. An image of a second anti-Alliance party leaflet distributed in East Belfast was shared and condemned by several tweeters, while another contributor asserted that it was a 'sad day for democracy' when Naomi Long's East Belfast constituency office had to be protected by 18 police vehicles. There were also a few tweets from citizens expressing support for UUP MLA for Lagan Valley Basil McCrea in January 2013, a period in which he faced disciplinary action from his party for contradicting its position on the flag issue by supporting the designated days protocol. However, these were outliers in a discursive space that was dominated by voices critical of unionist political representatives, in particular for their failure to address the zero-sum notions of identity that underpinned the flag protests.

#Flegs: inoffensive wordplay or reinforcing (negative) stereotypes of working-class loyalists?

A somewhat existential debate about the hashtag began on 20 January 2013. Journalist Eamonn Mallie revealed that he and his colleagues had refrained from using #flegs as they felt it was "designed to offend", and asked others what they thought of this stance.[33] Several citizens echoed these sentiments and criticised journalists for using a hashtag that was 'condescending' and 'demeaning' towards the protesters. PUP leader John Kyle was among those to highlight the 'middle-class snobbery' perpetuated by the #flegs hashtag. One tweeter noted that those who opposed the #flegs protests appeared to be as sectarian as those who supported them. However, there were nearly three times as many tweets in the corpus defending the hashtag as a humorous response to the flag dispute. Mick Fealty was among those to respond to Mallie's tweet explaining that he had used "#flegs with gusto, on the basis of its currency to discuss the current political situation in Northern Ireland on the microblogging site".[34] Political activist Áine McGrath noted that 'Twitter vigilantes' were focusing on the hashtag while she and others were more bothered by the "display of #flegs on NI's lamp posts!"[35] Many tweeters in the corpus felt that it was an inoffensive 'play on dialect' and provided much needed 'comic relief' from the 'sorry saga' of the flag protests. It was also praised for being a unique identifier for social media discussion about the protests, with one tweet suggesting that it was one of the 'few things' uniting people during the protests. Somewhat ironically, this succinctly captured the 'othering' of working-class loyalists that was so heavily criticised by John Kyle and others.

There were certainly some signs that #flegs contributors were perpetuating negative stereotypes of working-class loyalists. Both republicans and seemingly unaffiliated citizens referred to the protesters variously as 'illiterate thugs', 'knuckledraggers' and suggested they were unemployed and had nothing better to do. While the term 'chav' wasn't present in the corpus, loyalists were often portrayed as possessing the same negative traits of racism, laziness and violence that dominate media representations of the white working class in Great Britain (Jones, 2011; Tyler, 2013). Hopes were expressed that the "dole cunts" would freeze in the inclement weather conditions and that the PSNI would use snow ploughs to clear them off the roads. There were also a few tweets comparing the protesters to guests on the *Jeremy Kyle Show* and the stars of MTV reality television show *Geordie Shore*, both of which were associated with the 'chav' stereotype. Many offensive remarks about the physical appearance and attire of the protesters were also made. For instance, the publication of images of suspected loyalist rioters in several local newspapers was met with a number of sneery comments about how they could at least have afforded a decent haircut. There was also some evidence of sectarianism in tweets demonising loyalists as 'English colonists' and 'huns'. However, the vast majority of these offensive posts about loyalists were not retweeted during the period of data collection. This was in contrast to tweets that sought to either embarrass or shame individual loyalists. For example, one of the most shared posts in the corpus (retweeted 28 times) contained a screenshot of a comment on a loyalist Facebook page urging supporters to 'raise a toast' to the British Army on the anniversary of the 1972 Bloody Sunday massacre. The online shaming of working-class loyalists will be discussed further in Chapter 5 but it is worth noting here that #flegs tweeters focused more on the poor spelling and grammar of loyalists than the hate speech

found on their Facebook pages. Author, and former republican prisoner, Tim Brannigan was among those to highlight their "reckless
disregard for punctuation" in a tweet mocking an anti-Alliance party
leaflet distributed to Belfast shopkeepers.[36] Although these tweets
may have been designed to build some form of bonhomie with other
#flegs contributors, they contributed to the 'othering' of working-class
loyalists by characterising them as 'uneducated bigots' detached from
the rest of society.

Nevertheless, irreverent humour was much more prevalent in the
corpus than tweets reinforcing negative portrayals of working-class
loyalists. There was an unashamed lack of respect for authority figures
in many of the memes hashtagged #flegs. The most shared image
(retweeted 28 times) was a picture of Queen Elizabeth II captioned
"Do I Look Like I Give a Fuck", presumably in reference to the flag
dispute. Parody accounts were a prominent vehicle for such irreverence, with a fabricated story about the Queen being deeply embarrassed by the protests posted on a parody *Sky News* account mistaken
for a real news story by several tweeters. Other digital artefacts found
in the dataset included a flag protest themed version of the *Dmitri
Finds Out* meme and *Belfast Bigot/No Surrender*, in which footage
of a woman shouting "No Surrender" through a broken window at
Belfast City Hall was superimposed over a reindeer.[37] The latter's
focus on an individual loyalist protester was exceptional in a corpus
punctuated by memes that were typically irreverent rather than offensive. These invariably revolved around the Union Flag itself. For
example, a meme advertising the fictional 'Fleg Specs' (containing an
image of Queen Elizabeth II and a dog wearing glasses with Union
Flags imposed upon them) was shared by several tweeters. Citizens
often shared images of food products and advertising billboards that
had Union Flags on them, which they joked reminded them of the
protests. There were also many puns offering no commentary on the
legitimacy of the protests that were congruent with the defence that
#flegs was an innocuous play on dialect. These included tweets show-
ing pictures of snowmen holding Union Flags captioned #snowsur-
render, and suggestions that those tweeting about the weather should
be referring to 'sneagh' rather than snow. Overall, the study suggested
that the hashtag was, to paraphrase one of Liz Fawcett's tweets on the
matter, "not designed to offend" but was certainly patronising towards
loyalists at times.[38]

Conclusion

Northern Ireland Twitter was unsurprisingly critical of the flag protests. Hashtags such as #flegs constituted important conversation markers on the microblogging platform for those affected by the protests. Although mainstream media were often lambasted for giving airtime to unelected loyalist representatives such as Bryson and Frazer, they remained influential sources of information on a hashtag that functioned as a news stream co-curated by citizens and professional journalists. The hashtag was also utilised by citizens to 'dual screen' debates about the flag dispute on programmes such as *Nolan Live*. Such hybrid media events revealed the high level of political partisanship and animosity towards the protesters during this period. While there was limited evidence to support the notion that #flegs was disrupting the central role of the news media in the Northern Irish information ecosystem, there were certainly some signs that the hashtag was 'presencing' critical voices that were ignored by mainstream media and political elites. Loyalist culture war narratives and claims of 'political policing' were invariably dismissed by tweeters, who felt that the PSNI should be taking stronger action against the protesters. Most notably, the 'sousveillance' footage of a 42-year-old man being arrested in East Belfast, shared via LPPU and other loyalist social media accounts, was fact-checked with reference to media coverage of the incident. The legitimacy of protests that blocked arterial routes across the region was also called into question by citizens and researchers who shared links to legal texts defining the rights of peaceful assembly and protest. There was also much incredulity at loyalist claims that the protests were largely peaceful and that the violent scenes in East Belfast were caused by the 'PSNIRA'.

The affective dimension of #flegs was much more significant than its role as a news stream. These were networked publics connected by their anger and frustration at the disruption caused by the flag protests. Unionist political representatives were accused of inflaming sectarian tensions around the issue and abdicating responsibility for the economic and reputational harm inflicted upon Northern Ireland as a result of the protests. However, it was Bryson and Frazer who bore the brunt of this anger on #flegs. The study found evidence of ad hominem and even homophobic abuse towards Jamie Bryson and Willie Frazer, much of which 'played the man, not the ball'. Suspected bot accounts were part of a campaign to 'troll' loyalists on Twitter and shape conversations about the flag dispute on the hashtag. This genre of #flegs tweets was notable for the sectarian and offensive language used by some tweeters to portray working-class loyalists as 'uneducated bigots'. Certainly, references to loyalists being unemployed appeared to lend support for this critique of the hashtag. As per the chav stereotype of white working-class communities in mainland Britain, flag protesters were portrayed as variously lazy, racist and violent. However, the analysis suggested that the public expression hosted on the hashtag was more often than not irreverent, rather than malicious. Hence the memes and puns that were the most widely shared in the corpus typically revolved around a play on dialect, as opposed to the online shaming of working-class loyalists associated with groups such as LAD during this period. Those viewing the hashtag between January and March 2013 were more likely to find pictures of snowmen holding Union Flags rather than tweets mocking the appearance of protest leaders such as Bryson. This reflected the polysemic nature of #flegs; while some used the conversation marker to express their anger at the protesters in an abusive and vitriolic manner, others saw it as 'comic relief' from the daily disruption they caused.

Notes

1 C. Young, "Flags Crisis – Loyalists planning 'Operation Standstill'", *Irish News*, 11 January 2013, p. 6.
2 G. McDonald and S. Cunningham, "Business – International investors put off by flag protests", *Irish News*, 5 March 2013.
3 For more on these hashtags, see here: https://knowyourmeme.com/memes/events/northern-ireland-flag-protests-2012-13 (accessed 10 January 2018).
4 Twitter justified the change on the basis that it would stop people having to "cram their thoughts into 140 characters". For more on this, see: https://blog.twitter.com/official/en_us/topics/product/2017/Giving-you-more-characters-to-express-yourself.html (accessed 10 January 2018).
5 D. McAleese, "Blockades And Riots On Road To Nowhere; Mass exodus from city, then protests turn to violence", *Belfast Telegraph*, 12 January 2013.
6 S. McGonagle, "Flag Protests – Visitors take to website to discuss Belfast fears", *Irish News*, 9 February 2013.
7 A. Fox, "Flag protests continue on countdown to Operation Standstill', *News Letter*, 7 January 2013, available at: www.newsletter.co.uk/news/

flag-protests-continue-on-countdown-to-operation-standstill-1-4652861 (accessed 10 May 2018).

8 "Revealed: Union Flag 'Operation Standstill' Plan To Bring Province To A Halt On Friday", *Belfast Daily*, 8 January 2013, available at: www.belfastdaily.co.uk/2013/01/08/revealed-union-flag-operation-standstill-plan-to-bring-province-to-a-halt-on-friday/ (accessed 10 May 2018).

9 Turkington was interviewed about #OperationSitin in several local news outlets, including UTV. For more, see: www.itv.com/news/update/2013-01-11/belfast-hits-back-with-operation-sit-in/ (accessed 10 May 2018).

10 Adam Turkington, "People of Belfast Be not afraid. Our eateries are well stocked & the kegs are full. This is the weekend. You know the drill #OperationSitIn," 11 January 2013, 11.08 p.m., Tweet.

11 For more on this, see: https://washdiplomat.com/index.php?option=com_content&view=article&id=12121:northern-ireland-punches-above-its-weight-in-digital-diplomacy&catid=1533&Itemid=428 (accessed 10 November 2018).

12 The campaign received the Digital Tourism Think Tank Award in 2013. For more on the campaign, see: www.thinkdigital.travel/opinion/backin-belfast-campaign/ (accessed 10 May 2018).

13 For more on the campaign, see "Digital Tourism Think Tank: Backin' Belfast", 7 February 2013, available at: https://thinkdigital.travel/awards 2013/backinbelfastcompressed.pdf (accessed 10 March 2018).

14 This critique of 'Backin' Belfast' appeared on the Love Belfast blog a few months after the campaign. For more, see: "Who's #BackinBelfast now? Or is the £1.5 million advertising budget spent? Time to #takebackthecity", 9 May 2013, available at: https://lovebelfast.co.uk/whos-backinbelfast-now-or-is-the-1-5-million-advertising-budget-spent-time-to-takebackthecity/ (accessed 10 May 2018).

15 C. Barnes, "PR Guru behind 'Love Belfast' brand is corrupt cop and shameless fraudster", *Sunday Life*, 24 March 2014, available at: www.belfasttelegraph.co.uk/sunday-life/news/pr-guru-behind-love-belfast-brand-is-corrupt-cop-and-shameless-fraudster-30118498.html (accessed 10 March 2018).

16 Hugh Odling-Smee, "I'm wearing a celtic shirt and Union Jack pants. Hedging my bets, and showing dignity and respect for everyone's identity. #flegs", 3 December 2012, 12.48 p.m., Tweet.

17 Allison Morris, "Re: Loyalist claims media not covering flag protests fairly since #flegs I've been threatened 6 times if we can't work safely we cant cover", 26 January 2013, 11:45 p.m., Tweet.

18 Stephen Murphy, "Dick back from @LaSourceBeauty All ready for the weekend #backinbelfast wearing his 35 #flegs", 8.34 p.m., Tweet.

19 Matt Johnston, "@ericn131 I'm not blaming anyone. Shop owners are saying they were coping with the recession, the #flegs have finished them off", 8 February 2013, 12:48 p.m., Tweet.

20 Faith and Pride, "Unfortunately, due to the expected civil disobedience, Faith, Pride, and Chat tomorrow is cancelled:(#flegs #FPC)", 24 January 2013, 11:33 p.m., Tweet.

21 Kevin Sharkey, "#protests are blocking Woodstock link, Donegall Road at Broadway, Shore road Mt. Vernon #flegs", 18 January 2013, 6.12 p.m., Tweet.

22 *News Letter*, "People's Forum accuses PSNI of political policing – Headlines – Belfast Newsletter http://t.co/8pNkJerB #flegs", 22 January 2013, 7.59 p.m., Tweet.

23 Marie Broderick, "#Flegs This could have been written for all the fleg protesters and rioters", 1 February 2013, 12:46 a.m., Tweet.

24 Breandan Clarke, "@ornayoung @mickfealty @eamonnmallie Yep,#flegs is a mere bagatelle. Issue is one of #equality and how unionist/loyalist psyche can't adjust", 20 January 2013, 10:23 a.m., Tweet.

25 Dara Gallagher, "In NI 'Sensible policing' means battering crap out of Nats/Republicans. Heavy handed policing is doing same to #flegs protestor", 30 January 2013, 11:13 p.m., Tweet.

26 This statement was from the hearing that led to a judicial review of the legality of the flag protests. For more on this, see: www.belfastdaily. co.uk/2013/02/01/nationalist-resident-granted-leave-over-union-flag-protests/ (accessed 10 October 2018).

27 Aoife Nolan, "Impt reading for #flegs fans: Full statement by UN Special Rapporteur on peaceful assembly on UK visit http://t.co/bN9bh8rE", 24 January 2013, 9.46 a.m., Tweet.

28 Ryan Wilkinson, "Only in Belfast! Lol #flegs #fashionpolice", 16 February 2013, 12:51 p.m., Tweet.

29 Chris Ryder, "I do hope police and the courts lavishly reward the jail-wish of Bryson and his #flegs ilk by handing them long and generous sentences", 23 January 2013, 11.15 a.m., Tweet.

30 Hurling is a sport traditionally associated with Irish nationalism. 'Erin go Bragh' translates into 'Ireland Forever' and is frequently used to express allegiance to Ireland.

31 For more on this, see Nolan (2014).

32 Frazer stated that he had been diagnosed with cancer of the stomach and bowel in an interview in March 2013. He died from cancer in June 2019. For more, see here: www.belfasttelegraph.co.uk/opinion/columnists/willie-frazer-cancer-death-threats-and-my-gaa-secret-30056375.html (accessed 10 November 2018).

33 Eamonn Mallie, "#flag Throughout the 'Union flag' controversy col-
    leagues & I refused to use #fleg. We feel #fleg is designed to offend.
    What do you think?', 20 January 2013, 9.37 a.m., Tweet.
34 Mick Fealty, "@ornayoung @EamonnMallie. @yeronlyman confirms
    your suspicions. I've been using #flegs with gusto, on the basis of its cur-
    rency", 20 January 2013, 10:09 a.m., Tweet.
35 Áine McGrath, "'Twitter vigilantes' don't like the display of hashtag
    #flegs in public. Personally, I don't like the display of #flegs on NI's lamp
    posts!", 20 January 2013, 11.24 a.m., Tweet.
36 Tim Brannigan, "Loyalist protesters open a new front by showing a reck-
    less disregard for punctuation. #flegs #Belfast http://t.co/C3tRZQ8E,"
    22 January 2013, 11:05 p.m., Tweet.
37 For an overview of memes shared during the flag protests, see: https://
    knowyourmeme.com/memes/events/northern-ireland-flag-protests-
    2012–13 (accessed 10 December 2018).
38 Liz Fawcett, "@EamonnMallie I prompted Twitter debate on this previ-
    ously Eamonn. #flegs not necess designed to offend but is patronising",
    20 January 2013, 9.54 a.m., Tweet.

4

PSNIRA vs peaceful protesters? YouTube, sousveillance and the policing of the flag protests

In a press conference on 18 November 2013, PSNI Detective Superintendent (DS) Sean Wright confirmed that there had been 440 arrests, and a further 560 people reported to the Public Prosecution Service, as a result of the two police investigations into the flag protests that took place between December 2012 and March 2013. Operations Dulcet and Titan saw PSNI officers analyse 1,500 images obtained from nearly 1,800 hours of CCTV footage in order to identify those suspected of engaging in criminal or antisocial behaviour.[1] Nevertheless, critics argued that the police had misinterpreted the legislation covering freedom of assembly by facilitating these unlawful street protests across the region. Nationalist and republican political representatives such as Sinn Féin MLA (and policing spokesman) Gerry Kelly lambasted the 'incompetent' policing operation; Anthony McIntyre, a republican writer and former Provisional IRA prisoner, contrasted the 'passivity' of the PSNI during the flag protests to their use of "dogs, armed men's fists and batons" against the nationalist residents peacefully protesting against a contentious Orange Order parade in North Belfast a few months earlier.[2] These allegations of 'political policing' echoed the claims made by the flag protesters that they had been 'brutalised' by the 'PSNIRA', who were said to be complicit in Sinn Féin's culture war against unionist and loyalist culture. Most of these allegations related to the police response to the violent clashes between nationalists and loyalist flag protesters near the Short Strand/Lower Newtownards Road interface in East Belfast. The police were accused not only of being heavy-handed towards the men, women and children participating in these demonstrations, but also of failing to protect them from being attacked by nationalist rioters during the unrest on 12 January 2013. This was part of a broader narrative suggesting that working-class loyalist communities had no confidence in the PSNI as an 'impartial' police service.

Mainstream news media narratives on the protests provided little succour to working-class loyalists who claimed they had been the victims of political policing. The content analysis conducted as part of this book found that policing was the most prominent theme in the *Belfast Telegraph* and *Irish News* coverage of the protests in January 2013 (see Appendix 1, Figures A1.1 and A1.2). Much of this coverage revolved around statements from senior PSNI officers, such as DS Sean Wright, confirming details of the police's ongoing efforts to arrest and charge those responsible for the flag-protest related violence. Only 3.66 per cent of *Belfast Telegraph* and 2.3 per cent of *Irish News* articles published in the same month referred to loyalist allegations that the PSNI had been heavy-handed. These articles typically carried statements from protesters alleging that they had been maltreated by the PSNI, which journalists were unable to substantiate or verify. The exception to this was an article published in the *Sunday Life* on 27 January referring to a video posted on YouTube purporting to show a man being the victim of an unprovoked assault by the PSNI outside the Wyse Byse store in East Belfast. It noted that it was "unclear why the altercation took place" and confirmed that a 42-year-old man had been arrested for assaulting a police officer and resisting arrest.[3] In contrast, a higher percentage of articles in both newspapers that month (7.06 per cent and 8.05 per cent respectively) suggested the PSNI had been too lenient in its handling of the protests.

The majority of newspaper articles analysed held the flag protesters responsible for the related unrest. This was particularly evident in January 2013, when 66.67 per cent of articles in the *Irish News* and 82.35 per cent of those in the *Belfast Telegraph/Sunday Life* focused on their culpability for the region-wide disruption and the violence seen in East Belfast (see Appendix 1, Figures A1.1 and A1.2). Many of these carried statements from the PSNI confirming the number of officers injured during violent clashes with loyalist rioters.[4] Indeed, PSNI Chief Constable Matt Baggott and Assistant Chief Constable Will Kerr were among the most quoted actors in coverage of the protests in January 2013. The former was particularly prominent in the *Belfast Telegraph* that month, appearing in 9.76 per cent of articles as he justified the police response to the violence in East Belfast (see

Appendix 1, Table A1.3). The newspapers also extensively covered criminal justice proceedings, especially in January and February 2013 when there was a significant increase in the number of cases involving loyalists charged with public order offences. Quotes from District Judges questioned the claims by the defendants that they had engaged in 'peaceful protest', as demonstrated by Justice McCloskey's remarks that the "vast majority of this kind of behaviour" was "thuggish rioting".[5] It was in this context that social media afforded loyalists opportunities to counter these narratives and focus attention on the 'heavy-handed' policing they blamed for the violence.

This chapter will focus specifically on the sousveillance (or inverse surveillance) footage shared by eyewitnesses to highlight the alleged police brutality towards the flag protesters. A key research question here was the extent to which this content elicited sympathy for loyalist claims that the police operation had sparked the isolated incidents of violence at the peak of the flag protest movement. It does so by reviewing the relevant literature on sousveillance and social media, analysing how the policing operation was framed by the news media, and presenting the findings from a thematic analysis of 1,586 comments posted in response to 36 YouTube videos posted by eyewitnesses to the flag protests between December 2012 and March 2013.

Sousveillance as a response to the 'surveillance society'

The ubiquity of smartphones, providing high-speed connectivity to the Internet via 3G, 4G and 5G broadband cellular networks, has provided unprecedented opportunities for recording eyewitness perspectives that focus attention on the conduct of authority figures. YouTube, the world's most popular video-sharing website, has provided an important repository for such content while also providing a platform for community formation around such issues (Burgess and Green, 2018). This chapter focuses on how the affordances of social media empower citizens to engage in sousveillance (translated into English as 'to watch from below'). It can be broadly defined as 'inverse surveillance' that empowers citizens through their use of technology to "access and collect data about their surveillance" (Mann et al., 2003: 333). The 'surveillance society' was said to be disrupted by people's use of body-worn cameras for sousveillance, which was conceptualised as "the many watching the few" (Mann, 2013: 1). The rationale for this 'undersight' was that data generated by the surveillance of private citizens by entities in positions of power lacked 'integrity' and provided evidence that was "less than the full truth" (Mann, 2017: 3). There were two forms of sousveillance originally identified by Steve Mann in the early 2000s: personal, which referred to the use of cameras at "eye-level for human-centred recording of personal experiences", while hierarchical was a more purposive, political activity documenting the actions of authority figures such as the police (Mann, 2004: 1). The former did not necessarily involve a political agenda whereas the latter shared the 'injunction to care' that was an integral component of 'media witnessing', the term used to capture the ways in which digital media transform people's capacity to bear witness to events and encourage others to engage with their perspectives (Allan, 2013). Moreover, there is a significant overlap between the conceptual frameworks of hierarchical sousveillance and citizen journalism, the process whereby citizens play an active role in the "collecting, reporting, analysing and disseminating news and information" (Bowman and Willis, 2003: 9). Citizens themselves are more likely to use the latter to describe their use of technology to 'watch the watchers' due to the frequency with which it is invoked by journalists to characterise such activity.

Yet, irrespective of intentionality, the recording of personal experiences in public spaces can contribute to 'equiveillance', defined as an "equilibrium (balance) between surveillance and sousveillance" (Mann, 2004: 627). Mann argued that a 'Veillance' society was inevitable due to the growth in citizens' use of smartphones for sousveillance (Mann, 2017). However, there are two caveats in relation to this sur/sousveillance distinction that should be noted. First, sousveillance was not primarily conceived by Mann as a mechanism to document incidents of police brutality. The feedback loops created by citizen sousveillance were said to be equally capable of capturing evidence of police officers "doing acts of good", as demonstrated by footage of New York Police Department (NYPD) officer Larry DePrimo purchasing a pair of shoes for a homeless man in November 2012 (Mann, 2013: 4). Furthermore, the emergence of a proleptical environment, in which citizens anticipate antagonistic interactions with police and thus record them, could potentially lead to some officers becoming self-disciplining subjects (Singh, 2017). This Foucauldian 'inverse panopticon' could militate against police misconduct during their interactions with citizens, irrespective of whether they are being recorded or not.

Second, it was anticipated that all forms of surveillance would increase in 'Veillance' societies in which these technologies are increasingly ubiquitous and embedded into architectures (Murakami Wood, 2015). This was illustrated by Mann's 'Veillance Plane', an 'eight-point compass' showing how the amount of surveillance and sousveillance in a physical space could be added or subtracted through, for example, an increase in the number people recording footage on smartphones. Both sousveillance and surveillance were conceptualised as orthogonal vectors in this model, with increases in one not necessarily being at the expense of another. Therefore, reductive analyses that frame sousveillance as a panacea for surveillance have been replaced by more contextualised approaches that recognise their coexistence within contemporary societies.

The efficacy of sousveillance in focusing attention on the actions of authority figures may ultimately depend upon the size of the network through which it is distributed, as well as the pervasiveness of hegemonic narratives on the legitimacy of the state and the police (Mann and Ferenbok, 2013). This was certainly the case in the most prominent example of sousveillance in the pre-social media era, the Rodney King assault. This revolved around video footage of four Los Angeles police officers assaulting Rodney King on 4 March 1991. George Holliday covertly captured the assault on the African-American taxi driver using his Sony Handycam and shared the video with local television station KTLA, which was later used as evidence in the trial of the police officers (Mann et al., 2003). The footage raised broader questions about police brutality towards African-Americans and the legitimacy of both local and national governments. It was repeatedly shown by US networks during the trial and subsequent acquittal of the defendants, which resulted in five nights of rioting in Los Angeles that left 50 people dead and 2,000 injured (Reis, 1995).

Sousveillance and social media

Social media and internet-enabled smartphones have been linked to an "intensification of sousveillance and the rise of sousveillance cultures" (Bakir, 2010: 23). These participatory media form part of a sousveillant assemblage that is comparable to the 'surveillant assemblage' developed in the 2000s to collect and monitor data on citizens (Bakir, 2010; Mann, 2017). While many social justice campaigners are cognisant of the privacy concerns raised by the use of online platforms, they continue to use sites such as Facebook and Twitter to focus attention on hierarchical sousveillance. Probably the most prominent examples of 'social media sousveillance' were deployed by Black Lives Matter, the campaign set up by activists Alicia Garza, Patrisse Cullors and Opal Tomet to highlight police killings of unarmed African-American citizens (Bonilla and Rosa, 2015). Emerging first in July 2013 as a hashtag and then transitioning into a much larger social justice movement, it shared distressing footage showing several of these controversial killings (Fischer and Mohrman, 2016). The eponymous hashtag was used to focus attention on these videos and highlight the NYPD's disregard for 'Black Lives' (Freelon et al., 2016a). Twitter debates surrounding such footage facilitated "large-scale informal learning" about the tensions between the police and Black communities, particularly among conservatives who acknowledged for the first time that these killings were 'unjust' (Freelon et al., 2016b: 79). In this sense, the integration of hierarchical sousveillance into a social justice campaign enabled non-elites to shape public discourse around race and law enforcement in the United States. Yet, the lack of punishment for these officers for violating established norms of 'good policing' suggests that the full potential of the proleptical environment has yet to be realised (Singh, 2017).

The increasingly important role of social media platforms in amplifying sousveillance may create other challenges for activists. Drawing on McLuhan's tetrad, Schaefer and Steinmetz (2014) argue that these practices are problematic due to the sheer volume of content available online, the frequency with which those with opposing views go off topic, and the distance between the viewer and its target. There has also been increasing evidence that both democratic and non-democratic states are forcing these companies to filter and suppress 'contentious' political content (Gillespie, 2018), including evidence of the maltreatment of citizens by the authorities. Moreover, the use of corporate social media to share such content contributes to the 'surveillance capitalism' that underpins these companies, which revolves around the profiling of user communities and the sharing of user data with third parties including national governments (Zuboff, 2018). Hence, these practices may produce outcomes far removed from the hierarchical and personal sousveillance originally conceived by Mann in the 2000s.

Viewers may not always agree that such footage is prima facie evidence of misconduct by authority figures such as the police. Take, for example, how YouTubers responded to videos showing alleged police brutality during the so-called 'Battle of Stokes Croft'. On 21 April 2011 there were violent clashes between the police and members of the public in the Stokes Croft district of Bristol, England in the aftermath of a controversial police raid on a local squat. Both local and national media were quick to frame the violence as a manifestation of the local campaign against the opening of a new Tesco supermarket in the area (People's Republic of Stokes Croft, 2012). Activists used social media to refute these allegations and blame the 'brutal' police dispersal of a peaceful protest for the violence (Hall, 2011). A key component of this strategy was the sharing of hierarchical sousveillance on YouTube, in support of claims by local residents that the police tactics were 'heavy-handed'. Analysis of comments posted under these videos provided little evidence to suggest that this footage had successfully focused attention on police 'brutality' (Reilly, 2014). The antisocial behaviour of the crowd was more heavily criticised than the actions of the police, with many commenters erroneously conflating the violence with the anti-Tesco campaign. Indeed, the results indicated that there was little rational debate about who was responsible for the violence, with the views of many commenters influenced by the media coverage of the riot (Reilly, 2015). This chapter adds to this emergent literature on social media and sousveillance by exploring whether a similar pattern of engagement was evident in relation to YouTube footage purporting to show 'heavy-handed' policing of the flag protests.

Conflicting narratives on policing of flag protests

Citizens are more likely to accept the authority of the police if they feel they have been treated fairly and respectfully by individual officers (Tyler, 2006; Worden and McLean, 2017). Nevertheless, public confidence in the police has typically been positively associated with the perceived legitimacy of governments in both democratic and non-democratic states (Kwak et al., 2012; Tyler and Fagan, 2008). Early political socialisation has been identified as a key factor shaping these attitudes, with childhood distrust of these institutions unlikely to shift significantly in adulthood. Therefore, the police are often in a "no-win situation" where negative experiences of policing harden attitudes against them and positive interactions have a less pronounced effect (Worden and McLean, 2017: 488).

These trends were evident in the discourses of 'political policing' during the flag protests, which built on a long history of contention over the policing of dissent in Northern Ireland. During the 30-year sectarian conflict in Northern Ireland (known colloquially as 'The Troubles'), the minority Catholic community, who predominantly identified as Irish rather than British and supported reunification with the rest of Ireland, perceived that they were poorly treated by the RUC, a police force which was almost exclusively Protestant and viewed as an arm of the unionist-controlled Stormont government (Hearty, 2017). Republican paramilitaries such as PIRA engaged in an 'armed struggle' against the RUC and the British security forces in order to force a British withdrawal from Ireland. Meanwhile, unionists and loyalists, who self-identified as British and supported the existing union with Great Britain, viewed the security forces as a bulwark against this republican terrorism. While the 2007 St Andrews Agreement saw Sinn Féin, the political wing of the republican movement, make the historic decision to support the PSNI, loyalist and republican critics of the Agreement have continued to accuse them of 'political policing'. Dissident republicans have argued that the PSNI is in effect the RUC under another name, whereas some loyalist groups have claimed that the police service is a vehicle for the 'Sinn Féin/ IRA' war on unionist and loyalist culture (Hearty, 2017: 7). This was a widely held perception among the flag protesters, despite the fact that the PSNI appeared no more representative of working-class nationalists than their loyalist counterparts (O'Rawe, 2010).

It was in this context that the PSNI's decision to facilitate public demonstrations blocking roads across Northern Ireland proved particularly controversial. Senior police chiefs retrospectively justified this approach by claiming that any move to arrest protesters for blocking roads might have increased support for loyalist or republican terrorist organisations within both communities (Pennington and Lynch, 2015: 556). Nevertheless, the two main narratives relating to the policing of the flag protests were highly critical of the PSNI, albeit for different reasons. First, there were many unionists and nationalists who felt that the PSNI had simply not done enough to prevent loyalists from blocking roads and participating in illegal marches, such as those from East Belfast to the Belfast City Hall that occurred every Saturday throughout January 2013. Nationalist residents' groups such as the Greater Ardoyne Residents' Collective (GARC) argued this was yet further evidence that the PSNI was a de facto 'unionist police force', which used "dogs, armed men's fists and batons" against nationalist residents engaged in peaceful protests but appeared unwilling to take any action against the 'armed masked men' participating in illegal loyalist roadblocks.[6] The PSNI Chief Constable Matt Baggott rejected this characterisation and argued that forcibly removing protesters from the streets might have further escalated tensions in areas such as East Belfast.[7] He also promised that those responsible for the protest-related violence would be arrested and prosecuted as part of Operation Dulcet.[8]

The legal basis for the PSNI strategy of non-intervention during unlawful public demonstrations was undermined by a judicial review brought against them by a Short Strand resident, under the pseudonym DB, in April 2014. Mr Justice Treacy ruled that the police had misinterpreted the Northern Ireland Public Processions Act (1988) and the Police (NI) Act (2000), which they believed limited their ability to prevent these illegal street protests or arrest those who participated in them. He criticised Baggott and his team of senior officers for "unjustified enforcement inertia" that resulted in very few prosecutions of those involved in the protests.[9] The PSNI successfully appealed against the ruling a few months later; a team of three judges led by Lord Chief Justice Sir Declan Morgan concluded that the police had taken appropriate steps to protect the Short Strand residents and not undermined the 1998 and 2000 Acts, as Treacy had asserted in his original judgment.[10] DB, the appellant, successfully challenged this decision in the Supreme Court in February 2017, with Lord Justice Kerr stating that the "PSNI misconstrued their legal powers to stop parades passing through or adjacent to the Short Strand area."[11] This spate of legal actions makes clear that there was a certain degree of confusion as to what constituted legal and illegal behaviour, not only in relation to the actions of the protesters but also to the ways in which the police responded to these incidents. The flag protesters themselves also appeared unsure whether their blocking of roads constituted a legal form of political protest or not (INTERCOMM and Byrne, 2013).

Loyalist activists argued that the PSNI were 'heavy-handed' in their policing of the protests. This narrative was often informed by direct or indirect experiences of the crowd control tactics deployed by the police. Focus groups revealed that there was a widely held perception among loyalists that the PSNI were "overly aggressive, antagonistic and confrontational" towards the protesters (INTERCOMM and Byrne, 2013: 10). There was much criticism on social media of the police tactics from those who had witnessed their use of water cannon and plastic baton rounds to disperse crowds in East Belfast. Protest leader Jamie Bryson used his own Facebook page to condemn what he viewed as the PSNI 'bloodlust' towards Protestants, positing that it might be partly explained by the fact that a large number of their officers were Roman Catholic.[12] This affectively charged language conformed to a long-established pattern of 'whataboutery' in Northern Irish politics. Loyalists complained that they had been subject to police brutality during the flag protests while a 'light touch' approach had been adopted towards the policing of protests organised by nationalist residents' groups. There were also complaints about a biased local media that focused only on violence perpetrated by loyalist mobs, with very little coverage of the protests being attacked by nationalist residents (INTERCOMM and Byrne, 2013). Yet, no charges were brought against any PSNI officer, nor did any of the independent bodies responsible for reviewing the policing operation conclude that the protesters had been 'brutalised.' For example, only 21 of 133 cases reported to the Office of the Police Ombudsman resulted in recommendations being made to the PSNI; only four of these formally or informally censured individual officers for their conduct during the protests, with 14 being categorised as 'Substantiated No Further Action.'[13]

Drawing on the literature reviewed above, the following research questions were investigated:

1. How did commenters respond to sousveillance footage shared on YouTube?
2. Were the comments congruent with the assumed expectations of those who uploaded this content?

A qualitative thematic analysis of comments on YouTube footage of the policing of the union flag protests was conducted by two researchers between October 2014 and January 2015.[14] Several terms relating to

PSNI actions during the protests were entered into the link analysis software Webometric Analyst (http://lexiurl.wlv.ac.uk) in order to identify a corpus of 53 videos uploaded to the video-sharing site between 3 December 2012 and 31 March 2013, regarded as the high-water mark of the flag protest movement. The next step was to remove content that did not conform to the requirements of the study, such as news media coverage or footage that did not focus specifically on the policing of the protests. This resulted in a final corpus of 46 videos, which had been uploaded between 21 December 2012 and 10 March 2013. While the primary focus was on how commenters responded to this footage, it should be noted that this content was produced and shared by just 24 YouTubers. Closer inspection of the metadata revealed that one YouTuber was responsible for uploading 19 of the videos, just over 40.4 per cent of the corpus. All of these eyewitnesses appeared to have spontaneously used their smartphones to engage in sousveillance, as demonstrated by the short runtime of many of these videos. The average length was just 2 minutes 43 seconds, with the shortest one (*PSNI Ruin Peaceful Protest Again 8/1/13*) just 8 seconds long and the longest one (*Sectarian Republican Nationalist Extremists Attack Protestants At Shortstrand*) coming in at 12 minutes 52 seconds.

While the themes in these videos will be elaborated below, the characteristics of the corpus illustrate the difficulties for researchers seeking to assess how citizens engage with content shared on You-Tube. Nearly a quarter of the corpus (10 videos) had been viewed multiple times but received no comments from those who had watched them. This left a total of 36 videos that conformed to the requirements of the study by virtue of having been commented on. A total of 1,586 comments were identified across the corpus, of which 1,109 (70 per cent) were linked to just three videos (*Belfast ambush 5th jan filmed by Jim Dowson Britain First, Belfast flag protest attacked by PSNI*, and *Newtownards Road East Belfast rioting 5th Jan 2013 after peaceful protest*). The long tail distribution of social media activity observed in flag protest-related Twitter hashtags was replicated to a certain degree here too. Although there were 576 unique commenters identified in the corpus, the 50 most frequent contributors accounted for 414 (26.1 per cent) of these posts. It should also be noted that the comments section below videos with more than one post tended to be dominated by conversations between a small number of YouTubers. Most notably, 288 of the 479 comments generated by *Belfast ambush*

5ᵗʰ jan filmed by Jim Dowson Britain First were posted 'in reply to' those from other commenters. This provided further evidence of the small but highly engaged group of viewers who commented on such content on the video-sharing website.

There was some evidence to corroborate the claims made in previous research that more people choose to 'watch' or 'lurk' online content rather than offer commentary (see Thelwall et al., 2012 for example). The 'ratio' of views to comments was as low as 42:1 in the case of videos such as *Belfast flag protest attacked by PSNI* (see Table 4.1). In the case of videos such as *PSNI Officer attacks photographer* the comment function had been disabled by the person responsible for uploading this footage. Some comments had also been removed in the intervening period between the video being uploaded and the data collection in October 2014. For example, several comments in a conversation about the events shown in *PSNI Brutality on Innocent Man 26/1/13* were no longer available at the time of the study. However, an alternative explanation for this dearth of commentary could be that these videos were being contested elsewhere online. Several of the videos in the corpus showed the alleged PSNI maltreatment of a 42-year-old man in January 2013, which had been vociferously debated by supporters and opponents of the protests on LPPU. For the sake of brevity, I will not repeat the key findings from Chapter 2 here, but it should be noted that critics of the flag protest movement took to the LPPU page to dismiss claims that the middle-aged man (not a pensioner as claimed by loyalists) had been 'brutalised' by the PSNI. These public Facebook pages functioned as a hub for the sharing of content about the flag protests that emerged elsewhere in what was becoming an increasingly networked media ecology. Although this does not shed light on whether 'watchers' were sympathetic to loyalist claims, it serves to underline the importance of cross- platform analysis in assessing the impact and significance of these digital acts.

It was clear from the study that loyalist activists intended to capture sousveillance footage that exposed 'political' policing. Nearly all of these videos showed crowds of eyewitnesses using their mobile phones to record images of police officers allegedly violating the right of loyalists to peacefully protest. For example, *PSNI treatment of residents* showed PSNI officers with dogs 'kettling' loyalist residents after violence broke out prior to a football fixture between North Belfast rivals Cliftonville and Crusaders. Loyalists were heard expressing their

Table 4.1 Characteristics of flag protest videos, 21 December 2012–10 March 2013.

Video	Date	Views	Comments	Commenters
PSNI block peaceful protest (www.youtube.com/watch?v=38zPoiI2GI4)	21 Dec	472	2	2
PSNI disrupting a peaceful protest (www.youtube.com/watch?v=u9k6Hk_qsek)	22 Dec	1486	5	5
PSNI intimidate peaceful protest with dogs (www.youtube.com/watch?v=SflXSzT2ANo)	22 Dec	3360	9	4
PSNI try to arrest innocent protester (www.youtube.com/watch?v=XOy0bCqbjF0)	29 Dec	15079	38	25
PSNI Refusing To Let Protestants Go Home! (www.youtube.com/watch?v=POh2dwOf1fY)	1 Jan	2663	2	2
Police brutality at peaceful protest in Carrickfergus 02-01-2013 (www.youtube.com/watch?v=hfRbERaYf5Q)	3 Jan	3240	11	7
HD Police heavy handed tactics in east Belfast (www.youtube.com/watch?v=XPy6VO-Hxlg)	5 Jan	5709	7	6
Police heavy handed tactics at Belfast city hall (www.youtube.com/watch?v=t73RCFCjp0w)	5 Jan	3223	3	3
Belfast ambush 5th Jan (filmed by Jim Dowson Britain First) (www.youtube.com/watch?v=gswXMPO_HAM)	5 Jan	32496	479	146
Newtownards Road East Belfast rioting 5th Jan 2013 after peaceful protest (Video no longer available as of 26 November 2019)	5 Jan	67111	313	199

Table 4.1 (continued)

Video	Date	Views	Comments	Commenters
PSNI/dogs attack peaceful protest 5/1/13 (www.youtube.com/watch?v=KzJKErprM)	6 Jan	12245	56	44
Peaceful protest attacked by nationalists 5/1/13 (www.youtube.com/watch?v=auXJ16HXsqA)	6 Jan	10959	26	20
Belfast flag protest attacked by PSNI (www.youtube.com/watch?v=7GOSlb7XABY)	6 Jan	13194	317	70
Peaceful protest ruined by PSNI 6/1/13 (www.youtube.com/watch?v=uAf4tx7l4zY)	6 Jan	5695	13	12
PSNI stop peaceful protest-brutality 5/1/13 (www.youtube.com/watch?v=mvnaXSDOMD0)	6 Jan	6204	29	20
PSNIRA baton charging peaceful protesters (www.youtube.com/watch?v=COodZ2IUW8w)	6 Jan	653	1	1
Short strand and PSNI attack Protesters Sat 5th Jan 2013 (www.youtube.com/watch?v=2_vCUA3FXmk)	7 Jan	4519	14	13
Nationalists Attack Peaceful Protest 7/1/13 (www.youtube.com/watch?v=XrF2eRgw-Uk)	7 Jan	2284	4	4
PSNI Ruin Peaceful Protest Again 8/1/13 (www.youtube.com/watch?v=fb4ueMi6eBI)	8 Jan	4755	3	3
psni officer go's to hit a man with his baton when another officer pulls him back 7 1 2013 (www.youtube.com/watch?v=PNcKw7AaW9I)	10 Jan	1843	1	1

(Continued)

Table 4.1 (continued)

Video	Date	Views	Comments	Commenters
Sectarian Republican Nationalist Extremists Attack Protestants At Shortstrand (www.youtube.com/watch?v=vKRheNLDHtA)	12 Jan	18672	76	50
East Belfast Verses PSNI/SFIRA,12/01/13, (Part3). (www.youtube.com/watch?v=i_ws8rppT_8)	12 Jan	878	6	5
Political Policing In Northern Ireland (www.youtube.com/watch?v=6QjGWKEaW7E)	14 Jan	608	2	2
PSNI brutality @shaftsbury square protest (www.youtube.com/watch?v=OWuJPrFBY1s)	14 Jan	9496	22	17
Newtownards Road, East Belfast RIOTING 5th January 2013 After Peaceful Protest (Video no longer available as of 26 November 2019)	18 Jan	5389	7	5
East Belfast 26th January 2013 (www.youtube.com/watch?v=mrNsXlrhyV0)	26 Jan	3362	16	13
PSNI Brutality – Harassment 26/1/13 (www.youtube.com/watch?v=0EP5S4l_9JQ)	26 Jan	2315	9	8
PSNI Brutality (www.youtube.com/watch?v=5R9P00fYgZU)	26 Jan	1112	5	3
PSNI Heavy Handed in East Belfast Part 1 (www.youtube.com/watch?v=aOY4xS_ARLU)	26 Jan	1939	2	1

Table 4.1 (continued)

Video	Date	Views	Comments	Commenters
PSNI Heavy Handed in East Belfast Part 3 (www.youtube.com/watch?v=p68RiLC0orQ)	26 Jan	348	1	1
PSNI officer Baton Drawn Despite no sign of trouble at city hall (www.youtube.com/watch?v=O9RIJymRbpg)	26 Jan	1180	6	6
PSNI Brutality On Innocent Man 26/1/13 (www.youtube.com/watch?v=P7RCAFNKHPg)	27 Jan	849	5	4
PSNI Dont Know What They Are Doing 26/1/13 (www.youtube.com/watch?v=nViu4MiLD9Q)	27 Jan	1824	1	1
PSNI Block Me From Going Home 9/2/13 (www.youtube.com/watch?v=xGRQLHFNpfM)	9 Feb	3094	4	4
PSNI treatment of residents (www.youtube.com/watch?v=EwpE3fKUTJQ)	16 Feb	4952	5	5
Double standards by the psni (www.youtube.com/watch?v=WVIduhd5haw)	2 Mar	2654	86	12

(All videos accessed 26 November 2019.)

anger at an alleged assault by a PSNI officer on a member of their group, with one yelling "we have got his number" in reference to the alleged perpetrator. This was one of a number of attacks that it was claimed had occurred off-camera. *Belfast ambush 5th jan filmed by Jim Dowson Britain First*, the most commented-upon video in the corpus, saw loyalist leaders Dowson and Bryson condemn the PSNI for their heavy-handed approach towards loyalists after they had been 'ambushed' by the Short Strand residents. A third man appeared on camera claiming he had been struck on the head by a bottle thrown by nationalists on the Newtownards Road. However, it was notable that none of those who spoke on camera appeared fearful of being attacked by the riot police, who were positioned a few feet away.

Despite many accusations of police brutality being made in these videos, no evidence of the 'unprovoked assaults' appeared to have been caught on camera. The arrest of an unidentified man in East Belfast on 26 January was among those events documented in *East Belfast 26th January 2013*. It showed three police officers forcibly holding down and handcuffing the man. In the background two women yelled at the police officers "get the fuck off him". Yet, there was no conclusive evidence suggesting that the police were 'heavy-handed.' This was typical of many videos in the corpus whose contents did not correspond to what was suggested in their provocative descriptions. In the case of *PSNI brutality at shaftsbury [sic] square protest*, for example, the poor picture quality meant that it was impossible to tell who was responsible for the brawl witnessed by this eyewitness. A chaotic picture also emerged from *New-townards Road East Belfast rioting 5th Jan 2013 after peaceful protest*, which was produced by photojournalist company 'Frontline Freelance Media'.[15] Despite numerous shots of baton-wielding police officers and police Land Rovers blocking the path of loyalist protesters, this footage disorientated the viewer rather than providing evidence of police brutality.

Although these eyewitnesses intended to highlight police brutality, the videos raised more questions about the conduct of loyalists. They frequently used expletives to express their anger at the police, as demonstrated by footage showing several people shouting loudly that the PSNI were a "fucking disgrace" (*PSNI Heavy Handed in East Belfast Part 1*). The videos provided evidence of the violence endured by police officers during these incidents. Loyalist defiance of PSNI efforts to break up these street protests invariably gave way to a wave of missiles and other objects being thrown at the lines of advancing Tactical Support

Group officers in attendance. One video, which focused on the efforts of police officers with dogs to disperse protesters from the Newtownards Road, captured the moment when loyalists used flagpoles to attack the police (*PSNI/dogs attack peaceful protest 5/1/13*). There were also numerous examples of loyalists threatening members of the 'PSNIRA', including one scene in which a protester asked a police officer to take off their uniform and fight them "so we can see who is a big man now" (*PSNI treatment of residents*) and another in which a loyalist yelled "you listen to me wanker or you'll suffer the consequences" at a police officer (*PSNI Heavy Handed in East Belfast Part 1*).

Overall, the analysis corroborated the findings of a Police Ombudsman investigation into 170 hours of YouTube footage of the protests, which concluded that the PSNI had shown great restraint in the face of loyalist provocation (Nolan et al., 2014: 79). One potential explanation for this was that these officers were fully aware that they were being recorded by both eyewitnesses and professional journalists, and had been trained not to react to any extreme provocation from the protesters. In effect, these officers were self-disciplining subjects, who were fully aware that their actions might be recorded and shared online, and acted accordingly (Singh, 2017).

The majority of comments were unsympathetic to loyalist claims that they had been the victims of PSNI brutality in the events captured on camera. Analysis of the comment threads under each of the 36 videos analysed showed that 20 (or 55.6 per cent) were dominated by comments criticising the loyalists, with seven (19.4 per cent) agreeing that the PSNI were heavy-handed and nine evenly split between the two positions (25 per cent). These themes will be elaborated in more detail below. As per the ethical stance outlined in the Introduction, the focus here will be on what was said rather than on who said it. Therefore, commenters are not identified by username and their posts are paraphrased or quoted in such a way as to protect their anonymity.

Results and discussion

Loyalist narratives on 'political policing' dismissed by most commenters

A small minority of commenters expressed support for the claims made in these videos about PSNI brutality towards the protesters.

The 'PSNIRA' were condemned for being a 'political police force' that favoured the nationalist Short Strand residents over the working-class loyalists; one commenter characterised this as a form of 'treason' that violated the officers' oath to the Queen. Acronyms such as ACAB (all cops are bastards) were frequently used by these YouTubers to convey their outrage at the policing tactics shown in these videos. In many cases they repeated the accusations made by loyalists in this footage. Most notably, it was argued that the PSNI had no right to stop and search the middle-aged man being restrained by several police officers in one video (*PSNI Brutality-Harassment 26/1/13*). It should be noted that many of these pro-loyalist commenters claimed to have witnessed the incidents depicted; these eyewitnesses often elaborated on their claims of police brutality when faced with criticism in the comments sections below these videos. Clearly it was not possible to verify whether they had actually been present during these events.

Loyalist commenters directed much vitriol at the 'PSNI scum' who 'lost it' during the confrontations with protesters in Carrickfergus and East Belfast; the police were also heavily criticised by some commenters for their failure to intervene when the protesters were attacked by the "vermin" in Short Strand (*East Belfast 26th January 2013*). Such negative views of the PSNI were also evident in the comments section of *PSNI try to arrest innocent protester*, the video in the corpus that generated the most pro-loyalist comments. The 'PSNIRA' were accused of supporting "IRA Marxists" and provoking violence so they could arrest the protesters; one eyewitness even claimed that a police officer had tried to steal his camera during the fracas. Self-identified loyalist commenters accepted this version of events and suggested that it was important to film these incidents in order to hold the PSNI accountable for their actions. This was one of a few comments that acknowledged how such footage might help shape public opinion about the policing of the protests. Two comments in the corpus compared one incident, in which a PSNI tactical support group officer was accused of knocking a loyalist protester to the ground, to the "man in England" who had been assaulted by the police (*PSNI Pushing Protestants Out Of Their Own Area*). This was presumably a reference to the video of an unprovoked assault by a Metropolitan police officer upon Ian Tomlinson during the London anti-G20 protests in April 2009, which resulted in the death of the newspaper vendor a few hours later. Yet, not all loyalist commenters engaged with this content as a form of sousveillance. There were a handful of comments that poked fun at the PSNI and mocked their calls in these videos for the protesters to disperse.

The overwhelming majority of comments refuted accusations that the PSNI were heavy-handed in dealing with the protesters. In the case of the East Belfast man whose arrest was the focus of several videos, one commenter joked about the "42-year-old pensioner" in reference to the fact that he was not as old as loyalists had claimed on various online platforms. Congruent with how many responded to this footage on LPPUB (see Chapter 2), there was much bemusement about loyalist claims that this footage constituted evidence that they had been 'brutalised' by the police, with one telling loyalists to 'grow up' and dismissing claims that the PSNI had 'intimidated' protesters (*PSNI intimidate Peaceful Protest With Dogs*). A handful of commenters referred to incidents such as Bloody Sunday and the policing of nationalist residents during the Ardoyne parade dispute as evidence that loyalists had no idea what it was like to be oppressed by state forces (*peaceful protest ruined by psni 6/1/13*). This 'whataboutery' saw self-identified nationalists and republicans claim they were the true victims of 'political policing'. There were also many comments challenging the assertions made by the eyewitnesses responsible for uploading this 'sousveillance' footage. For example, in *PSNI officer Baton Drawn Despite no sign of trouble at city hall* one commenter disputed its title, noting that the baton was still in the officer's holster. There was a similar response to the footage of loyalist clashes with the PSNI in Shaftesbury Square, with one commenter suggesting that images of "black shadowy figures" running around could hardly be considered evidence of the police brutality mentioned in the video's title (*PSNI brutality @ shaftsbury square protest*). In some cases, the lack of visual evidence to corroborate claims that loyalists were the victims of unprovoked violence was used to cast doubt upon their veracity. For example, a man who claimed on camera he had been injured by a bottle thrown from the Short Strand district was called a "liar" (*Belfast ambush 5th jan filmed by Jim Dowson Britain First*).

Nearly all of these commenters condemned the behaviour of the loyalists rather than the PSNI officers that were supposed to be the focus of this sousveillance. They questioned whether genuinely peaceful protesters would throw bricks at the police and expressed sympathy for the "poor PSNI" officers. Loyalists were characterised as sectarian for the anti-Catholic comments heard in the background of several videos. Some even contended that this abuse merited more aggressive policing actions than those documented in this footage, with the forcible restraint of a middle-aged man in East Belfast justified on the basis that he must have done something to deserve it. A few commenters argued that the PSNI should have acted more decisively to prevent protesters from blocking roads and arrested those refusing to disperse when asked to do so. There was little compassion given to loyalists injured during the protest-related violence, as demonstrated by the commenters who mocked footage of an unconscious man being carried into the back of a police vehicle to receive medical attention (*PSNI Heavy Handed in East Belfast Part 3*). Indeed, there were a few commenters who took great pleasure in the fact that loyalists had been hurt during these clashes with the police.

Working-class loyalists are frequently dehumanised and mocked by commenters

Bryson and Dowson were unsurprisingly subjected to many ad hominem attacks from critics of the flag protests; as in #flegs (see Chapter 3), the former's speech impediment was ridiculed in an excoriating riposte to his allegation that the PSNI was a 'Catholic' force, while the latter was labelled a racist due to his BNP links. However, for the most part, these offensive remarks were more indiscriminate in nature. Sectarianism was observed in the comment threads of half (18) of the videos in the study. For example, the comments under *PSNI Refusing to Let Protestant Home!* saw protesters derided as "stupid Orange bastards!" prompting angry responses from loyalists who warned republicans to keep their "irish fenian views" to themselves. A similar pattern emerged in the comments section below videos such as *Sectarian Republican Nationalist Extremists Attack Protestants At Shortstrand*, where loyalists were mocked for being frightened of being outnumbered by Catholics due to recent demographic changes within Northern Ireland. These vitriolic exchanges saw a small number of loyalists react angrily to suggestions that the video showed republican residents defending their community from an extremist loyalist mob. One of these commenters went as far as to call for a napalm attack to ethnically cleanse the Short Strand, which echoed a comment from a critic of the flag protests who suggested the PSNI shoot loyalists who blocked roads. Both were examples of hate speech that might have led to prosecutions under legislation such as Section 127 of the UK Communications Act 2003.[16]

The analysis revealed that the loyalists were more often than not the targets of sectarian abuse in the comment sections below these videos. One manifestation of this was the tendency for some commenters to refer to the protesters and their supporters as 'huns'. There were also a couple of instances in which critics mocked the spelling and grammar of loyalists in their responses to these videos. Most notably one commenter, who claimed he was one of the PSNI officers present during these events, asserted that nobody cared about "proda stants [sic] bastards" (*East Belfast 26th January 2013*). Clearly it was difficult to verify this claim, but the spelling and grammar errors suggested the post was inauthentic and part of the broader movement on social media portraying working-class loyalists as poorly educated (see Chapter 3). The analysis of these YouTube comments provided further empirical evidence of the ways in which online platforms were used to dehumanise working-class loyalist communities. A constant refrain of these commenters was that these were 'mouthy', 'uneducated', 'worthless' people who were either unable or unwilling to recognise that these were not sousveillance videos providing evidence of the 'unprovoked brutality' of the PSNI. In many cases it was suggested that those protesting were either unemployed or members of loyalist paramilitary organisations such as the UDA or UVF who engaged in criminal activities such as drug dealing. The flag protesters caught on camera were also often depicted as 'chavs', with one commenter asserting that "these are chavs, they are not people" (*PSNI Brutality-Harassment 26/1/13*). Overall, it appeared that loyalist efforts to expose police brutality had made minimal impact on the opinions of this small but vocal section of the 'online audience' and may in fact have reinforced their prejudices against the protesters.

Comments threads provide opportunities for informal learning?

There were two areas in which these comment threads appeared to facilitate some form of informal learning among loyalists. First, there was some clarification over the legality of the public demonstrations and marches that caused widespread disruption across Northern Ireland during this period. One commenter responded to the scenes shown in *East Belfast 26th January 2013* by arguing that loyalists were clearly not fully aware of the legal definition of peaceful protest; for example, they were reminded of the importance of not blocking roads and footpaths, as well as acting in a respectful and non-threatening manner, during the regular demonstrations at Belfast City Hall. It was also confirmed that marches on public roads and highways were technically illegal except in those circumstances when the police had been notified of the route normally twenty-eight days in advance. Second, there was a debate over whether the eyewitnesses should be sharing footage that revealed the faces of serving PSNI officers. The eyewitness responsible for *PSNI intimidate peaceful protest with dogs* argued with one commenter over whether this made the officers depicted more vulnerable to attack by dissident republican terrorist organisations, such as the recently formed 'Real IRA'. They offered to remove the footage on the condition that the PSNI take down the images of loyalists they wished to question in connection with protest-related violence, which had circulated in the mainstream media. Both seemed unaware of the fact that, under Section 58a of the UK Terrorism Act (2000), police officers did indeed have the power to stop eyewitnesses from recording them if they believed that the footage could be used for the purposes of terrorism. Yet, it was hard to tell whether the sharing of such information via social media actually altered the behaviour of loyalists, both collectively and individually. The announcement on 31 January that Operation Standstill would transition from blocking roads to white line protests occurred shortly after a meeting between the UPF and representatives from the PSNI.[17] It was reasonable to presume that this dialogue about the legality of the protests was more likely to have influenced the change in strategy, as opposed to the advice proffered by a YouTube commenter. There were also no responses within the comments threads that shed light on whether this advice was likely to be adhered to in the future, nor any digital traces indicating how 'lurkers/watchers' interpreted and acted upon this guidance. Nevertheless, there certainly appeared to be an effort by a few commenters to use the communicative spaces opened up by the videos to encourage informal learning about these issues among the protesters.

Conclusion

A key question in this chapter was the extent to which this 'sousveillance' footage enabled loyalists to counter media narratives blaming them for the flag-protest related violence throughout this period. The provocative descriptions of these videos, as well as the views of the pro-loyalist 'viewertariat', portrayed these protesters as the victims of 'political' and 'heavy-handed' policing. In some cases, this was a direct response to comments that mocked and dehumanised working-class loyalist communities. Yet, congruent with previous research (Reilly, 2015), they focused attention on the antisocial behaviour of the protesters rather than the alleged police brutality. There was simply no evidence to corroborate claims that protesters had been the victims of 'unprovoked assaults' by police officers, who appeared aware that they were being filmed and had been trained not to react to the provocation of the crowd. While it is beyond the remit of this book to examine whether a proleptical policing environment exists in contemporary Northern Ireland, these officers were self-disciplining when interacting with protesters, some of whom were recording these events on their mobile phones. Conversely, there were many examples of loyalists threatening police officers, which was held up as further evidence that they were to blame for unrest in areas such as East Belfast. In this regard, the study provided further evidence of how the use of social media for 'cop watching' might have had unintended negative consequences for activists.

As with Black Lives Matter, YouTube provided communicative spaces for informal learning, particularly about the legality of street protests and police powers to stop people recording footage that might aid terrorism. It was possible that viewers who did not leave comments may have developed their knowledge in these areas. However, the 'trolling' of working-class loyalists within these comment threads militated against the video-sharing platform facilitating deeper conversations about why they felt they were the victims of 'political policing'. This was congruent with previous research into video activism, which suggested that back and forth exchanges between those with opposing viewpoints were inevitable during the short period in which they paid attention to such footage.

The views of these commenters reflected broader discourses about the legitimacy of policing in the deeply divided society (or lack thereof). Those who perceived the 'PSNIRA' as being complicit in

Sinn Féin's 'culture war' were likely to believe the allegations of police brutality made by Bryson and Dowson in these videos, irrespective of the lack of corroborative evidence therein. Pro-loyalist comments in the corpus reflected how these communities were increasingly dissatisfied with the Stormont Assembly and disputed the legitimacy of the 'PSNIRA', who they accused of 'political policing'. The same might be said for critics of the protests watching videos showing loyalists threatening PSNI officers. The lack of visual evidence of 'police brutality' reinforced their views that these allegations were fabricated and that loyalists were the aggressors in confrontations with the police. This was perhaps to be expected given that activist content uploaded on YouTube typically polarises commenters. Congruent with recent research disputing the notion that social media facilitate "hermetically sealed echo chambers" (Bruns, 2019), the video-sharing site exposed these commenters to oppositional viewpoints on policing within this divided society. However, long-established perceptions of the PSNI's legitimacy (or lack thereof) were unlikely to be altered as a result of these communicative exchanges.

This chapter has illustrated the problematic nature of exploring sousveillance, or imagined sousveillance as was the case here, through the collection and analysis of 'easy', publicly available data. No generalisations could be made about the impact and reach of this sousveillance footage based on the contributions of the viewertariat active in these comments sections. These conversations were dominated by a small number of YouTubers who had strongly held opinions on the legitimacy of both the flag protests and the policing operation. The ratio of views to comments raised questions about the representativeness of this group when compared with the overall audience who watched this content. It was highly likely that these videos were being scrutinised on private Facebook pages and other online platforms that lay beyond the reach of the researcher. Future research should ideally adopt a cross-platform approach to examine how sousveillance footage uploaded to YouTube 'travels' between these online platforms and is interpreted by different audiences therein. Yet, the triangulation of social media data generated by sousveillance may fail to fully capture the motivations of those who comment or just watch such footage. These are digital traces from which it may be difficult to infer attitudes, especially given the propensity of some social media users to 'troll' others online, which will be discussed in the next chapter.

Notes

1 DS Wright issued these statistics in a press conference in the run-up to the anniversary of the flag protests. For more information, see here: www.belfasttelegraph.co.uk/news/northern-ireland/psni-seek-names-for-150-faces-29768368.html (accessed 10 May 2018).

2 For more on this see: www.thepensivequill.com/2013/01/psni-differences-in-policing-loyalist.html (accessed 10 May 2018).

3 "Clashes With Police As Protesters Return From City Hall", *Sunday Life*, 27 January 2013, p. 6.

4 "Flag protests: Loyalist violence flares again in east Belfast", *Belfast Telegraph*, 5 January 2013, available at: www.belfasttelegraph.co.uk/news/northern-ireland/flag-protests-loyalist-violence-flares-again-in-east-belfast-29011514.html (accessed 10 May 2018).

5 "Flags Crisis – Judge hits out at 'thuggish rioting'", *Irish News*, 14 December 2012, p. 2.

6 The GARC statement has been reproduced by republican activist and writer Anthony McIntyre on his blog here: www.thepensivequill.com/2013/01/psni-differences-in-policing-loyalist.html (accessed 10 August 2014).

7 www.bbc.co.uk/news/uk-northern-ireland-21179876.

8 Baggott discussed the remit of the Operation during a Policing Board meeting in February 2013. Details of this can be accessed here: www.nipolicingboard.org.uk/policing-matters-2013 (accessed 10 August 2014).

9 www.bbc.co.uk/news/uk-northern-ireland-27189536 (accessed 10 August 2014).

10 www.belfasttelegraph.co.uk/news/northern-ireland/psni-win-union-flag-protest-appeal-30397882.html (accessed 10 August 2014).

11 For more on the decision, see: *DB v. Chief Constable of Police Service of Northern Ireland (Northern Ireland)* [2017] UKSC 7, Paragraph 81.

12 www.anphoblacht.com/contents/22873 (accessed 10 August 2014).

13 This information was obtained by the authors of the *The Flag Dispute: Anatomy of a Protest* report. It can be found here: https://pure.qub.ac.uk/portal/en/publications/the-flag-dispute-anatomy-of-a-protest (5eb2044d-4628–48a1-a23f-1fafebbb767d).html (accessed 10 April 2017).

14 An intercoder reliability check was conducted by the two coders on 10 per cent of the total corpus, with 90 per cent agreement reached at the first iteration.

15 Frontline Freelance Media is run by professional photojournalist Mark Winter. For more, see: http://frontlinefreelance.wixsite.com/ffmedia (accessed 26 November 2019).

16 Section 127 of the Act prohibits the use of a public electronic communications network to send "a message or other matter that is grossly

offensive or of an indecent, obscene or menacing character". For more, see: www.legislation.gov.uk/ukpga/2003/21/section/127 (accessed 10 May 2018).

17 The police spokesperson confirmed those involved in white line protests would only be arrested if they blocked traffic. For more on this, see here: www.newsletter.co.uk/news/police-welcome-forum-white-line-protest-vow-1–4741899 (accessed 10 April 2017).

5

Parody of esteem? LAD and the rise of 'silly citizenship'

Memes and parody accounts are examples of 'ritualised social media practices' that are frequently used to provide irreverent commentary on contentious political issues and hybrid media events (Highfield, 2016b). Hashtags such as #flegs hosted public expression about the flag protests that was more often than not irreverent rather than malicious. Much of this activity revolved around parody accounts, with self-styled 'sitcom' Loyalists Against Democracy (LAD) emerging as one of the most prominent critics of the protest movement.[1] There was a team of 'LAD-mins' responsible for maintaining its social media accounts, some of whom sought to court controversy while others claimed they were "trying to make a difference in this country [Northern Ireland]" (Smith, 2014). This was perhaps best summarised by blogger Alan Meban, who suggested that the group were at their 'strongest' when "lampooning loyalist tropes" and weakest when they were attacking "'players' in loyalism, academics or innocent bystanders" (Meban, 2013).

This chapter sets out to explore the role of LAD in contentious politics in Northern Ireland. The study will empirically investigate whether LAD's targeting of flag protesters was satirical, as well as the extent to which the parody group and its supporters framed working-class loyalists as 'social abjects'. It does so by analysing the origins of LAD, exploring the controversy over its campaign against "street fighting loyalists" and presenting the key findings of a qualitative analysis of comments posted on LAD's Facebook page (N = 35,721) and Twitter account (N = 3,061) between December 2012 and November 2013.

Equal opportunity satirists or trolls? The case of Loyalists Against Democracy

Social media enable citizens to playfully engage in public debates using memes, wordplay and parody accounts. While the 'silly citizenship' conceptualised by Hartley (2010; 2012) did not specify that these practices should be humorous, they are typically deployed by citizens to provide irreverent commentary during hybrid media events. They can also be used to shape public narratives on contentious political issues, as demonstrated by the collection of hashtags created in January 2013 to articulate public opposition to the flag protests (see Chapter 3). The research presented in this chapter builds on this by focusing specifically on the contribution of parody group Loyalists Against Democracy (LAD) to political debates on social media during this period. Parody accounts typically subvert stereotypes of groups and public figures in order to highlight behaviours they deem objectionable (Holbert, 2013; Simpson, 2003). This is often characterised as a form of 'trolling', especially when these accounts interact directly with their targets on platforms such as Twitter. Early work in this field emphasised the deception of 'trollers' who created false identities in order to post inflammatory comments online that sparked conflict with others (Baker, 2001; Cox, 2006). This has gradually given way to a reimagining of trolling as a more nebulous set of practices that include the harassment of public figures, 'lulz' that express amusement at other people's misfortune, and the use of often grotesque language to critique dominant cultural tropes (Nagle, 2017). Hence, scholars such as Phillips (2015: 134) have argued that there needs to be much more research into the "cultural information embedded in the shit trolls produce". This chapter will assess the nature of LAD's contribution to political debates on social media, with a view to interrogating claims by its critics that it was nothing more than a group of middle-class 'Internet trolls' mocking working-class loyalist communities.

LAD certainly sought to cultivate a reputation as an "equal opportunities satirist" during the widespread disruption caused by the union flag protests between December 2012 and March 2013 (Spencer, 2013a). The group defined themselves as both non-political and non-sectarian, with a primary objective to "satirise the extremist dickheads within society who are intent on dragging Northern Ireland back to the bad old days" (Loyalists Against Democracy, 2013).

Supporters such as blogger Brian John Spencer argued they were holding up a mirror to the "naked sectarianism, bare racism and transparent illoyalism of the protesters" (Spencer, 2013a). They were praised for articulating popular opposition to the flag protest movement and heralded by political commentator Newton Emerson as the "online sensation of the year" for their use of Facebook to share sectarian and offensive comments posted by loyalists online.[2] Such activity generated much hurt and anger among loyalists, who organised mass reporting campaigns to force Facebook to remove the group's page, which was published and unpublished six times between its launch on 10 December 2012 and 6 October 2013.[3] Somewhat ironically, it was suggested that the screenshots of offensive posts from loyalists shared on the group's Facebook page might have been the reason for its removal.[4] Loyalists speculated about the relationship between LAD and NI21, a new political party launched by former UUP MLAs Basil McCrea and John McAllister in June 2013. It was subsequently revealed that members of the parody group were responsible for NI21's party election broadcast that year.[5]

Facebook, Twitter and YouTube enabled the group, which described itself as a collective of men and women from both Catholic and Protestant backgrounds, to target key players in the protest movement, such as Jamie Bryson and Willie Frazer. They justified their anonymity (members usually posted using pseudonyms) on the basis that it gave them the necessary protection to pursue these targets online. Like contributors to #flegs (see Chapter 3), LAD condemned BBC NI presenter Stephen Nolan for giving airtime to these unelected representatives and failing to report on the unlawful nature of the street protests. In an interview in October 2016, John-Paul Whearty asserted that he had founded the parody group in December 2012 in order to counteract the inaccurate information about the flag protests circulated in mainstream media and target "anybody who holds themselves up as a public figure in Northern Ireland and puts across a point of view not really motivated by the best of intentions" (Ferguson, 2016). However, the group were perhaps best known for mimicking the 'dialect' of protesters, with one of the 'LAD-mins' describing how they performed the role of an "incoherent, hate-filled loyalist" when they posted updates on the group's social media profiles (Jones, 2014). While this appeared congruent with the 'playfulness' associated with silly citizenship, the resignation of LAD-min 'Winston Smith' in

April 2014 raised questions about the motives of some group members. He left LAD in acrimonious circumstances after being told that two controversial tweets, one of which celebrated the murder of dissident republican Tommy Crossan, were good publicity for the group's comedy brand (Smith, 2014). An interview with two other LADmins prior to Smith's departure provided further evidence of how the group viewed itself as a type of "entertainment platform" (McCann, 2014a). This was illustrated by their 'Parody of Esteem' branding that appeared not only on its Facebook and Twitter profiles, but also on the content it produced and disseminated online. For example, the group released a charity record – Last December by 'Paramilitary Wives' in December 2013. The parody of the Wham! Christmas hit 'Last Christmas' encouraged its supporters to donate to local charity SOS Bus NI.[6] T-shirts and other paraphernalia embossed with the LAD logo were also promoted via its social media profiles during this period.

Parody of esteem?

LAD's claims that it was speaking truth to power were contested by a number of commenters. Much of this criticism emerged in the Northern Ireland blogosphere throughout 2013, possibly due to the lack of media scrutiny of the group during its first year in existence. It was perhaps no surprise that its most vocal critics were community workers and researchers operating within working-class loyalist areas. The group was accused of reinforcing middle-class stereotypes of these communities through their constant focus on the poor spelling and grammar of those who left comments on public Facebook pages (Mulvenna, 2013; Simpson, 2013). They were labelled "self-loathing unionists", whose anonymity left them unaccountable for their bullying and 'online shaming' of these individuals (Magee, 2013a). In two blogposts entitled "Exposing Bigotry or exposing their own bigotry", researcher Dave Magee provided anonymised quotes from community workers, politicians, researchers and writers criticising LAD for their 'cruel' and 'snobbish' attacks upon working-class Protestants, unionists and loyalists (PUL was an acronym often used to describe 'pro-Union' communities in Northern Ireland). Although one community worker did describe LAD as a 'guilty pleasure', most interviewees felt that the group purposefully ignored sectarianism from republicans and liked to "suggest that working class PUL people are thick" (Magee,

2013b). The consensus among these commenters was that by 'sneering' at poorly spelt Facebook posts the group were ignoring the perceived erosion of loyalist culture underpinning the flag protests.

A broader critique of the group's campaign to 'expose loyalist bigotry' related to its 'othering' of working-class loyalist communities. Researchers including Gareth Mulvenna suggested that the representations of the flag protesters being circulated by LAD and others on social media were akin to the 'chav' stereotype used to demonise the white working class in England.[7] The depiction of working-class loyalists as unemployed, violent 'abjects' was comparable to the neo-liberal discourses that portrayed working-class people as an 'underclass' unworthy of inclusion within society (Tyler, 2013). The demonisation of the working class made it harder for people to empathise with them, therefore making it less likely that they would want to improve their living and working conditions (Jones, 2011). In effect, negative representations of groups such as asylum seekers and travellers in the news media were designed to portray these social groups as being 'unworthy' of British citizenship (Tyler, 2013). Despite much evidence of socio-economic deprivation within their communities, there was also little public sympathy for working-class loyalists. This reductive framing of loyalists as antagonistic, sectarian bigots was contested by groups such as the Northern Ireland Unionist Collective Group (NIUG), which used the same online platforms as LAD to facilitate intra-community dialogue about the flag protests. Participants used the NIUG social media accounts to present more positive representations of loyalist communities. Long (2018: 62) argued that the NIUG, as well as the new online newspaper *Loyalist Perspective*, constituted positive community responses to LAD's use of crude stereotypes to describe working-class loyalists. The research presented in this chapter will explore how working-class loyalists were depicted by the parody group on social media, and whether there were any changes in these representations after the flag protests dissipated in March 2013.

Specifically, it will explore two research questions related to the role of LAD in contentious politics in Northern Ireland during this period:

1. How did LAD use social media to frame contentious political issues between October 2012 and November 2013?
2. Did the role of the parody group in contentious politics evolve after the flag protests? If so, how?

These questions are explored through a qualitative thematic analysis of content extracted from the official LAD Facebook and Twitter accounts. Discovertext was used to collect posts in real time from its Facebook page between 10 December 2012 and 20 February 2013 (N = 35,721). This time period was selected because it coincided with the peak of the flag protest movement. It should be acknowledged that the page may have been unpublished several times during this period. Its moderation processes also meant that many comments may have been deleted and therefore unavailable during the period of data analysis.

A further phase of data collection was conducted in October 2013 in order to explore how the parody group was contributing to hybrid media events and contentious political debates after the flag protests. Discovertext was again used to collect tweets posted by the LAD Twitter account between 2 October and 21 November 2013 (N = 3,061). All data were analysed between January and March 2014.

LAD Facebook page, December 2012–March 2013

There were several noticeable 'spikes' in comments on the LAD Facebook page during this period (see Figure 5.1). Like LPPU (see Chapter 2), these coincided with the violence in East Belfast in the first week of January and the loyalist move to white line protests announced towards the end of the month.

Sample characteristics

There were 1,223 threads in the corpus with an average of 29 comments each. Page administrators were responsible for instigating the vast majority of these threads (83.7 per cent) and were the most frequent contributors to the page, posting 2,197 (6.15 per cent) of the total comments in the corpus. There were no observable differences between the themes found in these threads and those in the 445 posts that generated no responses (1.24 per cent). A total of 83 comments could not be coded as they had been removed in the intervening period between data collection and analysis. While the percentage of 'orphan' posts was broadly comparable to LPPU (see Chapter 2), fewer Facebookers started threads on the LAD page. One interpretation of this finding was that these social media users viewed the page

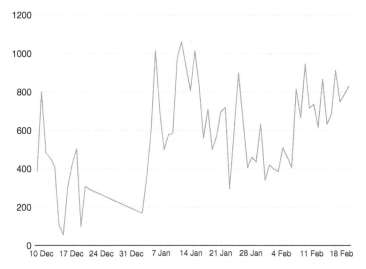

Figure 5.1 Number of comments posted on LAD Facebook page, December 2012–February 2013.

as an entertainment platform rather than a space for the contestation of the flag dispute.

LAD Facebook page provides space for mocking and shaming of 'cyber loyalists'

Results indicated that most of the threads on LAD's public Facebook page mocked the flag protesters. Indeed, 216 of these threads (17.67 per cent) revolved around the online shaming of loyalists, mainly for posting hate speech and poorly written comments on Facebook pages such as LPPU (see Figure 5.2). Sectarian remarks about the Short Strand residents, threats against a Translink bus driver who criticised the protests, praise for the Parachute Regiment's role in Bloody Sunday, and calls for the removal of Polish people from Northern Ireland, were highlighted by LAD, leading to calls for both Facebook and the PSNI to take firmer action against those responsible. Social services were urged to intervene in the case of a female loyalist who had posted a picture on Facebook that appeared to show her child holding a rifle and union flag. One of the longest comment threads in the sample

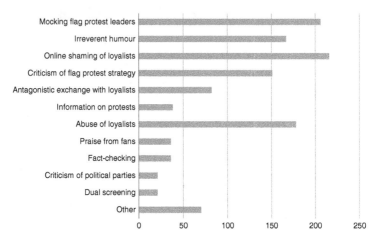

Figure 5.2 Main themes in threads on LAD Facebook page, December 2012–February 2013.

(N = 109) revolved around a screenshot of an LPPU post in which a protester boasted about having escaped from the 'cops' in the aftermath of rioting in East Belfast. While one LAD-min quipped that the PSNI would be monitoring the page, commenters noted that the loyalist's Facebook profile was fully public and that he was an ex-soldier. A threat to burn down St Matthew's Church near the Short Strand–Lower Newtownards Road interface was also screenshot, shared and roundly condemned by commenters. Those responsible for hate speech and threats on LPPU were frequently 'named and shamed' by LAD and its supporters. For example, one loyalist was identified as being responsible for threats against *Sunday World* editor Jim McDowell on a protest-related Facebook page, in retaliation for what they saw as the paper's negative coverage of the protests. In another thread a loyalist was shamed for her references to child abuse within the Catholic Church in a post on LPPU that erroneously claimed that the Union Flag had flown over City Hall for 106 years. This generated a wave of criticism, with the exception of one commenter, claiming to be a PSNI officer, who expressed support for her post. In response, several LAD supporters threatening to report him to his employers. This was illustrative of the antagonistic nature of the exchanges between critics and supporters of the protests on the page, albeit that these represented a very small proportion of the posts analysed in the study.

Commenters frequently characterised loyalists as sectarian, poorly educated bigots, with some going so far as to make misogynistic and disablist comments about those posting on LPPU. It should be noted that on a number of threads these remarks were challenged, with one commenter calling another's reference to Jim Dowson having Down's syndrome highly offensive. Nevertheless, the focus on spelling and grammar criticised by Dave Magee and others was very much in evidence here. One loyalist was labelled a 'flegtard' for referring to a 'border pole' [sic] in a post on LPPU. Others were shamed for misspelling locations such as 'Crumlin Road' while one loyalist was mocked for posting "two wrongs don't make a wright [sic]" on one of the flag protest pages. Sectarian remarks were screenshot and shared on the LAD page, presumably with the intention of shaming those responsible and highlighting the true nature of these 'street-fighting loyalists'. The Stephen Nolan audience, subjected to much abuse and mockery on #flegs, was described here as a group of "uneducated morons" in one thread, which criticised the BBC presenter for "licking their arses" and mocked the same woman fat-shamed on the hashtag. Indeed, the 'dual screening' evident on the LAD Facebook page focused on the same programmes being discussed on Twitter during this period. However, much of this online shaming was aimed at the administrators of public loyalist Facebook pages. LPPU admin 'Dan' bore the brunt of much of this abuse, with one thread revolving around his decision to support the TUV (see Chapter 2) leading to comments suggesting he was illiterate and had learning difficulties. His conspiracy theories about there being too many Catholics in the PSNI and planes being used to 'spy' on protesters were dismissed by LAD 'fans' who called him "inbred" and "simple". He was given the moniker 'Desperate Dan' for his post in January 2013 condemning the closure of the LPPU page in the aftermath of the J18 case, with many ridiculing his references to not surrendering to the IRA in "any shape or form". His claims that he could not protest due to work commitments led to derogative speculation that he was variously a benefit cheat, sex worker or employed in a burger bar.

Flag protest leaders mercilessly mocked by LAD supporters

Protest provocateurs, Bryson and Frazer in particular, were subjected to much derision on the LAD Facebook page. This abuse and mockery was identical to that seen in the #flegs (see Chapter 3). Bryson's media appearances, speeches at rallies and social media posts throughout January 2013 were ridiculed. A picture of him carrying a UVF flag during an Orange Order parade was also shared, leading many commenters to brand him a "hypocrite" in light of his claims that he was just a peaceful protester. These threads inevitably contained ad hominem abuse directed towards the North Down political activist. This abuse included references to him being a "pervert" and a "love child from the Jeremy Kyle Show", the latter resonating with the 'chav' stereotype of English working-class communities discussed earlier. Bryson's speech impediment was mocked by many commenters who compared him to the cartoon character Elmer Fudd; others used homophobic slurs and expressed their amusement at his 'high-pitched' voice during his various media appearances. Negative Amazon reviews of his novel *Four Men Had a Dream* were shared, much to the hilarity of LAD's supporters. The consensus among those commenting on the LAD page was that he was an attention-seeker who lacked intelligence and was badly out of his depth. This was perhaps best illustrated by several threads mocking his announcement of the name of the LPPU backup page; as one commentator noted, the "saviour of loyalism" and "Ulster's Mandela" did not appear to be very bright.

A similar story emerged in relation to the framing of Willie Frazer on the LAD Facebook page. The 'PIRA horsemeat conspiracy' was one of many stories about the South Armagh victims' campaigner shared by LAD for the amusement of its supporters in January 2013. Frazer's social media accounts also provided much material for LAD and its supporters to discredit or mock. For example, his argument with controversial comedian Frankie Boyle on Twitter led to jokes about Boyle being a member of the Provisional IRA if he was drawing the ire of the protest spokesperson. LAD supporters dismissed his call for more funding to be allocated to 'PUL communities', referring to the controversy over how his own victims' group (FAIR) had misused EU funds in the past. Like Bryson, he was frequently described as "paranoid" and a "conspiracy nut" for his allegations that protesters were being victimised by the 'PSNIRA'. His assertion that there had been tens of thousands of peaceful protesters on the streets was mocked for being untrue, as was his claim that loyalists were being interned and denied their human rights. Additionally, there was much ad hominem abuse directed towards Frazer; this focused on his physical appearance (many referring to him needing a "decent haircut"), and frequently used disablist and homophobic language to mock his 'lack of intelligence' and relationship with Bryson. Supporters were encouraged to 'troll' Frazer, with one LAD-min providing a link to his official Twitter account and a live *News Letter* web chat involving the victims' campaigner. In terms of the latter, LAD supporters were urged to post questions for Frazer, with many mocking his appearance and referring to the FAIR EU funding scandal. Whether intentional or not, the parody group was encouraging a social media 'pile on' that focused more on Bryson and Frazer than the issues underpinning the protests.

Loyalist culture war narrative and tactics challenged

While LAD may have self-identified as a 'sitcom', there was evidence to suggest that its Facebook page actually functioned as a space for its supporters to dispute the loyalist culture war narrative underpinning the protests. References to the "loyalist 'holocaust'" and the "PSNIRA" were held up as evidence of the conspiracy theories that fuelled the protest movement. Loyalists who claimed on LPPU that nationalists went out of their way to be offended by their marches were branded hypocrites in light of their response to the flag vote. The victim mentality of the protesters was frequently mocked, with commenters observing that they were ignorant of the economic and political disparities between Catholics and Protestants in Northern Ireland prior to the Troubles. Loyalists were said to be always blaming others for their perceived loss in cultural, economic and political rights. The 'sousveillance' footage showing the arrest of a man in East Belfast, much debated and shared on LPPU (see Chapter 2), was unsurprisingly given little credence on three threads analysed here. The unanimous opinion of LAD commenters was that the video failed to substantiate claims that the man had been the victim of an unprovoked and brutal attack, with many noting that Catholic residents in Ardoyne were frequently treated far worse during contentious Orange Order marches in North Belfast (to be discussed in Chapter 6). While comments made by Bryson, Dowson and Frazer were inevitably challenged for perpetuating these narratives of victimhood, groups such as the Ulster Political Research Group (UPRG) were also criticised for their statements blaming Sinn Féin for having orchestrated the flag dispute. As per #flegs, unionist and loyalist political representatives were condemned for failing to challenge the views of these 'supremacists', as well as raising tensions surrounding the flag vote that resulted in violence in East Belfast and the targeting of Alliance elected representatives.

The tactics adopted by the flag protesters were heavily criticised by LAD and its supporters. Claims by Bryson and Frazer that they were lawful and peaceful were dismissed, and the low turnout during Operation Shutdown ridiculed. Video footage appearing to show loyalists threatening *Irish News* journalist Allison Morris was also shared, condemned and cited as yet more evidence of the 'peaceful intimidation' employed by the protesters. LPPU updates about the decision to protest outside Facebook's Dublin HQ after its removal of the LPPU page, a planned demonstration in Derry/Londonderry on the anniversary of Bloody Sunday, and the move to white line protests, were copied and shared on the page for supporters to comment on. The latter was mocked by commenters who quipped that the protesters might try to snort the street markings, the implication being that loyalists were likely to consume illegal drugs and substances. This was in addition to the genuine concerns raised about the potential dangers of encouraging people to stand in the middle of the road, with the PSNI commitment to stop loyalists blocking roads broadly welcomed. While there was much mockery of these announcements (including one thread in which a LAD-min jokingly asked its supporters if they had any questions for the newly formed UPF which inevitably descended into offensive remarks about Bryson and Frazer), there was also evidence that the page was being used to share information that countered loyalist narratives. This included fact-checking claims by UPF spokespersons and LPPU commenters, such as a post about the Drumcree parade disputes in the 1990s which erroneously blamed five civilian deaths on the protests by the nationalist Garvaghy Road Residents' Coalition rather than the Loyalist Volunteer Force. There were also fact-checks of claims made on loyalist Facebook pages about the number of plastic baton rounds that had been discharged during the demonstrations, with LAD supporters confirming only two had been fired in the first month of protest-related violence.

Irreverent humour and building the LAD 'brand'

The irreverent humour evident in #flegs was also showcased on the LAD Facebook page. Much to the amusement of its supporters,

LAD-mins posted pictures of cars and houses decorated with union jacks, labelled the #flegsmobile and 'LAD Towers' respectively. Videos such as a skit about flags that featured on BBC Northern Ireland sitcom *Give My Head Peace* and a Lego version of an Eddie Izzard flag sketch were posted on the page, presumably to poke fun at the protesters. Memes such as *Dmitri Finds Out* and *Flegs specs* which had circulated on Twitter during this period, were also shared. Supporters were encouraged to create their own content using meme generators and resources such as a 'paint your own flag' sheet. They responded by making many jokes at the expense of the protesters. For example, one stated that if the flag was not restored above City Hall LAD would hold protests in the sky on Christmas Eve in order to disrupt traffic from "da north pole". Another joked that Catholics were appropriating loyalist culture by using the Red Hand of Ulster on Gaelic football tops, making fun of the fact that many loyalists did not appear to recognise the three Ulster counties situated in the Republic of Ireland. Loyalist protest leaders were compared to a boy band in another thread, which saw commenters suggest a variety of potential names for the group such as "LoyalZone" and "McFleg". There were also irreverent references to pop band Take That's set list at an upcoming gig in Belfast having protest-themed songs such as 'Relight my Fire', and Union J's appearance on the X Factor final, with many stating that the protesters must have been annoyed that they hadn't won the reality television contest. Loyalists were even compared to Chinese dissident Liu Xia, who was being held under house arrest by the authorities, presumably to ridicule their claims they were being interned. However, this often went further than #flegs in reinforcing negative stereotypes of working-class loyalists. Loyalists were depicted here as being offended by innocuous things such as the green man on a traffic light ('the IRA' preventing loyalists from crossing the road) and were ridiculed in ways that went far beyond the flegs puns and pictures of snowmen holding union flags being shared on Twitter during this period. While #flegs may have patronised loyalists at certain times, the study suggested that much of the humorous content on LAD's Facebook page was provocative and even offensive towards the flag protesters.

The LAD 'entertainment brand' was articulated through LAD-mins posting and interacting with supporters in character. All of its posts were riddled with intentional spelling and grammar errors parodying the updates on loyalist Facebook pages. LAD even went as far as to deny it was a parody page and presented itself as one of the main flag protest pages in posts condemning Facebook (labelled 'Taigbook' for its alleged republican sympathies) for closing down LPPU after the J18 case. The group jokingly condemned the UPF as a "waste of time" because it believed democracy worked and didn't allow members to use sectarian language. There were many other posts from LAD-mins poking fun at the protesters, such as one asking whether LAD were permitted to carry union flags in their hand luggage if they were to attend an upcoming demonstration in London. While this created some confusion among a handful of users who appeared to believe LAD were behind the flag protests, there was almost unanimous support for the parody group among commenters. Content from other parody accounts was regularly reposted on its Facebook page with supporters often responding to LAD-mins 'in character' themselves. There was also evidence of the group marketing itself as a comedy brand, as discussed in the aforementioned interview with Winston Smith a few months later. Most notably, they used their Facebook page to announce the release of a Christmas single, eliciting praise from supporters. LAD-mins were also keen to increase engagement with the page, encouraging fans to share their posts with their friends in order to show the world that "loyalists are against democracy". Solidarity for the group was frequently expressed in light of the mass reporting campaigns launched by loyalists to force Facebook to remove its page. Indeed, one thread on 21 December 2012 saw the group attribute a temporary absence from the platform to a "cyberhack BY SF.IRA", leading to praise from its supporters who welcomed its return. While it was possible that critical comments may have been deleted by one of the LAD-mins, the study suggested that the overwhelming majority of posts were supportive of its work as an 'entertainment platform' that also focused attention on the sectarianism associated with the flag protest movement.

LAD Twitter account, October–November 2013

A thematic analysis of 3,061 tweets posted by the LAD Twitter account between 9 October and 22 November 2013 was conducted in order to explore how the role of the parody group in contentious politics changed after the flag protests had petered out. There were several peaks in its Twitter activity coinciding with hybrid media

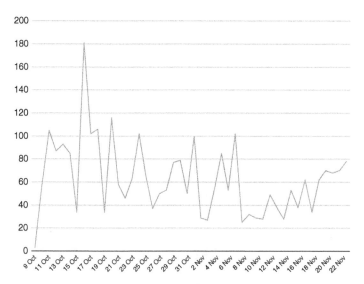

Figure 5.3 Number of tweets from LAD Twitter account, October–November 2013.

events (see Figure 5.3). These included a legal ruling that Health Minister Edwin Poots had displayed irrational religious bias in his decision to uphold a ban on blood donation from gay men (12 October), the airing of *The Disappeared*, a BBC Northern Ireland documentary on the 15 people murdered and buried secretly by the Provisional IRA during the Troubles (4 November), and the annual DUP party conference (22–23 November). It should be noted that the corpus included modified or quote tweets, retweets and those authored by the LAD-mins responsible for its account.

The majority of the corpus consisted of original tweets posted by LAD (67.1 per cent), followed by modified/retweets (20.52 per cent) and @replies to other tweeters (12.38 per cent). While the original tweets posted by the group will be investigated in further detail below, the group tended to retweet irreverent and humorous content posted by its supporters and other parody accounts on the microblogging platform (see Figure 5.4). They also shared tweets from supporters portraying loyalists as bigoted, irrational and unintelligent.

The group retweeted praise from fans, and shared posts from parody accounts (e.g. @Kokotheflegger) and supporters mocking the

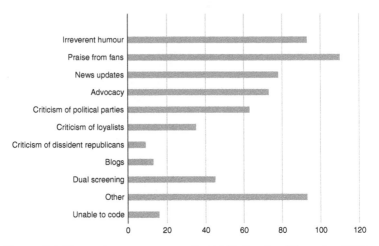

Figure 5.4 Themes in posts retweeted by LAD, October–November 2013.

protesters, such as Frazer's announcement that he was embarking on a charity 'bed push' through Belfast. There was also some evidence to support Whearty's claim they were "equal opportunity satirists". Tweets condemning violent dissident republicans who had sent letter bombs to politicians including NI Secretary of State Theresa Villiers were shared in October 2013. The group also retweeted posts promoting ongoing campaigns such as the initiative to save the Exploris aquarium in Portaferry from closure. Whereas 10 months earlier its Facebook page had focused on deconstructing the 'victim mentality' of flag protesters, its Twitter account focused the attention of its supporters on a variety of political issues, ranging from the plight of the Disappeared to calls for equal marriage in the contested polity.

Irreverent humour and memes an intrinsic component of LAD comedy brand

There were some continuities in terms of LAD's use of Facebook during the flag protests and its Twitter activity in late 2013, especially in terms of its 'in character' tweeting and use of irreverent humour to provide commentary on contentious political issues. The former was illustrated by its 'banter' with supporters. LAD-mins shared pictures of fans dressed as flag protesters on Twitter and plugged the imminent release of new content to the delight of its fans. They celebrated their tweet being mentioned on the BBC NI political discussion show *The View*, thanking the producers for making "six LAD-mins very happy".[8] However, the maintenance of the Twitter account by multiple volunteers, each of whom adopted a different loyalist persona, was not without controversy. Lewd remarks by one LAD-min about the appearances of both NI21 Chair Tina McKenzie and PUP activist Izzy Giles, as well as a caption meme featuring a picture of a woman in lingerie, caused a furore for which the group were later forced to apologise.

Elsewhere, there were references to #flegmas, 'celebrating' the upcoming anniversary of the flag protests, that were reminiscent of the #flegs wordplay seen on Twitter during the flag protests. The group invited suggestions from fans for loyalist-themed movies (#loyalistmovies) and asked for ideas about what they should condemn next, using the hashtag #LADcondemns. They jokingly claimed that a flag skit by comedian Jake O'Kane on BBC NI comedy panel show *The Blame Game* had been ripped off from LAD, offered to take tourists on a guided tour of murals across Belfast, and mocked the victim mentality of loyalists by suggesting that the bad weather must have been the fault of "themmuns" (presumably referring to republicans). They also offered to buy US envoy Richard Haas a pint in a tweet, hashtagged #peacethroughpissups, that poked fun at the lack of progress in the all-party talks to address conflict-legacy issues he was co-chairing with Professor Meghan O'Sullivan.[9]

Memes were more commonly deployed by the group during this period than during the flag protests. Indeed, just over 10 per cent of the tweets in the corpus were either videos or images mocking political representatives and the Protestant Coalition (PC), a newly formed loyalist political organisation that included Willie Frazer among its leaders. There were also a series of 'mural remixes' which saw popular television personalities such as TV game show host Roy Walker photoshopped into iconic images in support of paramilitary groups that featured on gable walls in working-class districts across Northern Ireland. There were much higher production values in the content produced by LAD here than in December 2012. For example, a parody of the English heavy metal band Motorhead's song *Ace of Spades* called *Waste of Space* was shared 10 times in the final four weeks of data collection.[10] Its lyrics condemned members of the Northern Ireland Assembly as "power-sharing jokers" who pandered to the extremes on both sides, and featured images of politicians such as UUP leader Mike Nesbitt nodding in synch to the lyrics. A similar remixing of the Boomtown Rats hit *I Don't like Mondays* (*I Don't like Lundys*) began with singer Bob Geldof's call for loyalists and republicans to 'grow up' and showed images of loyalists attacking the PSNI.[11] Parody party election broadcasts for the DUP and PC were created, mocking their leaders and policies, the former ending with the slogan "Aspire to Bitter" in a reference to the perceived intransigence and sectarianism of the largest pro-union party.[12] The group also used Twitter to share its *Flegger Watch* videos, which parodied UTV weather presenter Frank Mitchell's *Weather Watchers* segment by making humorous and often lewd references to towns in the region and signing off these segments with the loyalist slogan 'No Surrender'.[13] The other notable video shared was Undercover Ulster: Orgies, in which a television interview with Frazer was edited so that he appeared to be answering questions about a fictional swinging scene at the Twaddell peace camp.

Caption memes and remixes of pop culture icons were also used to attack the PC. To coincide with the annual BBC *Children in Need* telethon, there were a series of memes mocking Frazer and his colleagues as "brethren in need" and suggesting that the Twaddell camp was being organised in support of "Prodsey Bear" (a loyalist version of Pudsey, the famous mascot for the BBC campaign).[14] Other targets included PUP Cllr Billy Hutchinson, whose face was superimposed on the body of actress Uma Thurman in a *Pulp Fiction* poster renamed "PUP Fiction"; he also featured in a meme captioned 'Downton Abbey Centre' which poked fun at a picture of him dressed up as unionist leader Lord Edward Carson during a UVF commemoration event.[15] Although much of this content focused on unionists and loyalists, Sinn Féin representatives were not spared from memeification. Gerry Adams was depicted as hiding behind the sofa during the BBC documentary *The Disappeared* in one meme, with another featuring Queen Elizabeth II and Deputy First Minister Martin McGuinness in bed together drinking tea, which was captioned #disgrace presumably in reference to the poor spelling and grammar of loyalists on social media.[16] However, other memes shared by the group appeared to contravene Fealty's 'play the ball, not the man' rule. In particular, the 'separated at birth' meme appropriated by the group made disparaging comparisons between local politicians and popular culture icons. DUP Health Minister Edwin Poots was compared to the 'Pob' puppet from the eponymous Channel 4 children's show, and Mike Nesbitt was said to resemble Francis Griffin from US animated sitcom *Family Guy*.[17] Poots was also shown dressed as a vampire in a meme captioned "Straight blood only" in reference to the controversy over his support for the ban on blood donation from gay men.[18]

LAD forced to defend continued online shaming and mocking of loyalists

The online shaming of loyalists ('fleggers') was again evident on its Twitter account in October 2013, albeit that it was overshadowed by the irreverent humour and memes discussed above. Content posted on the PC Facebook page was frequently screenshot by LAD and shared on Twitter for the amusement of its followers. One loyalist commenter was mocked for her claims that the National Lottery was funding the Provisional IRA, while another was condemned for his apparent threat to "burn out foreigners" residing in East Belfast. However, unlike its Facebook page a few months earlier, this online shaming focused more on the social media posts attributed to the PC leadership rather than its supporters. For example, LAD linked to one of its own blogposts about a planned PC protest outside Belfast City Airport in response to unsubstantiated allegations that a local taxi firm had forced Protestant drivers to make way for their Catholic counterparts.[19] The parody group also issued corrections to disinformation spread on the PC Facebook page, in one case showing that a picture allegedly depicting the PSNI coming under attack from 'SF/IRA' had in fact been taken several months earlier. Bryson and Frazer continued to be the primary targets for the group's ire; the former was again mocked for negative Amazon reviews of his book while allegations that he had gone on hunger strike while in police custody were heavily ridiculed. The latter was nicknamed 'Wee Willie Taser' in reference to a picture he had posted on Facebook showing him inside an Army Saracen vehicle, with his claims that a paintbomb had been thrown at his house dismissed by a LAD-min who suggested that he had done it himself. There were noticeably fewer remarks about the appearance of the two protest provocateurs than 10 months earlier, with the exception of a few barbs about an image showing Frazer dressed as radical Muslim cleric Abu Hamza during a court appearance relating to his alleged incitement of violence during a flag protest rally in January 2013. LAD also mocked Bryson, comparing him to a monkey after he'd posted on social media about needing medical treatment for chest pains.

The group also used Twitter to refute accusations from other tweeters that it was elitist and defended their right to 'shine a light' on loyalist bigotry. The aforementioned blogposts by Dave Magee were dismissed by LAD in a Twitter 'spat' with the researcher;[20] Magee was mocked for his suggestion that 'homework clubs' could address some of the factors that caused the flag protests, and labelled a "flegger with a degree" after he accused the group of elitist snobbery. Indeed, researchers such as Queen's University Belfast's Professor John Brewer were condemned for being 'self-righteous' and obsessed with them. The group frequently highlighted their own working-class Catholic and Protestant members in response to claims from TUV activist Sammy Morrison and others that they only focused on loyalists. They pointed to examples such as their criticism of a dissident republican march in Castlederg, County Tyrone, and denied that they were perpetuating negative stereotypes of working-class loyalists on social media. However, they did acknowledge that it was harder to mock "faceless twats" who planted bombs in the night than groups such as the PC who broadcast their bigotry on social media.[21] Overall, it appeared that the group were not only fully aware of the critique of their online shaming of loyalists, but were actively using Twitter to justify their campaign of focusing on the sectarian hate speech of the PC.

LAD dual screen hybrid media events for their fans

The dual screening of political panel shows seen on the LAD Facebook page during the flag protests was also evident on its Twitter feed. The BBC NI documentary *The Disappeared* saw the group tweet and retweet posts criticising Gerry Adams for his evasive responses to questions about his role in the disappearance of Jean McConville in 1972. A tweet from the Sinn Féin leader asking people with information on the disappeared to contact him directly was described by the group as one of the most "ill-judged tweets of the year".[22] TUV leader Jim Allister was also condemned for using the documentary for political advantage. Somewhat inevitably, the radio and television programmes hosted by BBC presenter Stephen Nolan were also mentioned in the corpus. LAD 'rage tweeted' its responses to the discussion of the gay blood ban on the weekly television show, with the host criticised for providing a platform to "pompous" political commentator David Vance.[23] A BBC NI *Spotlight Special* highlighting the link between PUP representative Winston 'Winkie' Irvine and the UVF was also live-tweeted by the group, with a LAD-min mockingly expressing their surprise at the revelation that he had been a UVF Commander. They later shared the news that Irvine's appointment to a Policing and Community Safety Partnership was being reviewed in light of these allegations.

The party conferences were the other main focus of this dual screening. Much of the commentary on these revolved around irreverent observations about the parties' key personalities rather than their specific policy platforms. A LAD-min, who appeared to be attending the NI21 conference, shared pictures of its Deputy Leader John McAllister during his speech; they also joked that there weren't enough Rangers shirts and flags in the venue and that they were only there to stroke Basil McCrea's hair.[24] However, the hybrid media event that received the most attention was the annual DUP party conference between 22 and 23 November 2013. In addition to the alternative party election broadcast discussed earlier, this 'live-tweeting' consisted of humorous remarks made at the expense of speakers such as Diane Dodds; fictional quotes attributed to the MEP included "If it wasn't for our minister's you'd all be speaking German".[25] The speech by First Minister Peter Robinson was also 'remixed' by LAD so that he acknowledged the DUP's lack of accomplishments in office and made child-like jibes towards his opponents such as the "UUP are shit".[26] While much of this dual screening was irreverent and humorous, it nevertheless appeared to be informed by a critique of the actions and policies of these political parties. It also helped them connect with their fans on Twitter, many of whom expressed their amusement at how LAD was framing these events.

LAD speaking truth to power?

Congruent with the notion that satire should hold truth to power, the group focused much more on the actions of political parties during this period than it had during the flag protests. LAD mocked UKIP Cllr Henry Reilly for an editorial in which he challenged the scientific evidence base for climate change, and claimed he was under the influence of alcohol when he alleged the group were working for M15. He was also condemned for an article in which he asserted that homosexuality was a 'lifestyle' choice that he was "unable to condone". While PUP representatives including leader Dr John Kyle and Julie Ann Corr were praised for their unequivocal condemnation of attacks on Alliance party offices and their support for equal marriage, the party's support for a loyalist march marking a year since the controversial flag vote on 30 November was condemned. They were branded hypocrites for their previous support for a designated days flag protocol and their links to the UVF were heavily criticised. However, it was perhaps no surprise that the DUP was the main focus of LAD scrutiny during this period. South Belfast Cllr Ruth Patterson (given the moniker "Ronseal Roof" in light of her use of fake tan) was condemned for posting offensive social media comments about a republican parade in Castlederg in August 2013, and mocked for defecting from the DUP to the TUV. Health Minister Edwin Poots was something of a bête noire for the group on a range of issues including the gay blood ban, a funding shortage for care homes in the region, and his refusal to liberalise Northern Ireland's abortion laws to bring them in line with the rest of the UK. It was therefore no surprise that the group used #givepootstheboot to share a petition calling for his removal from office, and a link to a site entitled 'hasedwinpootsresignedyet', throughout this period. At the same time, the group tried to drum up support for #neveragain, a hashtag designed to highlight all those killed during the Troubles and to call for an end to sectarianism and violence in Northern Ireland. LAD pointed to the fact that Greysteel and Shankill, two of the atrocities they referred to in their tweets, were trending in Belfast. Local politicians were referred to as a "bunch of arseholes" for not joining the campaign.[27]

While some of the memes mentioned above did perhaps focus too much on the appearance of public figures such as Poots, it would be misleading to suggest that LAD was just 'playing the man, not the ball'. As discussed earlier, the group dual screened *The Disappeared* documentary and retweeted content criticising Gerry Adams's refusal to admit his membership of PIRA on the programme, and his seemingly dismissive responses to questions about Jean McConville. LAD added to the cacophony of voices urging him to retire from public life on the grounds that nobody would believe anything he would say "after that performance".[28] There were also signs that the parody group's social media presence was emerging as a focal point for the debate of contentious political issues that did not relate to the legacy of the conflict. In addition to focusing attention on the legal ruling on the gay blood ban, the group challenged the DUP's record on LGBT rights with reference to a story that its MLA Tom Buchanan had called homosexuality an abomination during a schools event hosted by the NI Assembly. The evidence in support of the human trafficking bill proposed by Lord Morrow, which was being debated in the Assembly during this period, was also contested by the parody group. DUP Cllrs Christopher Stalford, Peter Martin and Peter Weir were challenged on the merits of the proposals to criminalise the purchasing of sex, with the former's sarcastic reference to "happy hookers" heavily criticised. The DUP was accused of ignoring the views of sex workers themselves, as well as the evidence from countries such as Sweden that had introduced similar legislation. LAD argued that the Morrow proposals would push these issues further underground and asked the aforementioned DUP representatives to provide data in support of the proposals, a request that fell on deaf ears. In this way, the parody group appeared to take on a more activist stance in using an evidence base to challenge the main political parties on their agendas.

Conclusion

It was reasonable to presume that the flag protests would be the apotheosis of a comedy collective whose *raison d'être* was to satirise 'street fighting loyalists'. These protests were the largest mass mobilisation of loyalists since the mid-1990s, and also the first demonstrations of their kind to be contested on platforms such as Facebook and Twitter. The accessibility of public loyalist Facebook pages provided the parody group with plenty of material to work with in their mission to focus attention on the sectarianism of the protesters. Indeed, most of the threads on the LAD Facebook page shamed loyalists for their online hate speech. Threats to attack the nationalist residents of the Short Strand, which would result in LPPU being removed by Facebook after the J18 case, were highlighted and those responsible named and shamed. However, there was also evidence of the negative stereotyping of working-class loyalists that led some critics to accuse LAD of elitism. While a few of LAD's supporters did challenge these stereotypes, its Facebook page provided a space in which the 'other-ing' of loyalists who supported the protests was pervasive. They were labelled illiterate, violent bigots, and were shamed for their poor spelling and grammar in their social media posts. Commenters made a number of offensive remarks about LPPU administrators and audi-ence members during a Stephen Nolan television debate on the flag protests. The vilest abuse was reserved for protest provocateurs such as Bryson and Frazer. Their frequent media appearances during this period were mocked, with the latter's 'IRA horsemeat' conspiracy story the subject of much ridicule on the LAD Facebook page in January 2013. Much of this was ad hominem abuse that mocked their appearances, intellectual capabilities, and even included innuendos about their sexuality. It was therefore perhaps no surprise that the few exchanges between critics and supporters of the protest movement on the LAD page were antagonistic.

LAD embraced its burgeoning reputation as a focal point for the 'silent majority' who opposed 'street fighting loyalists' and the social conservativism of the DUP. The group's major contribution to con-tentious political debates broadly conformed to the 'silly citizenship' articulated by Hartley. LAD-mins live-tweeted events such as the annual DUP party conference 'in character', poking fun at the speak-ers while simultaneously critiquing their policies. Wordplay reminis-cent of the vernacular creativity seen in #flegs was used by the group and its fans to highlight what they saw as the absurdity of the demon-strations that were causing widespread disruption across the region. That is not to say that there wasn't a 'bite' to the increasingly sophis-ticated content created by the group and shared via its various social media accounts. There were many memes targeting the respective PC and UPF leaderships, which were provocative and often offensive towards its targets. However, LAD did increasingly speak truth to power in November 2013. Health Minister Edwin Poots was con-demned for his 'irrational' gay blood ban and for refusing to liberalise the repressive abortion laws in Northern Ireland. The DUP proposals for a Human Trafficking Bill were scrutinised and its representatives challenged on the evidence base to support its proposals to criminalise the purchasing of sex. While much of this activity focused on the largest unionist party and Poots, the PUP, Sinn Féin and TUV were also condemned by the group for their perceived political opportun-ism and hypocrisy during this period. LAD also appeared to play a key role in promoting social media advocacy campaigns such as #givepootstheboot and #neveragain on the microblogging site. Overall, LAD's repertoire appeared to have evolved from their online shaming of rank-and-file loyalists during the flag protests. Silly citizenship had become the modus operandi of its entertainment brand by the end of 2013, albeit that they continued to relentlessly target loyalist provocateurs such as Bryson and Frazer. LAD had emerged as a focal point for the debate of contentious political issues in the Northern Irish information ecosystem during this period. In this way, the parody group were speaking truth to power by holding political parties such as the DUP to account for their actions and introducing facts into key policy debates.

Notes

1 The group also went under the name LADFLEG. It is referred to here as LAD as this was its chosen moniker during this period.

2 Emerson's piece featured in the *Sunday Times*. It was later reproduced on LAD's blog and can be accessed here: http://loyalistsagainstdemocracy. blogspot.com/2013/09/real-online-wonder-of-year.html (accessed 10 August 2014).

3 For more on this, see: "LAD is dead. Long Live LAD", available at: http://loyalistsagainstdemocracy.blogspot.com/2013/10/lad-is-dead-long-live-lad.html (accessed 10 September 2018).

4 J. Ó Néill, "@LADFLEG versus #Facebook", 9 October 2013, http://sluggerotoole.com/2013/10/09/ladfleg-versus-facebook/ (accessed 10 September 2018).

5 John McAllister denied knowledge of LAD's involvement in NI21. For more, see: S. McBride, "'Key people' at LAD website worked for NI21", *News Letter*, 27 August 2014, available at: www.newsletter.co.uk/news/key-people-at-lad-website-worked-for-ni21-1-6261675 (accessed 10 November 2018).

6 SOS NI is a volunteer-centred organisation providing support to vulnerable people on the streets of Belfast. The video can be found here: www.facebook.com/BELFASTLAD/videos/189875524550740/ (accessed 10 December 2018).

7 Mulvenna (2013), p. 6.

8 LAD, "Oh the shame of it @PJMcFaddenDerry @AlexKane221b @bbctheview – You've made 6 dickheads very happy", 17 October 2013, 11.24 p.m., Tweet.

9 LAD, "Welcome back Dick. See you later for a session. #PeaceThrough-PissUps", 28 October 2013, 3.02 p.m., Tweet.

10 The "Waste of Space" video can be found on the LAD blog here: http://loyalistsagainstdemocracy.blogspot.com/2013/10/ (accessed 10 January 2019).

11 The definition of Lundys, provided at the start of the video is a term used by unionists and loyalists to describe a traitor or Catholic sympathiser, with reference to the actions of Robert Lundy during the Siege of Derry. For more on this, see here: www.youtube.com/watch?v=Gbda-1vT56s& fbclid=IwAR3K-8cKjYALbeElKrUVXmv5unr1dm7xZIZrgFZIksWQ1 eXS8xt4IvXyaJA (accessed 10 October 2018).

12 LAD, "DUP-Aspire to Bitter http://www.youtube.com/watch?v=-9nuc OIKs74...#dup13", 23 November 2013, 11.53 a.m., Tweet.

13 LAD, "Lets check in with Frank-Fleggerwatching: sunbeds: youtu.be/gjtruHLkFis," 21 October 2013, 5.49 p.m., Tweet.

14 LAD, "Don't forget to dig deep tonight for Brethren In Need with our old mate Prodsey Bear http://fb.me/1Vh6Trcoh", 15 November 2013, 9.00 p.m., Tweet.

15 LAD, "Downton was amazin tonight wasn't it? http://t.co/PaTZPWAlhi", 13 October 2013, 10.16 p.m., Tweet.

16 LAD, "#DISGRASE http://t.co/VT4ivCEMND http://t.co/CPEIN5 tm3m", 11 October 2013, 10.15 p.m., Tweet.

17 LAD, "Separated at birth? #GivePootsTheBoot special https://t.co/gta1gQUc2q http://t.co/HxLpsivIhC", 6 November 2013, 9.35 p.m., Tweet.

18 LAD, "Count Poots is on the prowl. Straight blood only", 31 October 2013, 8.50 p.m., Tweet.

19 For more on the taxi story, see here: http://loyalistsagainstdemocracy. blogspot.com/2013/10/taxi-for-protestant-coalition.html (accessed 21 January 2019).

20 LAD, "Come join @dgmagee as he attempts to get inside my mind with his blog LAD: part 1' http://t.co/LLRKKyBr9N," 13 October 2013, 4:45 p.m., Tweet.

21 LAD, "@brianjohnspencr @IGLivingstone @bartoncreeth How can you mock a faceless bunch of twats, that sneak about in the night planting hoax bombs?" 12 October 2013, 7:11 p.m., Tweet.

22 LAD, "Ill judged tweet of the year?" 4 November 2013, 11:45 p.m., Tweet.

23 LAD, "Dave Vance's @DVATW answer to everything 'Republicans'. A vile, pompous twat earning a living from the public purse pic.twitter. com/mUptAnoiCC", 31 October 2013, 12:15 a.m., Tweet.

24 LAD, "Looking forward to stroking Bazza's lovely hair at the #NI21 conference. #freshhaircut", 16 November 2013, 10:32 a.m., Tweet.

25 LAD, "'If it wasn't for our minister's you'd all be speaking German'
    @DianeDoddsMEP #dup13", 23 November 2013, 11:44 a.m., Tweet.
26 LAD, "'Nesbitt is crap, UUP are shi' Robinson #dup13", 23 November
    2013, 12:24 p.m., Tweet.
27 LAD, "Not one single politician, not a fucking single one has joined in
    on to say #NeverAgain What a bunch of arseholes," 30 October 2013,
    10:07 p.m., Tweet.
28 LAD, "@GerryAdamsSF Time you disappeared from public life Gezza.
    No-one's gonna believe a word you say after that performance", 5
    November 2013, 12:03 a.m., Tweet.

6

Twitter, affective publics and public demonstrations: the 2014 and 2015 Ardoyne parade disputes

From January 2013 onwards, social media platforms were used with increasing frequency to mobilise publics around contentious parades and protests in the deeply divided society. Most notably, social media provided communicative spaces for the contestation of the Northern Ireland Parades Commission decision to re-route the return leg of an Orange Order parade away from the nationalist district of Ardoyne in Belfast during July 2013. Loyalists framed the ruling as yet further evidence of the how policymakers were constantly 'appeasing' republicans through symbolic gestures such as the altering of the flag protocol for Belfast City Hall in December 2012. Meanwhile, nationalist and republican residents criticised the Orange Order for refusing to engage in meaningful talks to resolve the impasse, going so far as to suggest that the outward leg of the parade should face similar restrictions.

This chapter analyses how these affective publics both escalated and de-escalated tensions surrounding the Ardoyne parade and related protests. It examines how citizens used Twitter to respond to the contentious Orange Order parade in July 2014 and 2015. Like the flag protests, there remains a dearth of empirical research investigating the extent to which citizens co-created these news streams, or how they responded to media coverage of the dispute. This chapter addresses that gap in the literature by providing background on the contentious parade and presenting the results from a study of 44 newspaper articles and 7,388 #Ardoyne tweets posted during the 2014 and 2015 disputes. In particular, it will focus on how tweeters responded to any misinformation and disinformation shared that had the potential to inflame sectarian tensions and generate violence during this hybrid media event.

Ardoyne dispute as a manifestation of 'ethnic poker'

Both the nationalist Ardoyne residents and loyalist supporters of the Orange Order had competing claims in relation to the annual 12 July Orange parade. Many of the residents opposed the parade and expressed their desire for it be re-routed away from the Ardoyne shopfronts on the Crumlin Road. They were accused of being intolerant of unionist and loyalist culture by supporters of the Ligoniel Orange lodges, who claimed that they had a right to march on the arterial North Belfast route. In effect, the Ardoyne parade dispute was a 'bellwether' for the progress towards a shared society (or lack thereof). These tensions illustrate the 'ethnic poker' that has persisted within highly segregated working-class districts in North Belfast, where zero-sum perceptions of space and politics have led rival interface communities to "unrealistically up the ante" against each other (Neill, 2004: 205). Indeed, the competition over resources and territory during the Troubles was left largely intact by the Agreement's emphasis on 'parity of esteem' between the two ethnic blocs (Aughey, 2007).

It was therefore no surprise that the annual 12 July Orange Order parade in North Belfast continued to be a flashpoint in the post-Agreement era. The nationalist residents organised sit-down protests in July 2005 to prevent the parade from passing by the Ardoyne shopfronts on the Crumlin Road. Eight civilians and 105 police officers were injured as a result of the violence that flared after the protesters were forcibly removed to allow the return leg of the parade to proceed along its traditional route towards the city centre. The 2006 and 2007 parades passed off relatively peacefully due to an agreement between the newly formed Ardoyne Parades Dialogue Group (APDG) and the North-West Belfast Parades and Cultural Forum. However, this brought only temporary respite from the disturbances synonymous with the return leg of the parade. In July 2009, the Real IRA were blamed for a gun attack on PSNI officers and orchestrating a rioting involving nationalist youths in the aftermath of the evening parade.[1] Hopes that a solution similar to that agreed in 2006 and 2007 could be brokered were dealt a further blow by the non-compromising stance taken by the Crumlin Ardoyne Residents Association (CARA) and Greater Ardoyne Residents' Collective (GARC), who replaced the APDG as the representatives of the residents in 2010. GARC made their own applications to the Parades Commission for permission to host counter-demonstrations coinciding with the return leg of the parade during the next few years. The proscription of these protests helped focus media attention on how the police 'hemmed in' local residents who opposed the parade.

The Parades Commission, a quasi-judicial body created under the Public Processions (NI) Act 1998, categorised the Ardoyne parade as one of 213 contentious public demonstrations held in 2011, which accounted for only 5 per cent of the total number held that year.[2] They imposed restrictions on the parade from 2012 onwards in relation to its timing, the number of participants and the playing of music. These failed to prevent violent clashes between nationalist youths and the PSNI following the return legs of the 2011 and 2012 parades. This prompted the Commission to ban the return leg of the 2013 parade from passing by the Ardoyne shopfronts. Its written determination expressed disappointment at the failure of political representatives to broker a deal between the Orange Order and the Ardoyne residents, while acknowledging the difficulty balancing "the rights and responsibilities of all people involved and affected by the parade".[3] A total of 70 PSNI officers were injured during four consecutive nights of "animalistic" violence by loyalist rioters in North Belfast, which later spread to other areas such as Portadown.[4]

The 'largely peaceful' 2014 Ardoyne parade

In 2014, the Parades Commission again banned the return leg of the parade from the 800-metre stretch of road that passed by the Ardoyne shopfronts. The failure of political representatives on both sides to broker a solution to this impasse, highlighted by the continued presence of a loyalist protest camp in nearby Twaddell Avenue, led many observers to fear that there would be a repeat of the 2013 violence. Loyalists at the self-styled 'peace camp' were accused of ratcheting up sectarian tensions by organising evening band parades near the interface area. In August 2013 several broke through the police lines in an attempt to finish the parade that the Ligoniel Orange lodge had been unable to complete a month earlier (Donnelly, 2013).

Tensions in Ardoyne were raised in July 2014 when leaders of the main unionist political parties, together with loyalist representatives and the Orange Order, announced a 'graduated response' to the Parade Commission's decision to alter the route of the return parade for the second year in a row. Further details on this were released on the eve of the Twelfth, including plans for a 6-minute pause of all Orange marches the following day to represent the time it would take for the North Belfast march to return home via its traditional route.[5] In response, a member of GARC tried to obtain a high court injunction preventing the outward leg of the parade from passing the Ardoyne shops on the morning of the Twelfth.[6]

Social media was being used to both escalate and de-escalate tensions between nationalist residents and the Orange Order in the run-up to the Twelfth. Loyalists reacted angrily to the rumours suggesting that an image of Oscar Knox, a 5-year-old who had died from a rare form of childhood cancer, had been burnt on an 'Eleventh night' bonfire in Randalstown, County Antrim. A picture supposedly showing the bonfire began to circulate on Twitter late on 11 July, prompting many angry responses. These rumours were quickly refuted and condemned by loyalists, who 'named and shamed' two tweeters they believed responsible for starting them (Reilly, 2015). Evidence that the image had been digitally altered emerged later that evening. One tweet provided a link to the original image of the bonfire that had been taken by photographer Stephen Barnes in July 2013.[7] The image of Knox, that had caused so much anger among tweeters a few hours earlier, was clearly absent from the picture. It was noticeable that the number of tweets about the Knox incident sharply declined after visual counter-evidence was shared online. Moreover, both sides were praised for delivering one of the most peaceful Twelfths in recent memory.

Newspaper coverage focuses on 'graduated response' and appeals for calm

The Knox visual disinformation did not feature in the media coverage of the 2014 parade. A total of 24 articles addressing the Ardoyne parade between 8 and 14 July 2014 were identified. Just over two-thirds of these were published in the *Belfast Telegraph* and its sister publication the *Sunday Life* (see Appendix 2, Table A2.1). Previews of the contentious parade speculated about the 'graduated response' while also providing a platform for political representatives to appeal for calm. Hence, four representatives of the Orange Order featured in the top 10 most quoted actors in this dataset (see Appendix 2, Table A2.2). Statements from these leaders reiterated that any violence during the Twelfth would play into the hands of republicans, as well as harming their efforts to reverse the determination. On the eve of the Twelfth, Grand Master Edward Stevenson was among those to appeal for any demonstrations to be peaceful, warning those intent on violence to "stay away from our protests".[8] This echoed the sentiments of the Northern Ireland Executive, which issued a brief press release confirming that "the Executive agreed that all parades and parades-related protests should be lawful".[9]

There were many newspaper editorials calling for talks to find a permanent solution to the impasse. Most notably, the *Belfast Telegraph* proposed a commission, consisting of stakeholders from both sides, to broker a deal between the residents and the Orange Order.[10] The cost of policing parades and protests in the previous 20 months, estimated at £55 million, was often cited in articles calling for a peaceful solution.[11] Sinn Féin MLA Daithí McKay was among those to express concern about how an "unspecified political action" like the 'graduated response' might send out "negative signals to potential tourists".[12]

A recurring theme in this coverage was that the PSNI were prepared to deal with any parade or protest-related violence that might occur. Although an unnamed senior police source expressed "guarded optimism" about there being a peaceful outcome,[13] this was set against a backdrop of statements confirming the number of PSNI officers to be deployed in North Belfast and other potential flashpoint areas on the Twelfth. On 11 July, freelance journalist and author Brian Rowan reiterated that the PSNI "did not want to show their teeth" but confirmed that "50–60 public order units" were due to attend the Twelfth demonstrations, each equipped with 25 officers, "five land rovers, water cannon and dog teams".[14] This appeared to be part of a concerted effort to warn loyalists and nationalist residents that violence would be swiftly dealt with should tensions boil over. Furthermore, a spokesperson from the Parades Commission confirmed that proven breaches of its determination would influence future decisions on the contentious Ardoyne parade.[15]

In the days following the Twelfth (13–14 July), local newspapers provided a platform for politicians to congratulate both sides for delivering the most peaceful Twelfth in recent memory. Northern

Ireland Secretary of State Theresa Villiers commended the Orange Order and unionist leaders for their "intensive work" to ensure the parades passed off without incident, while acknowledging that nationalist leaders had "played their part in working hard to defuse local tensions".[16] North Belfast political representatives were less effusive in their praise for both sides, albeit for different reasons. DUP MP Nigel Dodds welcomed the behaviour of the Orange Order in the face of "severe provocation from republican elements" whereas SDLP MLA Alban Maginness praised the dignity shown by the Ardoyne residents and called on the Parades Commission to examine several breaches of its determination.[17] It was also noticeable that several violent incidents received scant coverage in these articles. This included the stabbing of a 28-year-old man after rival Catholic and Protestant gangs clashed on Ormeau Bridge in the south of the city, and the scuffles between nationalist residents and loyalists after bandsmen breached a Parade Commission ruling prohibiting the playing of music outside St Patrick's Church, just north of Belfast City Centre. The eight arrests and six men charged with public order offences in connection with these incidents, as well as an explosive device found at the Mallusk postal sorting office, were reported in one *Belfast Telegraph* article stating that "this year's Twelfth was peaceful".[18] Perhaps the most accurate summary was provided by PSNI Chief Constable George Hamilton, who said he was pleased that the day's Twelfth parades had passed off "largely successfully".[19]

The 2015 parade dispute

There was little progress made in efforts to resolve the parade impasse throughout the rest of the year. In the absence of such an agreement, the Parades Commission ruled that the 2015 parade would be subject to the same restrictions as in the previous year due to the "potential for public disorder".[20] They also placed limitations on a planned GARC protest against the outward leg of the parade, which, as in previous years, was permitted to follow its traditional route past the Ardoyne shops. GARC reacted angrily to their protest being restricted to 60 people, urging local residents to ignore the ruling and come out in force during the morning parade.[21] Loyalist groups such as the West Belfast Ulster Political Research Group (UPRG) claimed this was part of a republican strategy to provoke violent clashes between residents and the Orangemen, thus leading to the outward leg of the parade being re-routed in future years.

The 2015 parade was marred by loyalist rioting in North Belfast, as protesters faced off against PSNI officers preventing marchers from returning home via their traditional route. A total of 24 police officers were hurt after loyalists began to throw missiles at their lines, with erroneous rumours circulating online that PSNI Chief Constable George Hamilton was among those injured.[22] Baton rounds and water cannon were also deployed by officers in the nearby Woodvale Road as tensions flared shortly after the march arrived at the police barricade at 7.30 p.m. Tensions were further raised when Orangeman John Aughey drove his car into a crowd of residents who had gathered on the Crumlin Road during the stand-off between loyalists and the police. He was later charged with attempted murder for the attack, which resulted in a 16-year-old girl being seriously injured.[23] Images of PSNI officers and local residents lifting the car onto its side to free the girl were shared by eyewitnesses and journalists on Twitter. As in 2013, the violence was condemned by politicians from across the political divide. Having praised the behaviour of the Orange Order and residents a year earlier, Theresa Villiers described the attacks on police as disgraceful and accused the rioters of damaging Northern Ireland.[24]

Episodic framing of dispute dominates 2015 newspaper coverage

A total of 20 articles addressing the Ardoyne parade between 8–15 July were identified. Like the 2014 corpus, over two-thirds of these (70 per cent) were published in the *Belfast Telegraph* and its sister publication the *Sunday Life* (see Appendix 2, Table A2.3). These newspapers again provided the PSNI with the opportunity to reassure members of the public that they were prepared to deal with any breaches of the Parade Commission determination. PSNI Assistant Chief Constable Stephen Martin, one of the top 10 most quoted actors in the 2015 dataset (see Appendix 2, Table A2.4), confirmed that the police were ready for any trouble in an article published in the *Sunday Life*.[25] However, there was little optimism about a peaceful outcome in the week leading up to the Twelfth. Unionist and loyalist representatives quoted in this coverage expressed their anger and frustration at the Parades Commission for not allowing the return leg of the North Belfast parade to proceed along its traditional route. One article featured a speech by UPRG activist Gerard Solinas in which he stated "we thought that we should be rewarded for behaving as we were supposed to".[26] He channelled the flag protest narrative that the dispute was a 'lightning rod' for loyalist dissatisfaction with 'republican appeasement' and 'one-sided' historical enquiries that had overlooked atrocities such as the 1993 Shankill Road bombing.[27] Like the year before, media coverage leading up to the Twelfth focused on several court rulings relating to the contentious parade. For example, the *Belfast Telegraph* reported on the conviction of five members of the Pride of Ardoyne flute band for repeatedly breaching a Parade Commission determination by playing music at demonstrations at the Twaddell peace camp between February and May 2014.[28]

The episodic nature of the 2015 coverage was illustrated by the fact that 25 per cent of the articles focused on the Aughey incident. For the most part, these centred on eyewitness accounts confirming that he had lost control of the vehicle and that "police turned over the car onto its side to release the girl".[29] A number of these human-interest stories featured updates from the relatives of Phoebe Clawson, the victim of the attack. Newspapers additionally carried statements by PSNI spokespersons emphasising the role of their officers in tending to the stricken teenager after the attack, as well as providing updates on her condition.[30] This was against the backdrop of much criticism of Aughey being part of the 'small minority' who were "determined to return to the bad old days."[31]

The coverage of the parade impasse in the days following the Twelfth was dominated by appeals for calm after the violent scenes seen in the North Belfast interface. A spokesperson for the Orange Order echoed the statements made by Grand Master Edward Stevenson a year earlier, calling on those responsible to desist as the violence was "strengthening the hands of those who wish to further curtail our parades".[32] Nigel Dodds adopted a similar rhetorical stance to his 2014 statement calling for all protests to remain peaceful; the North Belfast MP condemned the "outrageous behaviour" of the Parades Commission and the way in which they "caved in to Republican violence and threats of violence".[33] Like the Solinas speech a few days earlier, this showed how unionists and loyalists believed that the Commission was biased against the expression of their culture.

While there was no evidence that social media was being used to source news in 2014, hybrid media logics were much more evident in the 2015 coverage. This began in the run-up to the Twelfth with an article in the *Belfast Telegraph* reproducing verbatim a statement posted by GARC on its Facebook page condemning the "disgraceful decision" of the Parades Commission to place restrictions on its counter-demonstrations. The fact-checking capacity of the local news media would be illustrated by an article written by Claire Williamson on the 14 July, which corrected rumours and misinformation spread on social media about the Chief Constable being injured during the violence. The source for this correction was a tweet from Hamilton in which he reassured members of the public that he was "safe and well".[34] Journalist John Monaghan also wrote a piece on how a Russia Today live feed showing the stand-off between loyalists and the police on the evening of the 13 July had been watched by 150,000 viewers. The footage captured using the Twitter Periscope application was held up by the *Irish News* journalist as evidence of the "how latest technology played a central role in Monday's event".[35]

The analysis above raised questions about what role, if any, tweeters had played in reducing the tensions surrounding the contentious parade in 2014 and 2015. Research indicates that social media has turbocharged the sharing of misinformation and disinformation (Wardle, 2017). In the Northern Irish context, it has been alleged that rumours spread on social media platforms have contributed to intercommunal violence in contested urban interface areas (Young, 2014). Therefore, this research focused specifically on how users responded to misinformation and disinformation circulated on Twitter.

There were three specific research questions that were investigated:

1. To what extent did critics and supporters of the Orange Order use Twitter to reduce sectarian tensions surrounding the Ardoyne parade in 2014 and 2015?
2. How did these tweeters respond to misinformation and disinformation relating to the contentious parade?
3. What role did professional journalists play in these information flows?

These research questions were explored through a critical thematic analysis of tweets posted during two periods: 11–14 July 2014, and 12–15 July 2015. The two selected periods included key events relating to the marching season in both years, including 'Eleventh night' bonfires and both legs of the annual Ardoyne Twelfth parade in North Belfast that caused such controversy. It should be noted that the 2015 demonstrations were on 13 July because Twelfth parades were not traditionally held on Sundays. It was anticipated that eye-witnesses would share their perspectives on these events within these time periods, referring to any rumours or disinformation circulating on the site.

The text-mining software tool Discovertext.com (www.discover-text.com) was again used to collect these tweets in real time during both periods of data collection. A keyword search was conducted using 'Ardoyne' in order to identify tweets referring to the North Belfast parade. A total of 7,388 tweets were identified, 1,842 in 2014 and 5,546 in 2015. These were plotted on a time-series graph, which revealed that 'Ardoyne' tweets peaked at 7 p.m. on the day of the Twelfth demonstrations in both years (see Figure 6.1). One explanation for this finding was that this spike in Twitter activity was the result of viewers of flagship television news programmes, such as *BBC Newsline* and *UTV Live Tonight*, turning to social media to follow what was happening during the return leg of the parade.

Both corpora were dominated by retweeted content (64 per cent in 2014; 55 per cent in 2015), followed by original tweets and @replies to other users (11 per cent in 2014; 6 per cent in 2015) (see Figure 6.2). One interpretation of this finding is that there was very little conversation between these tweeters in relation to the dispute. However, it should be acknowledged that responses to tweets that did not mention Ardoyne were not collected due to the keyword search used.

Geotagged tweets

There was a dearth of geotagged tweets in both corpora. In 2014, only 21 tweets (1.14 per cent) were tagged to specific locations by their respective authors. The majority (14) of these were within Northern Ireland, with six situated within 6.5 miles of the Ardoyne district. Other locations in this corpus included cities in Italy, Portugal, Republic of Ireland and Saudi Arabia. Despite its larger size, the 2015 corpus had fewer geotagged tweets than the 2014 dataset. Only four tweets (equivalent to 0.07 per cent of this corpus) contained geotagged locations, three of which were within 4 miles of the North

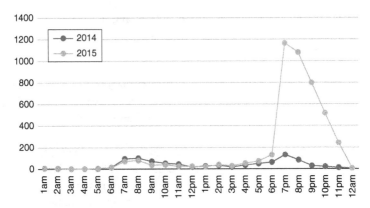

Figure 6.1 Tweets mentioning Ardoyne, 12 July 2014 and 13 July 2015.

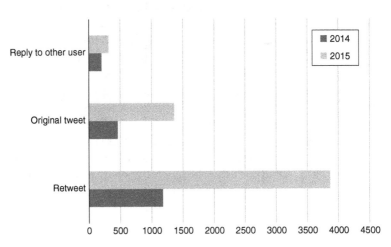

Figure 6.2 Classification of 'Ardoyne' tweets.

Belfast interface, with the other in Lisburn, a city 8 miles south-west of Belfast. One interpretation of these data might be that few of the 2014 and 2015 tweeters were present in Ardoyne. Most users retweeted content produced by eyewitnesses and professional journalists who were in attendance. However, it could also be argued that this finding is congruent with previous research that suggests that geotagging is not a common practice among tweeters due to privacy concerns (Malik et al., 2015).

Profile of Ardoyne tweeters

A long tail distribution of user activity was evident in both corpora. Of 1,025 tweeters identified in 2014, 717 (70 per cent) tweeted only once during the period of data collection. A similar distribution was also evident in the other corpus, with 1,648 out of 2,605 identified users (63 per cent) tweeting once between 12–15 July 2015. In contrast, the 50 most prolific contributors to both Twitter streams accounted for 23.78 per cent of tweets in 2014 and 16.97 per cent in 2015. This finding was congruent with the pattern of user activity in flag-protest related hashtags (see Chapter 3), as well as previous research into politicised debates about protests on Twitter (Bruns et al., 2016).

Analysis of the profiles of the top 50 tweeters revealed that a clear majority were citizens (see Figure 6.3). Although there were relatively few bloggers in both datasets, the most frequent contributors in 2014 and 2015 were Ardoyne Republican (@RepublicanUnity) and Brian John Spencer (@brianjohnspencr) respectively. Seven (14 per cent) of

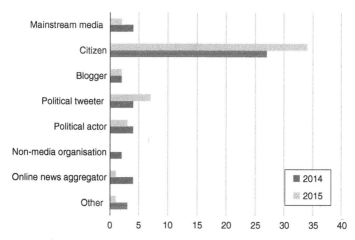

Figure 6.3 Top 50 'Ardoyne' tweeters by actor type.

the most prolific contributors in 2015 were political tweeters, although this group was less prominent the year before. Most of these self-identified as loyalists (three in 2014; four in 2015), compared with just one republican in both years. In contrast, both loyalist and republican political actors were equally represented in the 2014 top 50 (with 4 per cent respectively). While mainstream news media organisations such as the *Irish News*, and its journalist Allison Morris, featured among the most active tweeters in 2015, they were less prominent in 2014. Overall, there was some evidence to suggest that the same group of highly engaged users were dominating these Twitter streams, with 26 social media profiles ranking within the top 50 tweeters in both years. It should also be noted that a few of the top 50 #flegs tweeters were present in these corpora (one in 2014 and three in 2015 respectively).

A clear majority of the total Ardoyne tweeters (64.5 per cent in 2014; 74.31 per cent in 2015) were citizens who did not express politically opinions on their Twitter bios (see Figure 6.4). In contrast, there were relatively few political tweeters (11.71 per cent in 2014; 7.7 per cent in 2015), mainstream news media (7.22 per cent in 2014; 5.06 per cent in 2015), bloggers (2.73 per cent in 2014; 2.46 per cent in 2015), and non-media organisations such as the Northern Ireland Community Relations Council (2.34 per cent in 2014; 1.84 per cent

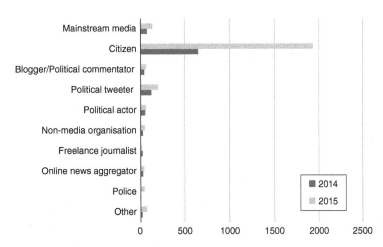

Figure 6.4 Ardoyne tweeters by actor type.

in 2015). Members of political parties including the Alliance Party, DUP, PUP, SDLP, TUV and UUP were present in both corpora (4.78 per cent in 2014; 2.34 per cent in 2015). Tweeters categorised as 'Other' (3.99 per cent in 2014; 3.15 per cent in 2015) included parody accounts, such as LAD and academic researchers.

Authors of retweeted content

There were some differences in terms of who was responsible for content retweeted in both corpora (see Figure 6.5). In 2014, 206 tweets were identified that had been retweeted 1,312 times during the period of data collection. Citizens were responsible for the largest proportion of these (31.7 per cent), closely followed by professional journalists and news media organisations (29.61 per cent). Representatives from six political parties (Alliance, DUP, Northern Ireland Conservatives, PUP, SDLP and Sinn Féin) were retweeted under 'Ardoyne' that year. Although some of these will be explored in more detail below, it is worth noting that the PUP (41.67 per cent) and Sinn Féin (25 per cent) accounted for the majority of party tweets that were retweeted. Political tweeters were responsible for nearly three times as many tweets as the representatives of the main political parties, with the majority self-identifying as loyalists (44.4 per cent) or republicans

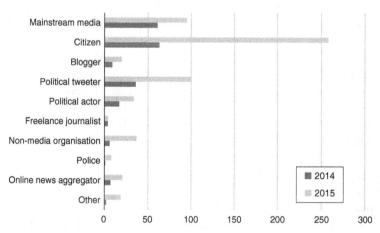

Figure 6.5 Authors of retweeted content in #Ardoyne.

(30.55 per cent). Many of these tweets were also attributed to the same accounts, with 129 unique users identified as responsible for these 206 tweets.

During the period of data collection in 2015, 596 tweets were retweeted 3,870 times. A larger proportion (258 tweets or 38.75 per cent) was authored by citizens compared with 2014, probably due to the larger number of tweets collected during this period. Political tweeters were responsible for more of this content than mainstream media and professional journalists, with most of these self-identifying as loyalist (35 per cent) or republicans (33 per cent). A total of 34 tweets were attributed to political actors, with the TUV and UUP represented along with the other five parties from the 2014 corpus. As per the previous year, the PUP (29.4 per cent) and Sinn Féin (23.53 per cent) accounted for the majority of these. There were, however, some differences between the two corpora that should be acknowledged. First, the PSNI, which had not been prominent in the 2014 corpus, were responsible for seven of these tweets in 2015. Second, bloggers such as Brian John Spencer and online news aggregators such as 24NI news (@24NI) were much more visible compared with the previous year. Finally, it should be acknowledged that there was some overlap between the authors of retweeted content in both 2014 and 2015. Providing yet further evidence of how these Twitter streams were dominated by a small group of highly active users, 344 unique users were identified as being responsible for these 596 tweets, 23 of whom had been responsible for retweeted content in 2014.

A small minority of the tweets in both corpora were deemed non-relevant to the study. Most notably, a picture posted by BBC Northern Ireland (BBC NI) television reporter Mark Simpson on 27 June 2014, showing a cross-community 'sleep-out' in Ardoyne, was retweeted 53 times during the first period of data collection. There were also a few tweets circulating in 2014 promoting community events, such as a family fun day at the Ardoyne GAA (Gaelic Athletic Association) club later that month. In 2015, non-relevant tweets included one referring to a mural in the district expressing support for Gaza and one praising local footballer Joe Gormley.

A critical thematic analysis of these tweets was conducted in two phases: August 2014 and March 2016. In addition to the difficulty of establishing the representativeness of these tweets and the attitudes of their authors, the dearth of geotagged tweets made it difficult to say for certain whether these tweeters were in a position to influence or report on events on the ground. Therefore, this study assessed the extent to which geographically dispersed affective publics appeared to be helping reduce sectarian tensions around the contentious parade.

Results and discussion

Ardoyne information flows on Twitter tend to originate from the mainstream media

Analysis of both corpora showed that the most heavily retweeted content was produced by professional journalists rather than citizens or other actors. In 2014, for instance, a picture posted by BBC NI reporter Mark Simpson, showing one of the Ligoniel lodges as they walked past a GARC observer, along with the text: "peaceful start to 12th July marches. No trouble as Orange Order parade passes Ardoyne shops" was shared 72 times.[36] The integral role of mainstream media in these information flows was further illustrated by the high number of retweets of seemingly mundane updates posted by journalists, particularly during the 2014 parade. For example, a tongue-in-cheek tweet from BBC NI journalist Kevin Sharkey showing two dogs greeting one another (captioned "Trouble in #Ardoyne"), was one of the most retweeted that year (19 times).[37] The real time coverage provided by journalists showed images of crash barriers, police personnel and vehicles put in place to enforce the Parade Commission's ruling in relation to the return leg of the parade. In the absence of violence, such content also illustrated how professional journalists, presumably deployed in North Belfast in the expectation of a recurrence of the violence seen in 2013, had very little to report on.

Further evidence of the role of journalists in structuring these information flows emerged during the 2015 parade. Reporters present at the scene were mainly drawn from local newspapers, such as the *Belfast Telegraph* and *Irish News*, and regional television news programmes produced by BBC NI and UTV. However, one of the most retweeted posts (120 retweets) in this corpus was Sky News Northern Ireland correspondent David Blevins' tweet featuring an image of protesters being soaked by a PSNI water cannon captioned: "BREAKING: Water canon deployed after police officer injured during disorder at

Ardoyne flashpoint, North Belfast".[38] Indeed, a recurring theme in tweets posted by journalists between 7 p.m. and 10 p.m. was the ferocity with which loyalists attacked police lines with bricks, bottles and even sections of the barricade erected to prevent them from passing by the Ardoyne shops.

Professional journalists also initiated most of the information flows during the outward leg of the parade. This included detailed descriptions of the heavy security presence in North Belfast, as well as reports on the arrest of two GARC protesters for assaulting a PSNI officer during the group's counter-demonstration that morning. The latter story in particular highlighted the role of mainstream media in shaping information flows about the parade. News of these arrests was first shared by journalists such as Allison Morris, who tweeted that apart from the arrests it had been a "fairly hassle free albeit wet morning".[39] Rebecca Black (*Belfast Telegraph*) provided subsequent updates confirming that two men had been arrested, rather than one as had originally been reported. The media framing of these arrests was in sharp contrast to that of the West Belfast UPRG, who tweeted "PSNI moving in against DISSIDENT SCUM at Ardoyne !! Several arrests being made !!", as well as sharing a picture of the police dispersing the counter-demonstration.[40] The tweet, posted at 9.10 a.m., was shared 17 times by those supportive of the Ligoniel Orange lodges, but not by any news organisation or professional journalist. This was in contrast to the higher number of retweets for content produced by professional journalists such as Morris and Black throughout the day. Overall, there was little evidence to suggest that either loyalists or the nationalist residents were initiating information flows that travelled further than their respective constituencies.

Several affective publics mobilised in response to the dispute

The few politicians in both corpora tweeting about Ardoyne appeared united in their support for a peaceful resolution to the parade dispute. Sinn Féin's Gerry Kelly[41] and the SDLP's Nichola Mallon[42] expressed similar sentiments in 2014 and 2015 respectively, hoping the day would remain peaceful after the outward leg passed off without incident. Few politicians proposed a solution to the impasse, with most only going so far as to suggest that there should be an 'agreement' at the local level. It was perhaps no surprise that several loyalist and unionist political representatives criticised the Parades Commission, with TUV leader Jim Allister and DUP Cllr Nigel Kells[43] expressing support for the Ligoniel lodges in their efforts to return home via their traditional route. PUP Cllr Julie Ann Corr was one of several representatives to condemn a decision by a Belfast court to convict five members of the Pride of Ardoyne flute band for violating the terms of a Parades Commission determination.

One interpretation of these findings might be that politicians were perpetuating zero-sum perceptions of space and politics in North Belfast, praising their own side while laying the blame for the impasse on the 'other' community. Yet, the same cannot be said for the vast majority of tweeters who appeared anxious about the threat of violent disorder in North Belfast. This anxiety appeared in many cases to stem from the reputational damage to Northern Ireland that would be caused by a repeat of the violence seen in 2013. A recurring theme in the 2015 corpus was that the rioting had brought shame and embarrassment to everyone living in Northern Ireland. Tweeters characterised the rioters as a "lawless mob" and urged both sides to work together to resolve the dispute. The Orange Order and unionist political leaders were criticised for failing to provide leadership for the "brainless thugs" attacking the police lines on the evening of 13 July. At the same time, the PSNI were praised for holding the line between the loyalists and the residents in North Belfast.

These were not the only publics evident in both corpora. A small but vocal minority of loyalist and republican tweeters used Twitter to share crude stereotypes of the 'other' community and to blame them for the dispute. Loyalists argued the decision to re-route the parade for the third consecutive year rewarded GARC, who were described as "dissident filth", in reference to their alleged links to dissident republican terrorist groups. The Mid Shankill Residents Group (@Mid_Shankill_RG) urged the people of Ardoyne to stand up against these "mindless sectarian bigots".[44] There were tweets in both 2014 and 2015 claiming that GARC "bussed in" protesters in order to swell the numbers at their counter-demonstrations. Loyalists were united in their belief that institutions such as the news media, the police and the judicial system favoured the residents over their community. The paucity of media coverage devoted to paint bomb attacks on the Twaddell peace camp on 12 July 2015 was held up as evidence of the 'war' against unionist and loyalist culture. It should also be noted that few of these tweets used sectarian language to describe the residents, with those that did being posted by accounts endorsing loyalist paramilitary groups such as the UDA.

A larger public was identified in each corpus that supported the nationalist residents and criticised the loyalist protesters. In 2014, several tweets mocking the Orange Order and its supporters for their inability to complete the return leg of the march were hashtagged #reroutetheflute. The 'graduated response' was also mocked in a meme showing leaders of the Orange Order and unionist politicians at its launch, captioned "The Last Supper". Loyalists were characterised as a "sectarian hate mob" that lacked the "muscle" to force their way through the police lines. Few of these tweeters praised the Orange Order for the role they played in ensuring the morning parade passed off without incident. Indeed, one predicted that it would probably "kick off" during the return parade later that evening.

These tweeters highlighted the sectarianism of the marchers as the reason for their continued opposition to the contentious parade. You-Tube footage of the violence seen in July 2013 was shared as evidence of the "sectarian hatred" that the nationalist residents were subjected to on the Twelfth. Pictures also circulated showing the names of several dead UVF members on the drum and banner of a flute band. The Orange Order was accused of "glorifying terrorism" through their decision to allow this band to lead the North Belfast parade. Supporters of the Orangemen responded quickly to this criticism, with one tweeter asserting that this drum skin had been used during a memorial parade and that it would likely be changed before the Ardoyne parade. However, a member of this band provided a different narrative on this image, tweeting that they were "proud" to display these names on their uniform and flags.

Blogger Ardoyne Republican (@RepublicanUnity), the most frequent contributor in the 2014 corpus, identified the "militarisation" of the Greater Ardoyne community as one of the reasons why GARC opposed "unwelcome marches", such as those of the Ligoniel Orange lodges.[45] This was presumably a reference to the heavy police presence in the area during the Twelfth each year. Contrary to the consensus view that the morning parade had passed off without incident, he confirmed that several breaches of the Parades Commission determination were going to be reported to the relevant authorities.[46] The United Protestant Voice (@unitedprotestan) responded by asking for evidence of these breaches and accusing GARC of participating in an unlawful protest against the parade.[47] There were also hostile exchanges between the republican blogger and the West Belfast UPRG in 2014. During one conversation, the former described the latter as the "supporters of UDA fascists" in response to their claims that the Ardoyne residents were being held to ransom by "deviant Republicans".[48] This was typical of the interactions between loyalists and republicans that were found in both corpora. However, it should be noted that these were few in number and most tweeters did not directly address others in this way.

The mocking of loyalist culture was even more pervasive in the 2015 corpus. The Orange Order were depicted as "sectarian clowns" and, in one case, there was a very personal attack on a loyalist woman alleged to have been dealing drugs in North Belfast. The increased vitriol against loyalists appeared to be linked to the aforementioned incident when John Aughey drove his car into a crowd of nationalist residents. Loyalists were heavily criticised for failing to condemn the attack and their claims that the residents had launched an unprovoked attacked on the vehicle. The other focal point was the Russia Today live feed showing the stand-off between loyalists and the police on the evening of 13 July. While many tweeters noted it just showed "people standing around", others mocked the appearance and behaviour of those who had gathered in front of the police lines. One tweeter suggested that the trouble was caused by drunk kids being 'egged on' by drunk women to throw objects at the police.

Twitter users move quickly to debunk rumours and disinformation

Misinformation and disinformation appeared to have a very short lifespan in both corpora. This was particularly evident in 2014, when both loyalists and republicans checked the veracity of claims made by each other on the microblogging site. Loyalists were accused of digitally altering pictures in order to portray GARC and the nationalist residents in a negative light. A picture of a protester holding a mock-up road sign indicating that the Orange Order was not welcome in the area began to circulate on Twitter shortly after 7.30 p.m. on 12 July. One tweeter suggested that this illustrated the intolerance of republicans and highlighted the 'unlawful' nature of the GARC counter-demonstrations. Within a few minutes visual evidence was shared on Twitter showing that the protester's placard proclaimed "Love Thy Neighbour", rather than the anti-Orange Order slogan in the doctored image. This was corroborated by an image of the same scene, taken and shared on Twitter by BBC NI journalist Kevin Sharkey a few hours earlier. The tweeter responsible for the photoshopped image was accused by others on the site of spreading lies about what was happening on the ground at Ardoyne. It was perhaps no surprise that the number of retweets of the altered image declined significantly after this revelation, in much the same way as the Oscar Knox rumour a few hours earlier.

A similar theme emerged in relation to the Ardoyne parade and counter-demonstrations in July 2015. Most notably, images taken from many different vantage points were used to support claims and counterclaims about the Aughey incident. West Belfast UPRG was one of several accounts to share reports that the republicans had attacked the car, with no reference to the attempted murder of the residents in attendance.[49] It should be noted that one of these tweeters had been responsible for the photoshopped image of the 'Love Thy Neighbour' placard the previous year. Elsewhere, there was much speculation about whether Phoebe Clawson had been trapped under the vehicle. The *Belfast Telegraph* coverage of the incident was queried due to its headline referring to a crash rather than the attempted murder of the Clawson. Within a few minutes of the incident, first reported by journalists including the BBC's Chris Buckler at 7.43 p.m., the PSNI confirmed that the teenager had been injured and that Aughey had been arrested at the scene.[50] It was a further two hours before local MLAs, such as Sinn Féin's Gerry Kelly, and the PSNI Chief Constable George Hamilton confirmed her injuries were not life- threatening.

The Chief Constable himself was the subject of misinformation spread on Twitter later that evening. Several viewers of the Russia Today live feed claimed that they had seen a senior police officer, resembling Hamilton, being injured by an object thrown by one of the rioters. Within a few hours, journalists such as the *Impartial Observer*'s Rodney Edwards tweeted to confirm that these reports were inaccurate. Hamilton later used his own Twitter account to thank members of the public for their best wishes and express his gratitude to the officers on duty in the interface area. Those viewing the feed also speculated about whether one of the PSNI officers injured on camera had lost his ear or not. Hybrid media logics meant that many professional journalists used Twitter to source stories like these for publications such as the *Belfast Telegraph*. Indeed, this was one of the clearest examples in the study of how citizens and professional journalists co-created news about the parade impasse.

There was one incident in particular that illustrates how citizens were using Twitter to prevent the spread of misinformation and disinformation that might incite violence during the North Belfast parade. One citizen tweeted a rumour that he had heard from an acquaintance suggesting that a deal had been put in place for the return leg of the parade to proceed via its traditional route past the Ardoyne shops. This tweet, shared a few days before the Twelfth, was only shared three times but clearly had the potential to raise tensions in Ardoyne. The same tweeter acknowledged that this information was untrue and apologised for spreading false information in a tweet posted on the morning of 13 July 2015. Clearly it was difficult to tell how many saw the original tweet, or how they responded to this false information. However, this corrective tweet showed how at least some tweeters were aware of the impact that such misinformation might have upon community relations in the interface area.

Conclusion

Several affective publics were mobilised on Twitter in relation to the Ardoyne parade dispute in 2014 and 2015. The majority of those who tweeted about the Ardoyne hashtag confirmed that 2014 had been the quietest Twelfth in recent years. The consensus among this public was that the Orange Order and the nationalist residents deserved much praise for ensuring that there was no repeat of the violence seen in 2013. A similar theme emerged from the 2015 corpus, with many condemning the violence, expressing support for the PSNI and urging both sides to talk to one another to resolve the dispute. That is not to say that there was much evidence of cross-community agreement on how it should be resolved. Rather, these were affective publics connected by zero-sum perceptions of the Ardoyne parade that existed long before the social media era. Republicans depicted the Orange Order as a "sectarian hate mob" and outlined the reasons why the contentious parade was not welcome in Ardoyne. Loyalists, in return, argued that the re-routing of the return leg of the parade was yet further evidence of republican bigotry towards their culture. What was perhaps surprising was that so few of these tweets used sectarian language in their attacks on members of the 'other' community. However, the limitations in the sampling strategy might partly explain this finding. It is also feasible that some tweeters may have deleted or removed offensive content shortly after it had been posted.

Twitter did not appear to provide the shared space that is required for reconciling the differences between loyalists and the nationalist residents' groups in Ardoyne. The same group of highly engaged users dominated both of these Twitter streams, with tweets from the news media being the most retweeted. There were no signs of the 'conflictual consensus' needed to resolve the parade dispute. However, Twitter might not be the most appropriate platform to facilitate intergroup contact and discussions about polarising issues such as parades and related protests. The complexities of such issues are unlikely to be explored through the exchange of messages that are restricted to just 280 characters. A related concern was the representativeness of the Twitter users who engage in such online debates. Research by the Pew Internet and American Life Project suggests that social media perpetuates the "spiral of silence", whereby people only speak in public about certain policy issues if they believe that their views are shared by others (Hampton et al., 2014). Therefore, generalisations about the attitudes of loyalists and republicans cannot be made based upon the themes that emerged from tweets addressing controversial issues such as the Parades Commission decision to ban the return leg of the parade from passing the Ardoyne shops.

Nevertheless, Twitter's most significant contribution to peacebuilding in Northern Ireland appears to lie in its empowerment of citizens to correct misinformation and disinformation. There were several examples of citizens using the site to expose those responsible for photoshopping images, such as with the Randalstown bonfire and the picture of a protester in Ardoyne. Mainstream media and politicians also benefited from the digital affordances of Twitter in their ability to issue corrective tweets about issues such as the reported injuries to Clawson in 2015. The relatively short lifespan of these rumours, not to mention the lack of mainstream media coverage they received, illustrate how effectively tweeters corrected disinformation during this period. It is reasonable to presume that this activity helped calm some tensions between these antagonistic groups, particularly in light of the negative impact upon community relations that rumours spread on social media had during the 2013 union flag protests. However, the violence seen in 2015 clearly demonstrates how the use of Twitter to correct rumours and disinformation may be insufficient to prevent the outbreak of violence in interface areas.

Notes

1 Local Sinn Féin MLA Gerry Kelly was among those to attribute the violence to the Real IRA. More details can be found here: www.theguardian.com/uk/2009/jul/14/belfast-riots-real-ira-blame (accessed 10 August 2014).

2 There was an increase in the number of contentious parades between 2010 and 2012, from 195 to 213. Full details can be found here: www. gov.uk/government/uploads/system/uploads/attachment_data/file/ 229060/0186.pdf (accessed 10 April 2017).

3 The determination stated that there should be no music played on the section of the Crumlin Road near Ardoyne. It can be viewed here: www. paradescommission.org/fs/files/det-earl-of-erne-lol-647–12july-20131. pdf (accessed 10 April 2017).

4 H. McDonald, "Northern Ireland violence leaves 70 police officers injured", *The Guardian*, 16 July 2013.

5 A. Rutherford, "Implement Belfast Telegraph's Ardoyne parade proposal, unionists urge", *Belfast Telegraph*, 11 July 2014, available at: www. belfasttelegraph.co.uk/news/northern-ireland/implement-belfast-telegraphs-ardoyne-parade-proposal-unionists-urge-30423154.html (accessed 10 June 2018).

6 More information on these legal challenges can be found here: www.bbc. co.uk/news/uk-northern-ireland-28264670 (accessed 10 August 2014).

7 The original image can be found at: www.demotix.com/news/2246569/ protestants-prepare-11th-night-bonfires-northern-ireland#media-2246528 (accessed 10 October 2014, no longer available).

8 Rutherford, "Implement Belfast Telegraph's Ardoyne parade proposal", *Belfast Telegraph*, 11 July 2014.

9 "Parades protests 'should be lawful'", *Belfast Telegraph*, 9 July 2014, available at: www.belfasttelegraph.co.uk/news/northern-ireland/parades-protests-should-be-lawful-30415689.html (accessed 10 June 2018).

10 L. Clarke, "Ardoyne parade proposal: It is an idea that just might offer a way forward", *Belfast Telegraph*, 11 July 2014, available at: www.belfasttelegraph. co.uk/opinion/columnists/archive/liam-clarke/ardoyne-parade-proposal-it-is-an-idea-that-just-might-offer-a-way-forward-30423170.html (accessed 8 June 2018).

11 A. Ferguson, "Can the Orange Order keep a lid on Twelfth tensions?", *Belfast Telegraph*, 12 July 2014, available at: www.belfasttelegraph.co.uk/

news/northern-ireland/can-the-orange-order-keep-a-lid-on-twelfth-tensions-30425523.html (accessed 10 June 2018).

12 J. Manley, "Appeals for peace as north awaits 'graduated response,'" *Irish News*, 8 July 2014, available at: www.irishnews.com/news/2014/07/08/news/appeals-for-peace-as-north-awaits-graduated-response--96294/ (accessed 10 June 2018).

13 "Hopes for peaceful parades, protest", *Belfast Telegraph*, 11 July 2014.

14 B. Rowan, "Ardoyne parade: police ready to act, but hope they won't have to", *Belfast Telegraph*, 11 July 2014, available at: www.belfasttelegraph.co.uk/opinion/columnists/archive/brian-rowan/ardoyne-parade-police-ready-to-act-but-hope-they-wont-have-to-30423152.html (accessed 1 June 2018).

15 C. Young, "Loyalist Protest – Prosecution Warning", *Irish News*, 12 July 2014, available at: www.irishnews.com/paywall/tsb/irishnews/irishnews/irishnews//news/2014/07/12/news/prosecution-warning-96615/content.html (accessed 10 May 2018).

16 "Praise for peaceful July 12 events", *Belfast Telegraph*, 13 July 2014.

17 J. Mulgrew, "Twelfth of July Orange Order marches in north Belfast pass off peacefully", *Belfast Telegraph*, 12 July 2014, available at: www.belfasttelegraph.co.uk/news/northern-ireland/twelfth-of-july-orange-order-marches-in-north-belfast-pass-off-peacefully-30426941.html (accessed 30 May 2018).

18 "Orange demo over parade restriction", *Belfast Telegraph*, 12 July 2014, available at: www.belfasttelegraph.co.uk/news/northern-ireland/orange-demo-over-parade-restriction-30425979.html (accessed 10 May 2018).

19 Mulgrew, "Twelfth of July Orange Order marches", *Belfast Telegraph*, 12 July 2014.

20 For more on the PC decision, see: www.belfastlive.co.uk/news/belfast-news/north-belfast-parade-barred-again-9596250 (accessed 10 August 2018).

21 This prompted an angry response from North Belfast MP Nigel Dodds. For more, see: www.newsletter.co.uk/news/ardoyne-residents-to-defy-parades-commission-restrictions-1-6845828 (accessed 10 August 2018).

22 The Chief Constable denied these rumours and expressed his concerns for the injured PSNI officers. For more, see: www.belfastlive.co.uk/news/belfast-news/north-belfast-parade-barred-again-9596250 (accessed 10 August 2018).

23 The 61-year-old was charged with two incidents of attempted murder. For more, see: www.theguardian.com/uk-news/2015/jul/14/attempted-murder-car-belfast-crash-marching-season (accessed 10 August 2018).

24 Villiers expressed her concern for the injured officers in the statement. For more, see: www.irishtimes.com/news/politics/orange-order-parades-all-sides-condemn-disgraceful-violence-1.2284398 (accessed 10 August 2018).

25 P. Devlin, "We're Now At Boiling Point […] Minor incident could tip flash-point at Ardoyne over the edge", *Sunday Life*, 12 July 2015, available at: www.highbeam.com/doc/1P2-38502987.html (accessed 10 September 2016, no longer available).

26 Devlin, "We're Now at Boiling Point", *Sunday Life*, 12 July 2015.

27 The Provisional IRA were responsible for the Shankill Road attack in 1993, which resulted in 10 fatalities after a bomb exploded in a fish and chip shop, and the La Mon restaurant bombing, which caused a fire that left 17 people dead and injured many more. For more on these incidents, see: Bew and Gillespie (1993).

28 A. McDonald, "Pride of Ardoyne Flute Band members convicted for playing music at north Belfast interface", *Belfast Telegraph*, 8 July 2015, available at: www.belfasttelegraph.co.uk/news/northern-ireland/pride-of-ardoyne-flute-band-members-convicted-for-playing-music-at-north-belfast-interface-31361830.html (accessed 30 May 2018).

29 G. Moriarty, "Missiles hurled as PSNI block parade; Orangemen prevented from parading past Ardoyne shops in north Belfast", *Irish Times*, 14 July 2015, available at: www.irishtimes.com/news/politics/orange-order-parades-missiles-hurled-as-psni-block-march-1.2283794 (accessed 10 May 2018).

30 R. Black, "Ardoyne crash girl's pain as driver charged with double murder bid", *Belfast Telegraph*, 15 July 2015, available at: www.belfasttelegraph.co.uk/news/northern-ireland/ardoyne-crash-girls-pain-as-driver-charged-with-double-murder-bid-31377800.html (accessed 10 May 2018).

31 D. McAleese, "Ardoyne: Teen girl trapped under car and 24 officers hurt as violence erupts at Belfast flashpoint", *Belfast Telegraph*, 14 July 2015, available at: www.belfasttelegraph.co.uk/news/twelfth/ardoyne-teen-girl-trapped-under-car-and-24-officers-hurt-as-violence-erupts-at-belfast-flashpoint-31374665.html (accessed 10 May 2018).

32 C. Williamson, "Twelfth 2015: Tense stand-off between police and loyalists after return route of Orange Order parade turns violent in north Belfast", *Belfast Telegraph*, 14 July 2015.

33 C. Cromie, "Twelfth 2015: DUP leaders condemn north Belfast rioters", *Belfast Telegraph*, 14 July 2015, www.belfasttelegraph.co.uk/news/northern-ireland/twelfth-2015-dup-leaders-condemn-north-belfast-rioters-31375817.html (accessed 10 May 2019).

34 Williamson, "Twelfth 2015", *Belfast Telegraph*, 14 July 2015.

35 J. Monaghan, "The Twelfth – 150,000 watched Ardoyne riots on live YouTube feed", *Irish News*, 15 July 2015.

36 Mark Simpson (@BBCMarkSimpson), "Peaceful start to 12th July marches. No trouble as Orange Order parade passes Ardoyne shops", 12 July 2014, 7.41 a.m., Tweet.

37 Kevin Sharkey (@tv_kevinsharkey), "Trouble in #Ardoyne", 12 July 2014, 8.53 p.m., Tweet.

38 David Blevins (@skydavidblevins), "BREAKING: Water canon deployed after police officer inured during disorder at Ardoyne flashpoint, North Belfast", 13 July 2015, 9.14 p.m., Tweet.

39 Allison Morris (@AllisonMorris1), "One man was arrested at shop fronts but apart from that fairly hassle free albeit wet morning #Ardoyne", 13 July 2015, 8.42 a.m., Tweet.

40 West Belfast UPRG (@WestBelfastUPRG), "PSNI moving in against DISSIDENT SCUM at Ardoyne !! Several arrests being made !!", 13 July 2015, 9.10 a.m., Tweet.

41 Gerry Kelly (@GerryKellyMLA), "The quietest 11th night in years and the morning parade passed Ardoyne, Mountainview and the Dales without trouble. Hope for calm day grows", 12 July 2014, 8.48 a.m., Tweet.

42 Nichola Mallon (@NicholaMallon), "Parade in Ardoyne passes off peacefully. Hopes are that the day stays peaceful. Resolution is possible – dialogue. http://t.co/yPtnhY9Es0", 13 July 2015, 8.01 a.m., Tweet.

43 Nigel Kells (@nigelkells), "I support @OrangeOrder graduated response. 6 minute parade delay might not seem like much, but it's all it would take in Ardoyne! #Tolerance", 10 July 2015, 11.20 a.m., Tweet.

44 Mid Shankill Residents Group (@Mid_Shankill_RG), "@WestBelfast-UPRG 2/2 Ardoyne need to stand up against these mindless sectarian bigots who clearly need to grow up", 12 July 2015, 7.14 p.m., Tweet.

45 Ardoyne Republican (@RepublicanUnity), "Militarising the Greater Ardoyne community has and continues to be one of key reasons why GARC oppose unwelcome marches though our area!", 12 July 2014, 6.14 p.m., Tweet.

46 Ardoyne Republican (@RepublicanUnity), "GARC Activists, Residents and Independent Observers logged a number of breaches of determination during this morning's march through Ardoyne", 12 July 2014, 2.42 p.m., Tweet.

47 UPV (@Unitedprotestan), "@RepublicanUnity breaches? For instance? Did these breaches involve an unlawful protest by Garc?", 12 July 2014, 3.49 p.m., Tweet.

48 Ardoyne Republican (@RepublicanUnity), "@WestBelfastUPRG More bullshite from the supporter of UDA fascists!", 7 July 2014, 8.57 p.m., Tweet.

49 West Belfast UPRG (@WestBelfastUPRG), "Republicans have over-turned a car at Ardoyne shopfronts !! http://t.co/AhfXLMSQZ6", 13 July 2015, 7.22 p.m., Tweet.
50 Victoria Stevely (@vstevely_utv), "Police clarify 16-year-old girl injured in Ardoyne crash – male driver of overturned car arrested at scene: http://t.co/9a2GhDSs9S", 13 July 2015, 8.02 p.m., Tweet.

Conclusion

Throughout this book I have argued that the flag protests marked a watershed moment in terms of contentious politics in Northern Ireland; henceforth social media provided communicative spaces in which citizens made rights claims in this deeply divided society. The extent to which these nascent acts of 'digital citizenship' contribute to peacebuilding ultimately depends on the socio-political context in which such claims are made. During periods of political instability, for instance, affective publics mobilised via online platforms may *help and hinder* efforts to moderate the sectarian tensions caused by contentious public demonstrations. The 2014 and 2015 Ardoyne parade disputes suggest that social media's most significant contribution to building peace in Northern Ireland might lie in its empowerment of citizens to correct misinformation and disinformation that might spark intercommunal violence. Whether these information flows directly influence the course of events on the ground remains to be seen. There was no identifiable causal link between the misinformation and disinformation shared on Facebook, Twitter and YouTube and the civil disturbances that occurred during these contentious public demonstrations, nor between the correction of false information and the absence or moderation of violence during such incidents. That is not to say that such information flows didn't indirectly contribute to the rioting seen in January 2013 and July 2015. Certainly, digital citizens recognised that false information about these public demonstrations *could* have a negative impact on community relations, as demonstrated by the tweeter who apologised for sharing misinformation about a deal being struck to enable the Pride of Ardoyne to return home via their traditional route. It is also conceivable that misinformation and disinformation shared on private Facebook pages and encrypted messaging apps may have directly contributed to the violence during these contentious episodes. Yet, previous research indicated that protesters, for the most part, distrusted information shared on social media (Nolan et al., 2014: 79). In the case of the flag protest movement, LPPU page administrators attempted to verify reports that Garda An Síochána officers had been deployed in Belfast, which was misinformation that clearly had the potential to exacerbate tensions surrounding the policing of the protests. While acknowledging that this project analysed 'easy' rather than 'hard' data (Burgess and Bruns, 2015), the evidence here was that social media enabled online commenters to debate contentious political issues rather than influence those with the power to resolve them.

Little sign of conflictual consensus emerging between affective publics

There seemed little prospect of a 'conflictual' cross-community consensus emerging via social media in relation to how to address the contentiousness of these public demonstrations. For instance, the 'sousveillance' footage shared on YouTube during the flag protests was dismissed on the grounds that it provided insufficient evidence of PSNI 'brutality', with most commenters suggesting that the police should have taken stronger action to prevent the protesters from blocking roads. This was congruent with newspaper coverage of the protests, which gave little credence to loyalist claims that they were being brutalised by the PSNI. While Facebook and YouTube did provide opportunities for loyalists to learn about the legality of street protests, antagonistic interactions with critics militated against the large-scale informal learning about policing seen during Black Lives Matter (Freelon et al., 2016a). This was perhaps to be expected given that the flag protests and the Ardoyne parade dispute were symptomatic of the lack of progress made towards a shared society since the 1998 Agreement. These were hybrid media events defined by political contentiousness, differentiated from previous mass mobilisations by citizens' use of social media to contest their legitimacy. Facebook, Twitter and YouTube were 'battlegrounds' in which citizens disputed the perceived grievances of working-class loyalist communities who felt left behind by the Stormont Assembly and that their culture was under attack by 'Sinn Féin/IRA' and the 'PSNIRA'.

#Flegs demonstrated how affective publics, 'discursively rendered' by the shared emotions communicated via Twitter hashtags (Papacharissi, 2014), militate against efforts to promote reconciliation within a deeply divided society. The affective dimension of this hashtag overshadowed its other key function as a news stream co-curated by citizens and professional journalists. #Flegs 'presenced' the views of critics of the flag protests who felt they were under-represented in media coverage of the public demonstrations that caused such widespread disruption between December 2012 and March 2013. Although there was an irreverence and black humour in many of these tweets, there were also ad hominem attacks on protest provocateurs such as Bryson and Frazer. LAD was part of a vanguard using social media to portray loyalists as 'uneducated bigots' and shaming them for their poor spelling and grammar. These were shared spaces in the sense that members of both communities could freely access and contribute to them, but they appeared to reinforce divisions between anti-Agreement loyalists and their critics.

This feeds into the ongoing debate over whether social media platforms create 'filter bubbles' and 'echo chambers', in which the algorithmic curation of newsfeeds and the tendency of people to predominantly engage with like-minded individuals reinforce pre-existing opinions. The empirical investigation of these claims has been a primary focus of Internet studies for the past decade. For example, one study found that people are exposed to ideologically diverse opinion courtesy of the sharing of content produced by traditional media on Facebook, albeit that they are still most likely to click on those stories that are congruent with their opinions (Bakshy et al., 2015). This corroborated the characterisation of news consumption as a performance or ritual confirming rather than challenging people's world views (Carey, 1992). More recent research conducted by Dubois and Blank (2018) argued that much of the evidence for the echo chamber thesis was based on studies of news consumption on one social media platform, namely Twitter. They contended that political information-seeking and news consumption practices were invariably conducted across multiple platforms; those with diverse media diets and an interest in politics were less likely to find themselves in echo chambers due to their constant exposure to alternative viewpoints. Bruns (2019: 76) goes as far as to suggest that online platforms are "powerful engines of context collapse" that expose their predominantly apolitical users to views that they might find undesirable. Yet, there is already some evidence to suggest that 'civic-minded' citizens share tabloid news via their social media accounts, irrespective of its accuracy, to spark debate with others. While the intentional sharing of fabricated news may be subject to the correction of other social media users, many "democratically dysfunctional news sharing behaviours" on these platforms are left unchallenged (Chadwick et al., 2018). Therefore, further research is needed to explore the factors that motivate citizens to comment and share information about contentious public demonstrations on these platforms.

Information crisis or (dysfunctional) politics as usual?

In June 2019, fabricated stories on Facebook were linked to a Russian campaign to exacerbate Anglo–Irish tensions caused by Brexit (Carswell, 2019), as well as an attempt by conspiracy theorists to frame the murder of journalist Lyra McKee as a false flag operation.[1] The use of social media to spread such misinformation and disinformation could be viewed as yet further evidence of the 'information crisis' threatening contemporary liberal democracies. Certainly, three of the five 'evils' of the information crisis identified by the LSE Truth, Trust and Technology (T3) Commission (2018) appear to be evident in Northern Ireland to varying degrees. First, *apathy* can be seen in the significant decline in public confidence in Northern Ireland's political institutions over the past decade, probably due to scandals such as 'Irisgate' and the renewable heating incentive scheme. Fewer than one third (32 per cent) of respondents in the 2015 Northern Ireland Life and Times Survey said that they trusted the Northern Ireland Assembly to work in their best interests, compared with 60 per cent when the DUP and Sinn Féin formed a power-sharing Executive in 2007.[2] There has also been a considerable drop in the percentage of 18–24 year-olds who stated they were fairly satisfied with how their MLAs were doing their jobs (from 32 per cent in 2007 to just 7 per cent in 2014). This correlates with a similar percentage point increase in the number of participants within this group who were very dissatisfied with the performance of their MLAs, which rose from 7 per cent to 34 per cent in the same period. There has also been a fivefold increase in the percentage of respondents aged 65 and over who were very dissatisfied with their elected representatives, rising from 9 per cent in 2007 to 48 per cent in 2014.[3] Such trends echo the findings of research conducted by the Edelman Trust across 27 countries in 2018, which showed that only 47 per cent of participants trusted government and media institutions.[4] Yet, conversely, there has been no clear indication that voter turnout is being negatively affected by this increasing public dissatisfaction with political representatives. The fall-out from the renewable heat incentive scandal, as well as the political machinations about the status of Northern Ireland post-Brexit, has energised voters in recent elections. Most notably, turnout in the 2017 Northern Ireland Assembly Election rose by nearly 10 per cent compared with the year before (from 54.91 to 64.78 per cent), with a more modest 3.9 per cent year-on-year increase reported during the 2017 UK General Election.[5] Moreover, the apathy towards the main political parties does not equate to a "complete abstention from political and civic activity", as demonstrated by the new forms of political activism emerging on issues such as marriage equality (Hayward and McManus, 2019: 152).

There is also mixed evidence to suggest that the 'evil' of *confusion*, caused by the rapid growth and diversification of media platforms, has taken root in Northern Ireland. As discussed in Chapter 1, citizens in the deeply divided society are increasingly unsure over what and whom to believe, particularly in relation to online information. While this trend might have been expected to continue in the wake of polarisation caused by the 2016 UK EU referendum, recent surveys suggest a renewal of public trust in local mainstream media. A YouGov survey in March 2018 found that most participants (31 per cent) believed that local newspapers were the most trustworthy source of information about their local area, with just 3 per cent trusting social media.[6] These results were congruent with findings of the 2018 UK Edelman Trust Barometer, which pointed to a significant increase in public trust in traditional media in the UK during this period (from 48 per cent in 2017 to 61 per cent in 2018). In contrast, social media was only trusted by 24 per cent of respondents with many calling for greater regulation of companies such as Facebook.[7] A similar trend has emerged from research into disinformation across EU member states. While concerns remain about media bias and sensationalism, citizens continue to express higher levels of public trust in professional journalists as news sources than content shared by unverified sources on social media (European Commission, 2018;

Newman and Fletcher, 2017). This apparent resurgence in public faith in traditional media correlates with an increasing cynicism about the commitment of social media companies to clamp down on 'antisocial' behaviour on their respective platforms.

The LSE T3 project identified *fragmentation*, in which the "pool of agreed facts on which to base societal choices is diminishing", as the third evil of the information crisis (LSE, 2018: 11). Such a 'pool' has arguably never existed in a society divided along sectarian lines, with no middle ground between the two main narratives on its constitutional status. Northern Ireland has a long history of both pro-government and anti-state propaganda being disseminated via both mainstream and alternative media. There is already a high degree of public scepticism about the former's impartiality in light of their perceived complicity in UK government propaganda campaigns during and after the Troubles, particularly among dissident loyalists and republicans. Twenty years after the Agreement, it remains a deeply divided society in which competing narratives over the conflict and its constitutional status remain deeply entrenched. Therefore, the ebb and flow of misinformation and disinformation during contentious public demonstrations should be attributed to the failure of its consociational political institutions to satisfactorily address their root causes. Hayward and Komarova (2014) argue that efforts to resolve contentious parades such as Ardoyne have been undermined by the fixed "interpretative horizons" of both sides, which are the product of a dysfunctional political system in which openness to alternative interpretations is limited by the actions of ethnopolitical elites.[8] Since 2007, the DUP and Sinn Féin's electoral dominance has been based on their operationalisation of ethno-sectarian differences, leaving little room for compromise on issues such as how to deal with contentious public demonstrations (McGarry and O'Leary, 1995). This has fed into ongoing concerns about the democratic deficit in Northern Ireland, exacerbated by the suspension of the Assembly between 16 January 2017 and 11 January 2020. The conflation of 'post-conflict' politics with de-democratising tendencies, particularly among socially conservative younger people, has also increased the divide between political elites and citizens (Lehner and McGrattan, 2018). This suggests that misinformation and disinformation shared on social media is unlikely to significantly affect public perceptions of contentious political issues in what remains a divided and contested polity.

Indirect effects of online incivility may make it harder to promote reconciliation in divided societies

By definition, an inclusive approach towards peacebuilding requires grass-roots organisations from each ethnic bloc to work together to build positive cross-community relationships. The affective publics mobilised on sites such as Twitter during this period did not conform to these requirements and were not representative of the broader population. Leaving aside the difficulties in sampling social media data discussed in the Introduction, a long tail distribution of online comments was evident across all the data analysed here. For instance, no generalisations about the attitudes of citizens in the 'post-conflict' society could be drawn from content generated by 'Northern Ireland Twitter', which, like the blogosphere (see Chapter 1), consisted of a small but highly engaged group of citizens, commenters and journalists predominantly speaking to one another online. This was illustrated by the finding that the same 26 Twitter accounts, the majority of whom were citizens, were among the top 50 most prolific tweeters in the Ardoyne corpora in 2014 and 2015. One explanation for this might be the 'spiral of silence'. Difficult conversations between Catholics and Protestants about the recognition of their respective cultural rights might have been taking place on private Facebook pages away from the prying eyes of other social media users. Nevertheless, the incivility of the discourses circulating on social media during this period was unlikely to reconcile anti-Agreement loyalists with their critics. The negative stereotyping of loyalists as 'inbred sectarian bigots' directly contradicted one of the key tenets of the reconciliation framework articulated by Hamber and Kelly (2004), namely that individuals treat each other as human beings rather than anonymous members of an outgroup. Although this activity was attributed to a relatively small group of digital citizens, the extended/indirect contact hypothesis suggested that any antagonistic interactions between Catholics and Protestants on social media were likely to increase prejudice towards outgroups among their respective social networks. Future research should build on these findings by using focus groups and questionnaires to longitudinally explore whether attitudes towards outgroups are directly or indirectly shaped by cross-community interactions on social media, as well as those experienced vicariously. In particular, it should investigate how communities within deeply divided societies engage with one another both online and offline, with a view to examining the potential use of social media to build a more inclusive, positive peace.

Might a Citizens' Assembly help address contentious parades and protests in Northern Ireland?

Irrespective of the nature of intergroup contact on these platforms, one should be wary of the 'bullshit' peddled by corporate social media to convince users that they are a force for global peace. As discussed in the Introduction, initiatives such as *Peace on Facebook* have proved to be quixotic projects. Thus far there are few signs that exposure to the views held by outgroups on corporate social media, whether accidental or intentional, can bridge sectarian divides in Northern Ireland. Although some citizens may work to counteract misinformation and disinformation that inflames sectarian tensions around contentious public demonstrations, they do not appear to be working together to resolve their root causes. Conversely, there is overwhelming evidence suggesting that positive direct contacts with members of the 'other' community remains the most effective way of fostering reconciliation in contested entities such as Northern Ireland. Deliberative polls (DP) have been proposed as an innovative democratic mechanism that could encourage cross-community participation in decision-making within deeply divided societies. A successful pilot in January 2007 saw a broadly representative sample of 127 parents from Omagh, County Tyrone spend a day discussing issues facing primary and post-primary schools in the area.[9] Results showed increased support for religious mixing within local schools, with participants reporting much more favourable perceptions of outgroups as a result of their participation. For example, the percentage who believed that Catholics were 'trustworthy' rose from 50 per cent to 62 per cent in surveys conducted before and after the DP, with a similar result reported for Protestants (from 50 per cent to 60 per cent) (Fishkin, 2009: 167). While acknowledging that political elites might not heed its results, the researchers behind the DP noted that such "civil, constructive discussion between communities" could not only inform policy but facilitate greater levels of mutual understanding in these contexts (Luskin et al., 2014: 133).

The next major deliberative exercise in Northern Ireland occurred in Belfast over two weekends in October and November 2018. The

Citizens' Assembly for Northern Ireland brought together a 'mini-public' of 77 participants, broadly representative of Northern Irish society, to discuss the future of adult social care in Northern Ireland. They produced a list of 27 recommendations in this policy area, ranging from the abolition of compulsory zero-hour contracts for care workers to providing greater support such as a 24-hour advice line for unpaid carers.[10] Like the Omagh DP a decade earlier, participants felt that there was a high degree of mutual respect in the discussions, with 97 per cent favouring the use of Citizens' Assemblies to inform policy-making in other areas.[11] It should be acknowledged that, at the time of writing, there was no data available on the attitudes of participants towards members of the 'other' community. It should also be acknowledged that issues such as education and social care are not conflict-legacy issues that polarise opinion along sectarian lines. Nevertheless, Citizens' Assemblies might provide a forum in which both sides could respectfully discuss competing claims and make recommendations about how future contentious parades should be dealt with by the PSNI and other statutory bodies. The evidence to date suggests that talks between the Orange Order and nationalist residents have often failed to deliver long-term solutions to these disputes. For example, the deal struck in September 2016, permitting the Ligoniel Orange Lodges to complete the Ardoyne parade, was a temporary arrangement to enable a "process between the lodges and CARA to seek agreement on future return parades".[12] Future research should empirically explore whether the Citizens' Assembly model might facilitate the difficult conversations needed in order address the zero-sum perceptions held by members of both communities in relation to contentious public demonstrations.

From LAD to Border Irish: the irresistible rise of silly citizenship?

One of the key findings of this book was that Northern Irish citizens used social media, and Twitter in particular, to playfully engage with these contentious parades and protests. This 'silly' citizenship first came to prominence when tweeters shared memes and wordplay in order to express their opposition to the flag protests between December 2012 and March 2013. #Flegs, one of the most popular hashtags, was characterised as an inoffensive play on local dialect that provided a welcome distraction from the economic and reputational harm being inflicted upon this divided society. Parody accounts such as @BattMaggott poked fun at public figures as part of their efforts to highlight the failure of political elites and the PSNI to rein in the 'street fighting loyalists'. The shaming of loyalists for their poor spelling and grammar proved more divisive and was symptomatic of the high levels of political polarisation during this period. Bloggers debated whether this was merely black humour making light of the situation, or if it reinforced negative portrayals of working-class loyalists as a 'social underclass'. Much of this discussion centred around the online activity of LAD, the standard -bearer for this new mode of citizenship in Northern Ireland. Despite claiming to being satirists, the parody group often used offensive language to describe protest provocateurs such as Jamie Bryson and Willie Frazer. During the peak of the protests they frequently mocked the appearance of loyalist protesters, going as far as to 'fat-shame' loyalist women appearing on local television programmes about the demonstrations.

The departure of 'Winston Smith' from the group demonstrated that not all LAD-mins favoured this approach. By November 2013, its main focus was on scrutinising the actions of politicians rather than shaming working-class loyalists for their spelling mistakes. That is not to say that the group had completely forsaken the infantile humour with which it had become synonymous a few months earlier. Memes comparing politicians such as Edwin Poots to characters from children's television shows were notable for 'playing the man, not the ball' by focusing on physical appearances rather than policies. They continued to ridicule the Facebook posts and tweets of Bryson and Frazer and frequently shared them for the amusement of their supporters. Yet, LAD's activism on a number of equality and social issues suggested that they were, in the words of blogger Alan Meban, increasingly focused on the "actions, behaviours, contradictions and characters" within politics requiring scrutiny.[13] Memes of Sinn Féin leader Gerry Adams hiding behind the sofa were shared during the broadcast of the BBC documentary *The Disappeared*, with LAD criticising his answers to questions about his role in the abduction and murder of Jean McConville in December 1972. However, the DUP remained the primary target of both the group's 'silly citizenship' and its political activism. The group live-tweeted the 2013 DUP party conference 'in character' in order to poke fun at the speakers and critique their policy positions. They lent their support to hashtag campaigns such as #givepootstheboot that sought to oust the beleaguered health minister from office. They also emerged as a focal point for contentious political debates on Twitter about the human trafficking bill that was being proposed in the Stormont Assembly. The group shared relevant information and statistics from countries such as Sweden as part of their critique of the proposals. In this way, they were holding the DUP responsible for their actions and seeking to promote an evidence-based approach towards policy in this area. The group's repertoire of contention appeared to have evolved from the flag protests insofar as it now combined playful forms of political engagement alongside the fact-checking associated with traditional forms of online activism.

LAD has continued to straddle this divide between 'silly' and 'serious' forms of citizenship in the past few years. In terms of the former, the parody group promoted hashtags such as #votetillyouboke to encourage citizens to vote down the ballot in local and European elections held under the single transferrable vote system between 2014 and 2019.[14] Specifically, they urged supporters to vote for parties other than the DUP and Sinn Féin, who they blamed for the political paralysis within the Assembly. The group were also at the forefront of #gaycake, which came to prominence in June 2014 when news broke about the Northern Ireland Equality Commission's case against Ashers Baking Company for their refusal to bake a cake for Gareth Lee, a gay rights activist, because it carried a slogan supporting equal marriage. This hashtag contained both 'playful' and antagonistic responses to Ashers and their supporters within the DUP, sparked by the ruling in May 2015 that the bakery had discriminated against Lee on the basis of his sexual orientation and political beliefs.[15]

LAD's most significant interventions during this period revolved around the online shaming of public figures for their use of offensive hate speech. Jolene Bunting, the first TUV candidate to be elected to Belfast City Council in May 2014, was shamed for using sectarian language to describe Catholics and selling drug paraphernalia on Facebook. LAD criticised party leader Jim Allister for his unwavering support for Bunting in light of these posts.[16] This was overshadowed by the furore caused by a video uploaded to the group's YouTube channel in the same month, which showed Pastor James McConnell making a number of offensive remarks about Muslims during a sermon held in a Belfast church. #Pastorgate received extensive coverage in the local news media in the wake of ill-judged remarks by First Minister Peter Robinson defending the pastor's reputation, in which he shared his own distrust of Islamic doctrine but claimed that he would still trust Muslims "to go to the shops" for him (Manley, 2014). The parody group used a combination of memes, jokes and "sincere messages" to condemn McConnell and Robinson's remarks, while expressing their support for an anti-racism rally held at Belfast City Hall on 31 May (Soares, 2015: 48). They have also held Sinn Féin representatives to account for their social media posts. Most notably, they drew attention to a controversial video posted online in January 2018 by West Tyrone MP Barry McElduff, in which he appeared to mock the victims of the 1976 Kingsmill massacre (Reilly, 2018). These incidents illustrate how the parody group was increasingly scrutinising the behaviour of authority figures rather than seeking to shame those without power and agency. However, LAD's social media sites would disappear in June 2020, with founder Whearty distancing himself from the group's increasingly 'republican direction'.[17]

Others have followed in LAD's footsteps in using irreverent humour to speak truth to power on social media. For example, *Nelson McCausland Looking at Things* (https://nelsonmccauslandlooking atthings.tumblr.com) and Twitter accounts such as @MLAsAndThe Like poked fun at photographs of politicians attending public events. 'Paul', the creator of the latter, told the *Belfast Telegraph* that he was 'apolitical' and shared these images for his own amusement (White, 2019). Such acts of silly citizenship have been increasingly prevalent since the 2016 UK EU referendum, which saw the UK vote to leave the European Union by a narrow margin despite 56 per cent of voters in Northern Ireland choosing to remain within the bloc.[18] Tweeters found playful ways to channel their anger and frustration at the implications of Brexit for the peace process. Their primary targets were the political proponents of Brexit such as the DUP, TUV and the European Research Group within the Conservative Party. All were accused of peddling quixotic technological solutions to prevent a hard border being reintroduced on the island of Ireland, which looked increasingly likely due to the insistence of the Westminster government that the UK leave the customs union and European Single Market (ESM).[19] Probably the most well-known of these was The Irish Border (@BorderIrish), which was set up in February 2018 and accumulated over 80,000 followers on Twitter before it was 'retired' on 31 January 2020, the day on which the UK officially left the EU. Tweets from the account were written 'in character', as if the border between Northern Ireland the Republic of Ireland was an actual person. Like @MLAsAndTheLike, the person behind this account chose to remain anonymous and based the profile on an account dedicated to a river in New Zealand (White, 2019). Its opposition to a hard border was reflected in its Twitter bio, which stated "I'm seamless & frictionless already, thanks. Bit scared of physical infrastructure".[20] @BorderIrish quickly gained a cult following due to its irreverent commentary on the Irish 'backstop', the proposals to align Northern Ireland with the customs union and ESM in order to avoid a hard border. The failure of the DUP and European Research Group to adequately address the border issue was one of its constant targets. For example, a remixed image, showing a boardroom meeting being overshadowed by a large elephant was humorously captioned "There's me at the Brexit negotiations".[21] Such was the popularity of @Border-Irish, it provided an explainer on the border issue for the BBC website and published a book on the same topic in late 2019.[22] Future work should build on research by exploring the contribution of both 'silly citizenship' and parody accounts to contentious political debates within deeply divided societies.

The price of digital citizenship in 'post-conflict' Northern Ireland?

Digital citizens have increasingly used social media to articulate their positions vis-à-vis campaigns for progressive social and political change in the 'post-conflict' society. Northern Ireland Twitter reacted angrily to the DUP's use of the Petition of Concern mechanism within the Assembly to block the introduction of equal civil marriage on five occasions between 2012 and 2015.[23] There was also much social media activism focused on extending reproductive rights available elsewhere in the UK to Northern Irish women. For example, the Now for NI campaign has used Facebook, Twitter and a website to highlight the plight of women who were forced to travel to England, Scotland or Wales in order to gain access to the abortion services legally prohibited in Northern Ireland.[24] Clearly it would be premature and perhaps even misleading to suggest that this represents de facto evidence that

Northern Irish social media users have been moving beyond the tribal politics of its recent past. A genre of Twitter accounts, such as On This Day the IRA (@OnThisDayPIRA), were created to remind tweeters about the atrocities committed by paramilitaries during the conflict. Interactions between supporters of the two main parties (the DUP and Sinn Féin) on the microblogging platform remain largely antagonistic, especially during contentious hybrid media events such as Orange Order parades in areas like North Belfast. So-called 'Shinner-bots' and 'loyalist keyboard warriors' have frequently been accused of using social media to continue the conflict by other means. This study found evidence to corroborate these claims during the flag protests, with the attempted use of 'bots' to flood #flegs with tweets condemning the protesters being seemingly unsuccessful. Yet, social media has undoubtedly provided communicative spaces for the contestation of political issues that do not specifically relate to the constitutional status of Northern Ireland. Platforms such as Facebook and Twitter have empowered citizens who were previously marginalised in debates over issues such as marriage equality and women's reproductive rights, while also providing unprecedented mobilisation resources for activists seeking legislative changes in these policy areas. The increasing importance of what Chadwick (2013) refers to as "hybrid media logics" may make it much harder for parties such as the DUP and Sinn Féin to ignore these rights claims in the future.

The narrative capacity afforded to digital citizens and social movements by social media may come at a heavy price. There was little sign of the respectful disagreement between former enemies synonymous with Mouffe's "agonistic pluralism" during the contentious episodes analysed in this book. Twitter hashtags were used to mock and disparage flag protesters, with groups such as LAD frequently accused of reinforcing negative stereotypes of working-class loyalist communities. While it was perhaps inevitable that there would be some sectarianism on social media during contentious public demonstrations in this deeply divided society, misogynistic and disablist language was also frequently used to describe those expressing support for the protests on LPPU or local news media. There was also controversy over LAD's inappropriate remarks about the appearances of politicians such as NI21 Chair Tina McKenzie, which forced the group to apologise for any offence they had caused. Such incidents appear typical of the abuse experienced by women on Twitter. The Amnesty #Toxic

Twitter report published in March 2018 was highly critical of the social media giant for its failure to deal with abuse promptly in accordance with its own rules. The report drew on interviews conducted with 86 women, six of whom were activists, journalists and politicians from Northern Ireland. Allison Morris, whose tweet about being threatened by loyalists during the flag protests was among the most retweeted in #flegs (see Chapter 3), explained how she had received "clear veiled threats" against her on Twitter.[25] Naomi Long, who became leader of the Alliance Party in October 2016, asserted that the platform had a "wholly ineffective process" for reporting abuse and suggested that the microblogging site was very often a hostile environment for women.[26] Future research on contentious politics within divided societies such as Northern Ireland should focus specifically on how the voices of women and other marginalised groups are represented in online debates about these issues. In particular, it should explore whether the perceived toxicity of social media prevents them from contesting these matters online.

Northern Irish digital citizens are enframed by sites such as Facebook and Twitter every time they avail of their services to perform citizenship. These are corporations sustained by the exploitation of user data, who strategically deploy the 'platform' metaphor to portray themselves as neutral tools. 'Bullshit' claims about the contribution of social media giants such as Facebook to world peace belie the fact that they benefit financially from the use of their platforms to share disinformation and hate speech. Furthermore, the tweaking of social media algorithms and architectures can have a significant impact on the visibility of digital acts, such as videos showing alleged police brutality against protesters. This may restrict the online audience available for dissident loyalists and republicans trying to undermine the Agreement, as well as those seeking to promote progressive social change such as the introduction of equal marriage in Northern Ireland. The extent to which citizens in this divided society are aware that social media companies monetise their data remains unclear. While research conducted in the UK has suggested that citizens see this as a price worth paying to gain access to online platforms (Hintz et al., 2018), there remains a dearth of evidence on how citizens in postconflict Northern Ireland perceive this surveillance capitalism. The research presented in this book certainly shows how its citizens were increasingly aware that these platforms were being surveilled by professional journalists and the PSNI. The J18 case resulted in LPPU page administrators warning commenters to be careful what they posted on the public Facebook page. Yet, there has been no empirical investigation of whether citizens in the divided society are aware of the surreptitious data collection practices employed by these companies. Future research should address this gap by examining whether citizens are aware of these social media materialities and, if so, whether they too are resigned to being subjects of this 'surveillance capitalism'. Focus groups and interviews should be conducted in order to explore whether an awareness of these data policies has a positive or negative impact on the use of social media platforms to perform citizenship in a deeply divided society.

Qualitative multi-platform studies are essential for understanding contemporary social movements

The study of political contention, by definition, involves examining the interactions between actors that have conflicting interests. While acknowledging that social movements are more than just communicative acts, ICTs have undoubtedly played a key role in the mobilisation of resources for contentious campaigns such as Occupy Wall Street over the past decade. Online platforms are important channels for activists to signal their capacity to disrupt politics as usual, allowing them to mobilise support from 'non-activists' who they would not reach via other forms of media activism (Tufekci, 2017; Zuckerman, 2015). As such, social media provide researchers with unprecedented opportunities to analyse the dynamics of both collective and connective action, providing new insight into what increases the 'spreadability' of activist content. The increasing importance of online platforms in contemporary social movements has coincided with the computational turn in the social sciences, which has seen social scientists embrace predominantly quantitative approaches to mine, scrape, and analyse 'big data'. This typically requires researchers to either learn how to use packages such as 'R', collaborate with computer or data scientists, or use 'off the shelf' software packages for the analysis of large datasets. This book project opted for the latter approach by using the text-mining software Discovertext to scrape data from public Facebook pages and Twitter hashtags used during contentious public demonstrations in Northern Ireland. While acknowledging the potential limitations of using 'black box' methods to sample social media data, as well as the usual caveats about non-hashtagged tweets and deleted comments being omitted, these data broadly reflected the online contestation of the flag protests and the Ardoyne parade dispute. These were 'small' rather than 'big' data when compared with the large social media datasets linked to high-profile social movements such as Black Lives Matter or Occupy Wall Street. Hence, it was possible to manually code each Facebook post, tweet and YouTube comment scraped during the period of data collection. The flexibility of the TA methodology allowed for more nuanced research findings that reflected on the origins of these contentious public demonstrations, as well as the failure of political elites to fully address the conflict legacy issues that contributed to them. Future research on contentious politics within divided societies should adopt a similar qualitative approach in order to fully capture the range of affective responses they elicit on sites such as Twitter.

This book also highlights the importance of applying cross-platform social media analysis to examine contentious hybrid media events. There were numerous examples of content posted on one platform being redistributed via another. For example, the YouTube video purporting to show PSNI 'brutality' against an East Belfast 'pensioner' was shared on the LPPU Facebook page as evidence of the heavy-handed policing being experienced by the flag protesters. This opened up new possibilities for comparing and contrasting how different audiences interpreted this 'sousveillance' footage. Moreover, the combination of these datasets avoided the inherent problems of relying exclusively on the 'low-hanging fruit' of Twitter hashtags. The microblogging site has been somewhat over-researched over the past decade due to the relative ease with which scholars can access data using the Search application programming interface (API). Burgess and Bruns (2015) argue that the commercialisation of Twitter data through the licensing of access to its Firehouse API has made it much harder for researchers to access hard data, such as longitudinal datasets. An additional problem with Internet studies' obsession with Twitter is the representativeness of its user base. Facebook remains the most used online platform across the globe, with Twitter tending to be most popular among men aged between 18 and 29 years old.[27] In the case of Northern Ireland, Twitter remains a minority interest and only a small but highly engaged group of users publicly commented on the Ardoyne dispute and the flag protests. It was therefore imperative that these results were combined with analyses of data gathered from the other two most popular online platforms in Northern Ireland, namely Facebook and YouTube. Clearly, this triangulation of easy data may not be able to provide the depth and richness offered by harder-to-reach data, such as posts on private Facebook pages, which would allow for a deeper exploration of how these parades and protests were contested on social media. There also needs to be a greater focus on how audiences make sense of these online interactions, which has been recognised as an under-researched area within social movement studies (Earl and Garrett, 2019: 98). Nevertheless, the approach taken in this book offers a framework for future research into how social media is used by citizens during contentious episodes in divided societies.

Notes

1 The false flag accusations were revealed by journalist Leona O'Neill, who criticised Facebook and Twitter for not doing more to protect her from these accusations. For more on this, see: www.theguardian.com/society/ 2019/jun/27/twitter-facebook-act-online-abuse-lyra-mckee-friend (accessed 27 June 2019).

2 The full dataset can be accessed here: www.ark.ac.uk/nilt/2015/Political_ Attitudes/NIAINTNI.html (accessed 10 October 2018).

3 These data can be viewed here: www.ark.ac.uk/nilt/2015/Political_ Attitudes/NIAINTNI.html (accessed 10 October 2018).

4 This cross-national survey was conducted in countries including China, Russia, and the US. For more on the results, see: www.edelman.com/ sites/g/files/aatuss191/files/2019-02/2019_Edelman_Trust_Barometer_ Global_Report.pdf (accessed 10 April 2019).

5 These statistics can be viewed here: www.eoni.org.uk/Elections/Election- results-and-statistics/Election-results-and-statistics-2003-onwards/ Elections-2017 (accessed 10 October 2018).

6 These results were from a YouGov survey commissioned by Local Media Works. A summary of its conclusions can be found here: www.localme- diauk.org/Consumer-Catalyst (accessed 10 May 2019).

7 Around 70 per cent of respondents felt these companies did not do enough to prevent "illegal and unethical" behaviours on their platforms. For more, see: http://www.edelman.co.uk/magazine/posts/edelman-trust- barometer-2018/ (accessed 10 September 2018).

8 An accommodation on the impasse was reached in July 2017. For more on this, see: www.irishnews.com/news/northernirelandnews/2017/07/13/

news/ardoyne-parade-passes-without-protest-for-first-time-in-almost-two-decades-1083148/ (accessed 20 April 2019).

9 There were more female than male participants in the DP.

10 A full list of the recommendations can be found here: www.involve.org. uk/sites/default/files/field/attachemnt/Recommendations%20%26%20 Resolutions%20of%20the%20Citizens%27%20Assembly%20for%20 Northern%20Ireland.pdf (accessed 10 May 2019).

11 A preliminary analysis of participant evaluations can be found here: https://citizensassemblyni.org/participant-evaluations-of-the-citizens-assembly-for-northern-ireland/ (accessed 10 May 2019).

12 The talks were facilitated by business leader Jim Roddy and Reverend Harold Good. For more on the deal, see here: www.bbc.co.uk/news/ uk-northern-ireland-37458065 (accessed 10 May 2019).

13 Alan in Belfast, "Interview with Loyalists Against Democracy" *Slugger O'Toole*, 9 December 2013.

14 This hashtag was used during Assembly, European Parliament and local government elections held during this period. For more on its role in the 2019 election, see here: www.irishtimes.com/news/politics/ni-council-election-results-due-from-friday-afternoon-1.3879023 (accessed 10 May 2019).

15 The case revolved around the fact that the bakery had taken payment from Lee and then refused to fulfil the order. It was subject to several legal challenges by Ashers. The UK Supreme Court eventually ruled that the bakery had not discriminated against Lee in October 2018. A chronology of the events can be found here: www.premier.org.uk/News/ UK/Ashers-bakery-victory-the-timeline (accessed 10 January 2019).

16 Screenshots of the posts from Bunting's Facebook page can still be found on the LAD blog: http://loyalistsagainstdemocracy.blogspot.com/ 2014/05/traditional-unionist-voice.html (accessed 10 May 2019).

17 www.newsletter.co.uk/news/politics/loyalists-against-democracy-lad-founder-it-was-my-stupidest-idea-ever-i-have-nothing-do-it-any-more-2927874 (accessed 16 November 2020).

18 For a breakdown of the Northern Ireland vote, see: www.bbc.co.uk/ news/uk-northern-ireland-36614443 (accessed 10 April 2019).

19 Senator George Mitchell, one of the architects of the Agreement, was among those to express concerns about the return to a hard border. See: www.independent.co.uk/news/uk/politics/brexit-latest-northern-ireland-border-serious-trouble-george-mitchell-good-friday-agreement-bbc-a8238111.html (accessed 10 April 2019).

20 Physical infrastructure refers to the likely introduction of border customs posts if a hard border was reintroduced.

21 The Irish Border, "There's me at the Brexit negotiations", 8 February 2018, 12:47 p.m., Tweet.

22 The explainer was written 'in character'. It can be found at: www.bbc. co.uk/news/newsbeat-46459904 (accessed 10 May 2019).

23 For an overview of the campaign, see the Rainbow Project website: www. rainbow-project.org/marriage-equality (accessed 10 May 2019).

24 Further information on Now for NI can be found at: https://nowforni. uk/about/ (accessed 10 May 2019).

25 The interview with Allison Morris can be viewed at: https://twitter. com/AmnestyNI/status/976434694546915328?ref_src=twsrc%5Etfw% 7Ctwcamp%5Etweetembed%7Ctwterm%5E976434694546915328& ref_url=https%3A%2F%2Fsluggerotoole.com%2F2018%2F03%2F21% 2Famnestys-toxictwitter-report-calls-for-rules-on-abuse-to-be-enforced%2F (accessed 10 May 2019).

26 A summary of the case studies in the report was provided by Alan Meban at: https://sluggerotoole.com/2018/03/21/amnestys-toxictwitter-report- calls-for-rules-on-abuse-to-be-enforced/ (accessed 10 March 2019).

27 A summary of Twitter demographics in 2018 can be found at: https:// blog.hootsuite.com/twitter-demographics/ (accessed 10 May 2019).

Appendix 1

Content analysis of newspaper coverage of flag protests

The sample was created by using LexisNexis to search for articles that contained major mentions of 'flag protest'. These were reviewed manually before being included in the study.

Table A1.1 Number of articles from three newspapers analysed, December 2012–February 2013.

Newspaper	December 2012	January 2013	February 2013
Belfast Telegraph/Sunday Life	46	85	11
Irish News	32	87	44
News Letter	20	15	7

Table A1.2 Actors quoted in *Belfast Telegraph/Sunday Life* coverage of protests, December 2012.

	Number of articles	Percentage
Billy Hutchinson (PUP)	6	13.04
Assistant Chief Constable Will Kerr	5	10.87
PSNI spokesperson	5	10.87
Jim Allister MLA (TUV)	2	4.35
Chief Constable Matt Baggott	2	4.35
District Judge Fiona Bagnall	2	4.35
Stewart Dickson MLA (AP)	2	4.35
David Ford MLA (AP)	2	4.35
Johnny Harvey (UPV)	2	4.35
Gerry Kelly MLA (SF)	2	4.35
Jackie McDonald	2	4.35
John Moore (SS Moore Sports)	2	4.35
Cllr Ruth Patterson (DUP)	2	4.35
Glyn Roberts (Chief Executive, Northern Ireland Independent Retail Trade Association)	2	4.35
Sammy Wilson MP (DUP)	2	4.35
Cllr Michael Carr (SDLP)	1	2.17
Hillary Clinton	1	2.17
Judith Cochrane MLA (AP)	1	2.17
Jeffrey Donaldson MP (DUP)	1	2.17
Cllr Sean Doran (SF)	1	2.17
Katrina Doran (fashion website editor)	1	2.17
Cllr Anthony Flynn (SF)	1	2.17
Arlene Foster MLA (DUP)	1	2.17
Willie Frazer	1	2.17
Adam Fullarton-Healey (businessman)	1	2.17
Janice Gault (NI Hotels Federation)	1	2.17
Paul Girvan MLA (DUP)	1	2.17
Paul Golding (Britain First)	1	2.17
Rev. Harold Good	1	2.17
Alan Hartwell (MD, Marketplace Europe)	1	2.17
Willie Hay MLA (DUP)	1	2.17
Cllr Terry Hearty (SF)	1	2.17
David Hyland (independent republican)	1	2.17
Lord John Kilclooney	1	2.17

Table A1.2 (continued)

	Number of articles	Percentage
Cllr John McArdle (SF)	1	2.17
Cllr Declan McAteer (SDLP)	1	2.17
Justice McCloskey	1	2.17
Chief Superintendent Alan McCrum	1	2.17
Conall McDevitt MLA (SDLP)	1	2.17
Donald McFetridge (retail analyst)	1	2.17
Cllr Jimmy McCreesh (SF)	1	2.17
Sarah McKeown (solicitor)	1	2.17
Sinead McLaughlin (Chief Executive of Londonderry Chamber of Commerce)	1	2.17
David McNarry MLA (UKIP)	1	2.17
Nichola Mallon MLA (SDLP)	1	2.17
Brendan Mulgrew (Public Relations agency)	1	2.17
Cllr Mick Murphy (SF)	1	2.17
Mike Nesbitt MLA (UUP)	1	2.17
Robin Newton MLA (DUP)	1	2.17
Office of First and Deputy First Minister (OFMDM)	1	2.17
Policing Board spokesperson	1	2.17
Edwin Poots MLA (DUP)	1	2.17
Fergal Rafferty (Foyleside Centre manager)	1	2.17
Peter Robinson MLA (DUP)	1	2.17
Cllr Jim Rodgers (UUP)	1	2.17
Steve Saunderson (Hawkin's Bazaar toy shop)	1	2.17
Cllr Christopher Stalford (DUP)	1	2.17
Value Cabs spokesperson	1	2.17
Jim Wilson	1	2.17

Table A1.3 Actors quoted in *Belfast Telegraph/Sunday Life* coverage of protests, January 2013.

	Number of articles	Percentage
Chief Constable Matt Baggott	8	9.76
Peter Robinson MLA (DUP)	7	8.54
PSNI spokesperson	7	8.54
Willie Frazer	5	6.1
Conall McDevitt MLA (SDLP)	5	6.1
Michael Copeland MLA (UUP)	4	4.88
Northern Ireland Secretary of State Theresa Villiers	4	4.88
Jamie Bryson	3	3.66
Billy Hutchinson (PUP)	3	3.66
Naomi Long MP (AP)	3	3.66
Terry Spence (Northern Ireland Police Federation)	3	3.66
Stewart Dickson MLA (AP)	2	2.44
Tanaiste Eamon Gilmore	2	2.44
Assistant Chief Constable George Hamilton	2	2.44
Martin McGuinness MLA (SF)	2	2.44
Cllr Leslie Mitchell (PUP)	2	2.44
Kate Nash	2	2.44
Mike Nesbitt MLA (UUP)	2	2.44
Robin Newton MLA (DUP)	2	2.44
Cllr Niall Ó Donnghaile (SF)	2	2.44
Parades Commission spokesperson	2	2.44
Detective Superintendent Sean Wright	2	2.44
Roger Bailie (psychologist)	1	1.22
British Army spokesperson	1	1.22
Rachel Brown (Gallery Café)	1	1.22
Judith Cochrane MLA (AP)	1	1.22
Jonathan Craig MLA (DUP)	1	1.22
Justice Deeney	1	1.22
Adeline Dinsmore (Ashfield Girls School)	1	1.22
Mark Durkan MP (SDLP)	1	1.22

Table A1.3 (continued)

	Number of articles	Percentage
Pat Dyer (St George's market stall holder)	1	1.22
Adam Fullarton-Healey	1	1.22
Joel Goodman (photographer)	1	1.22
Akim Hamadi (Le Bistro Salon)	1	1.22
Paul Hamill (Kainos)	1	1.22
Cllr Claire Hanna (SDLP)	1	1.22
Colin Hassard	1	1.22
Paula Hinchcliffe (St George's market stall holder)	1	1.22
Todd Kelman (GM, Belfast Giants)	1	1.22
Pat Kelly (solicitor)	1	1.22
Jenny Kennedy (St George's market stall holder)	1	1.22
Cllr John Kyle (PUP)	1	1.22
Gary Lightbody (Snow Patrol)	1	1.22
Raymond McCartney MLA (SF)	1	1.22
Justice McCloskey	1	1.22
Bob McCoubrey (Mourne Seafood)	1	1.22
District Judge Barney McElholm	1	1.22
Andy McMorran (Ashfield Boys' School),	1	1.22
Alban Magennis MLA (SDLP)	1	1.22
Matthew Pitts (Principal, Wellington College)	1	1.22
Cllr Jim Rodgers (UUP)	1	1.22
John Simpson (Economist)	1	1.22
Nigel Smyth (CBI)	1	1.22
Jimmy Spratt MLA (DUP)	1	1.22
Debbie Watters (NI Alternatives)	1	1.22
Andrew Webb (OCO Global)	1	1.22
David Weiniger (owner, Spires Restaurant)	1	1.22
Jim Wilson	1	1.22
Sammy Wilson MP (DUP)	1	1.22
Koulia Yiasouma (Include Youth)	1	1.22
Eva Zetterberg-Pettersson (teacher)	1	1.22

Table A1.4 Actors quoted in *Belfast Telegraph/Sunday Life* coverage of protests, February 2013.

	Number of articles	*Percentage*
Chief Constable Matt Baggott	3	27.27
Raymond Brady (co-proprietor, Chatters Coffee Shop)	1	9.09
Jamie Bryson	1	9.09
Gordon Dunne MLA (DUP)	1	9.09
Conall McDevitt MLA (SDLP)	1	9.09
Tony McGleenan QC	1	9.09
Patsy McGlone MLA (SDLP)	1	9.09
Paul McMahon (Castlecourt shopping centre manager)	1	9.09
PSNI spokesperson	1	9.09
Karen Quinlivan QC	1	9.09
Alan Revell (co-proprietor, Chatters Coffee Shop)	1	9.09
Justice Treacy	1	9.09
Detective Superintendent Sean Wright	1	9.09

Table A1.5 Actors quoted in *Irish News* coverage of protests, December 2012.

	Number of articles	*Percentage*
Gerry Kelly MLA (SF)	3	9.38
Cllr Tim Atwood (SDLP)	2	6.25
District Judge Fiona Bagnall	2	6.25
David Ford MLA (AP)	2	6.25
Willie Frazer	2	6.25
Justice McCloskey	2	6.25
PSNI spokesperson	2	6.25
Cllr Jim Rodgers (UUP)	2	6.25
Cllr Sean Begley (SF)	1	3.13
Hugh Black (Victoria Square manager)	1	3.13
Cllr Monica Digney (SF)	1	3.13
Seamus Dooley (NUJ)	1	3.13
Jim Dowson	1	3.13
DUP spokesperson	1	3.13

Table A1.5 (continued)

	Number of articles	Percentage
Cllr Billy Hamilton (independent unionist)	1	3.13
Ross Hussey MLA (UUP)	1	3.13
Billy Hutchinson	1	3.13
Assistant Chief Constable Dave Jones	1	3.13
Assistant Chief Constable Will Kerr	1	3.13
Danny Kinahan MLA (UUP)	1	3.13
Patricia Lewsley (NI Commissioner for Children and Young People)	1	3.13
Chris Lyttle MLA (AP)	1	3.13
Cllr Pat McCarthy (SDLP)	1	3.13
Conall McDevitt MLA (SDLP)	1	3.13
Alasdair McDonnell MP (SDLP)	1	3.13
Martin McGuinness MLA (SF)	1	3.13
Cllr Laura McNamee (AP)	1	3.13
Cllr Jim McVeigh (SF)	1	3.13
Mourne Seafood spokesperson	1	3.13
Cllr Gerardine Mulvenna (AP)	1	3.13
Northern Ireland Blood Transfusion Service spokesperson	1	3.13
OFMDFM	1	3.13
PUP spokesperson	1	3.13
Paul Rankin	1	3.13
Fergal Rafferty (Foyleside Centre manager)	1	3.13
Glyn Roberts (Chief Executive, Northern Ireland Independent Retail Trade Association)	1	3.13
Peter Robinson MLA (DUP)	1	3.13
Cllr Christopher Stalford (DUP)	1	3.13
Mervyn Storey MLA (DUP)	1	3.13

Table A1.6 Actors quoted in *Irish News* coverage of protests, January 2013.

	Number of articles mentioned	Percentage
Peter Robinson	8	9.2
Willie Frazer	8	9.2
PSNI spokesperson	6	6.9
Chief Constable Matt Baggott	5	5.75
Martin McGuinness	5	5.75
David Ford MLA (AP)	4	4.6
Northern Ireland Secretary of State Theresa Villiers	4	4.6
Jamie Bryson	3	3.45
Mike Nesbitt MLA (UUP)	3	3.45
Terry Spence	3	3.45
Gerry Adams TD (SF)	2	2.3
Judith Cochrane MLA (AP)	2	2.3
Michael Copeland MLA (UUP)	2	2.3
Sean Crowe TD (SF)	2	2.3
Stewart Dickson MLA (AP)	2	2.3
Facebook spokesperson	2	2.3
Tanaiste Eamon Gilmore	2	2.3
ACC George Hamilton	2	2.3
William Humphrey MLA (DUP)	2	2.3
Pat Kelly	2	2.3
Kieran McCarthy MLA (AP)	2	2.3
Conall McDevitt MLA (SDLP)	2	2.3
Jim Allister MLA (TUV)	1	1.15
An Garda Síochána spokesperson	1	1.15
Rev. David Armstrong	1	1.15
Cllr Tim Atwood (SDLP)	1	1.15
District Judge Fiona Bagnall	1	1.15
BBC spokesperson	1	1.15
BBC Trust spokesperson	1	1.15
Dennis Boyd (defence barrister)	1	1.15
Niall Collins TD (FF)	1	1.15
Rev. John Cunningham	1	1.15
Justice Deeney	1	1.15
DUP spokesperson	1	1.15
Department of Foreign Affairs spokesperson	1	1.15

Table A1.6 (continued)

	Number of articles mentioned	Percentage
Pat Doherty MP (SF)	1	1.15
Jeffrey Donaldson MP (DUP)	1	1.15
Noel Doran (Irish News Editor)	1	1.15
Paul Durant (Internet Service Providers Association)	1	1.15
David Fitzimons (Retail Excellence Ireland)	1	1.15
Arlene Foster MLA (DUP)	1	1.15
Rev. Mervyn Gibson	1	1.15
Peter Hopkins (Facebook Ireland Ltd)	1	1.15
Judge Horner	1	1.15
Ross Hussey MLA (UUP)	1	1.15
Billy Hutchinson	1	1.15
Gerry Kelly MLA (SF)	1	1.15
Cllr John Kyle (PUP)	1	1.15
Gary Lightbody	1	1.15
Nelson McCausland MLA (DUP)	1	1.15
Alasdair McDonnell MP (SDLP)	1	1.15
District Judge Barney McElholm	1	1.15
Cllr Ruairi McHugh (SF)	1	1.15
Stephen Magorrian (MD, Botanic Inns)	1	1.15
Conor Maguire (prosecution)	1	1.15
Gerald Nash TD (Labour)	1	1.15
Linda Nash	1	1.15
Stephen Nolan	1	1.15
Northern Ireland Electricity spokesperson	1	1.15
Northern Ireland Office spokesperson	1	1.15
Cllr Niall O'Donnghaile (SF)	1	1.15
Ofcom spokesperson	1	1.15
OFMDFM spokesperson	1	1.15
Parades Commission spokesperson	1	1.15
PSNI spokesperson	1	1.15
Brian Rea (Policing Board)	1	1.15
Nicola Roundtree (Barrister)	1	1.15
Alan Shatter TD	1	1.15
Sinn Féin spokesperson	1	1.15
Justice Stephens	1	1.15

(Continued)

Table A1.6 (continued)

	Number of articles mentioned	Percentage
Kyle Thompson (UKIP)	1	1.15
Translink spokesperson	1	1.15
William Ward (St Matthew's Church)	1	1.15
Jude Whyte (Victims and Survivors Forum)	1	1.15
Ken Wilkinson (PUP)	1	1.15
Detective Superintendent Sean Wright	1	1.15

Table A1.7 Actors quoted in *Irish News* coverage of protests, February 2013.

	Number of articles	Percentage
Jamie Bryson	3	8.82
Chief Constable Matt Baggott	2	5.88
Gordon Dunne MLA (DUP)	2	5.88
Willie Frazer	2	5.88
IFA spokesperson	2	5.88
Assistant Chief Constable Will Kerr	2	5.88
Chris Lyttle MLA (AP)	2	5.88
Peter Osborne (NICRC)	2	
Dennis Boyd	1	2.94
Judith Cochrane MLA (AP)	1	2.94
Crusaders FC spokesperson	1	2.94
John Dallat MLA (SDLP)	1	2.94
Gary Donnelly (32CSM)	1	2.94
Phil Flanagan MLA (SF)	1	2.94
David Ford MLA (AP)	1	2.94
Rev. Mervyn Gibson	1	2.94
Justice Horner	1	2.94
Cllr John Hussey (DUP)	1	2.94
Joe Jordan	1	2.94
Gerry Kelly MLA (SF)	1	2.94
David McClarty MLA	1	2.94
Justice McCloskey	1	2.94
Basil McCrea MLA (UUP)	1	2.94
Conall McDevitt MLA (SDLP)	1	2.94

Table A1.7 (continued)

	Number of articles	Percentage
Paul McMahon (Castlecourt manager)	1	2.94
Northern Ireland Water spokesperson	1	2.94
John O'Connor	1	2.94
Prof Michael O'Flaherty	1	2.94
PSNI spokesperson	1	2.94
Pat Ramsey MLA (SDLP)	1	2.94
Translink spokesperson	1	2.94
Ulster People's Forum spokesperson	1	2.94
Mark Winter	1	2.94
Detective Superintendent Sean Wright	1	2.94

Table A1.8 Actors quoted in *News Letter* coverage of protests, December 2012.

	Number of articles	Percentage
Peter Robinson	4	20
PSNI spokesperson	4	20
DUP-UUP joint statement	2	10
Padraig McShane	2	10
Alliance Party spokesperson	1	5
Jim Allister (TUV)	1	5
Jamie Bryson	1	5
Winston Irvine	1	5
Assistant Chief Constable Dave Jones	1	5
Assistant Chief Constable Will Kerr	1	5
Justice McCloskey	1	5
Robin Newton	1	5
Northern Ireland Secretary of State Theresa Villiers	1	5
Office of First and Deputy First Minister (OFMDM)	1	5
Strathclyde Police spokesperson	1	5

Table A1.9 Actors quoted in *News Letter* coverage of protests, January 2013.

	Number of articles	Percentage
Willie Frazer	3	20
Jamie Bryson	2	13.33
Peter Robinson	2	13.33
Niall Collins TD (Fianna Fáil)	1	6.67
Ian Coulter (CBI)	1	6.67
Stewart Dickson	1	6.67
DUP spokesperson	1	6.67
Billy Hutchinson	1	6.67
Jackie McDonald	1	6.67
PSNI spokesperson	1	6.67
Translink spokesperson	1	6.67
Ulster People's Forum spokesperson (unnamed)	1	6.67

Table A1.10 Actors quoted in *News Letter* coverage of protests, February 2013.

	Number of articles	Percentage
Willie Frazer	3	42.86
Jamie Bryson	2	28.57
Chief Constable Matt Baggott	1	14.29
Jim Dowson	1	14.29
Gordon Dunne (MLA)	1	14.29
Irish Football Association spokesperson	1	14.29
Joe Jordan	1	14.29
Paul McMahon (Castlecourt manager)	1	14.29

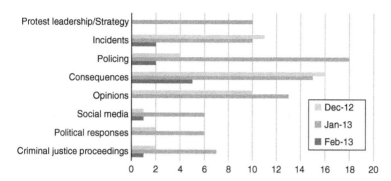

Figure A1.1 Main themes in *Belfast Telegraph* coverage of flag protests, December 2012–February 2013.

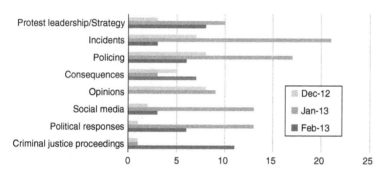

Figure A1.2 Main themes in *Irish News* coverage of flag protests, December 2012–February 2013.

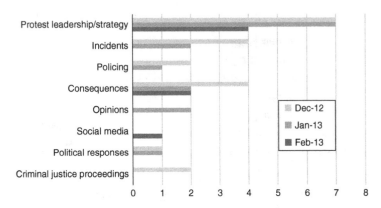

Figure A1.3 Main themes in *News Letter* coverage of flag protests, December 2012–February 2013.

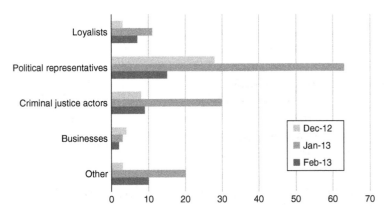

Figure A1.4 Actors quoted in *Irish News* coverage of flag protests, December 2012–February 2013.

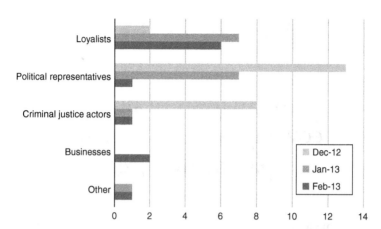

Figure A1.5 Actors quoted in *News Letter* coverage of protests, December 2012–February 2013.

Appendix 2

Content analysis of newspaper coverage of the Ardoyne parade disputes

A content analysis of newspaper coverage of the Ardoyne parade disputes was conducted between April and June 2018. The corpus (N = 44) was generated by searching for 'Ardoyne' in the 'Irish newspapers' catalogue within the LexisNexis database. Articles that didn't directly address the parade impasse, as well as letters from readers, were purposefully omitted from the study due the focus on how these newspapers framed the parade dispute in both years. It should be noted that there were no results for the *News Letter*, which was a surprising result given its position as one of the three most read newspapers in the region. Nevertheless, four papers that featured (*Belfast Telegraph*, *Irish News*, *Irish Times* and *Sunday Life*) were considered broadly representative of the media coverage of the disputes.

Table A2.1 Newspaper articles addressing Ardoyne parade dispute, 8–14 July 2014.

Date	Headline	Newspaper	Word Count
08/07/14	Parades, flags and the past – Appeals for peace as north awaits 'graduated response' – Ruling parties expected to meet today	*Irish News*	482
08/07/14	Ardoyne parade row: Escalation of tensions in no one's interest	*Belfast Telegraph*	368
09/07/14	Loyalist protests – Unionists' 'graduated response' details to be unveiled tomorrow	*Irish News*	481
09/07/14	Parades protests 'should be lawful'	*Belfast Telegraph*	116

Table A2.1 (continued)

Date	Headline	Newspaper	Word Count
09/07/14	Polarised views not confined to Ardoyne interface	*Belfast Telegraph*	575
09/07/14	Twelfth tension: What do Orangemen think about the Ardoyne crisis?	*Belfast Telegraph*	1965
09/07/14	After hours of critical Ardoyne parade talks, just 25 words from Stormont	*Belfast Telegraph*	827
09/07/14	Inter-unionist strains define response to march ban	*Irish Times*	808
10/07/14	Orange leaders discuss banning of Ardoyne parade	*Irish Times*	331
10/07/14	Orange Order: We can't guarantee parade protests will be peaceful	*Belfast Telegraph*	628
11/07/14	Implement Belfast Telegraph's Ardoyne proposal, unionists urge	*Belfast Telegraph*	714
11/07/14	Ardoyne parade impasse in north Belfast can be broken	*Belfast Telegraph*	353
11/07/14	Ardoyne parade: Police ready to act, but hope they won't have to	*Belfast Telegraph*	258
11/07/14	Ardoyne parade proposal: It is an idea that just might offer a way forward	*Belfast Telegraph*	684
11/07/14	Hope on the streets for a calm Twelfth	*Irish Times*	573
12/07/14	Opinion – Easy to work out who leads unionist group	*Irish News*	840
12/07/14	Loyalist Protests – Prosecution warning	*Irish News*	180
12/07/14	Hopes for peaceful parades protests	*Belfast Telegraph*	835
12/07/14	Can the Orange Order keep a lid on Twelfth tensions?	*Belfast Telegraph*	860
12/07/14	Orange demo over parade restriction	*Belfast Telegraph*	863
12/07/14	Twelfth of July Orange Order marches in north Belfast pass off peacefully	*Belfast Telegraph*	1106

(Continued)

Table A2.1 (continued)

Date	Headline	Newspaper	Word Count
12/07/14	PSNI PRAISE ALL SIDES AS DAY PASSES PEACEFULLY; TWELFTH NEWS ROUND-UP	*Sunday Life*	740
13/07/14	Praise for peaceful July 12 events	*Belfast Telegraph*	817
14/07/14	The Twelfth: Peaceful Ardoyne raises hope for deal; Pleas for Order to enter talks and finally resolve parades disputes	*Belfast Telegraph*	907

Table A2.2 Actors quoted in newspaper coverage of Ardoyne dispute, 8–14 July 2014.

Actor	Number of times quoted
PSNI Chief Constable George Hamilton	6
Police spokesperson (unnamed)	4
DUP MP Nigel Dodds	2
Orange Order Grand Chaplain Mervyn Gibson	2
SDLP MLA Alban Maginness	2
Orange Order Grand Secretary Drew Nelson	2
Orange Order Grand Master Edward Stevenson	2
Northern Ireland Secretary of State Theresa Villiers	2
SDLP MLA Alex Atwood	1
Orange Order Deputy Grand Master Spencer Beattie	1
Justice Minister David Ford	1
Belfast Centre Centre Manager Andrew Irvine	1
NI Attorney General John Larkin, QC	1
SDLP MP Alasdair McDonnell	1
Sinn Féin MLA Daithí McKay	1
Belfast Chamber of Trade and Commerce President, Paul McMahon	1

Table A2.2 (continued)

Actor	Number of times quoted
TUV press officer Sammy Morrison	1
Sinn Féin MLA John O'Dowd	1
First Minister Peter Robinson	1
Cooperation Ireland CEO Peter Sheridan	1
Spokesperson Ligoniel True Blues Lodge Stephen Shivers	1
DUP MP Sammy Wilson	1
NI Executive (statement)	1
Orange Order spokesperson (unnamed)	1
Parades Commission spokesperson (unnamed)	1
West Belfast loyalist (unnamed)	1

Table A2.3 Newspaper articles addressing Ardoyne parade dispute, 8–15 July 2015.

Date	Headline	Newspaper	Wordcount
08/07/2015	Pride of Ardoyne Flute Band members convicted for playing music at north Belfast interface	Belfast Telegraph	347
11/07/2015	Anger at Ardoyne group's call to flout Parades Commission ruling	Belfast Telegraph	449
12/07/2015	WE'RE NOW AT BOILING POINT; AHEAD OF THIS WEEKEND'S PARADES, TOP LOYALIST GIVES TENSE WARNING FOR THE TWELFTH 2015	Sunday Life	970
13/07/2015	Pleas for calm at flashpoint	Irish News	312
13/07/2015	Police hurt in Orange march clashes	Belfast Telegraph	905
14/07/2015	Missiles hurled as PSNI block parade; Orangemen prevented from parading past Ardoyne shops in north Belfast	Irish Times	398

(Continued)

Table A2.3 (continued)

Date	Headline	Newspaper	Wordcount
14/07/2015	The Twelfth – Eight police officers injured during riots	*Irish News*	424
14/07/2015	Man bailed on riot charges	*Belfast Telegraph*	115
14/07/2015	The inevitable violence at Ardoyne: stop blaming others and sort it out	*Belfast Telegraph*	392
14/07/2015	Ardoyne: Teen girl trapped under car and 24 officers hurt as violence erupts at Belfast flashpoint	*Belfast Telegraph*	882
14/07/2015	Twelfth 2015: Tense stand-off between police and loyalists after return route of Orange Order parade turns violent in north Belfast	*Belfast Telegraph*	885
14/07/2015	Twelfth 2015: DUP leaders condemn north Belfast rioters	*Belfast Telegraph*	629
14/07/2015	Twelfth 2015: Man arrested over attempted murder after girl hit by car at Ardoyne riot; Policeman's ear severed after being hit by masonry during violence	*Belfast Telegraph*	586
15/07/2015	The Twelfth – 150,000 watched Ardoyne riots on live YouTube feed	*Irish News*	292
15/07/2015	The Twelfth – The night trouble took everyone by surprise	*Irish News*	656
15/07/2015	Teen trapped under Orange bandsman's car has Irish army career hopes dashed	*Irish News*	383
15/07/2015	Officer's ear nearly severed in a night of frenzied violence in Ardoyne	*Belfast Telegraph*	678

Table A2.3 (continued)

Date	Headline	Newspaper	Wordcount
15/07/2015	Ardoyne crash girl's pain as driver charged with double murder bid	*Belfast Telegraph*	345
15/07/2015	Riot car murder bid charge Orangeman expresses 'profound regret'	*Belfast Telegraph*	623
15/07/2015	Twelfth 2015: Orangeman regrets 'attempted murder' car incident that broke 16-year-old girl's pelvis, is granted bail	*Belfast Telegraph*	887

Table A2.4 Actors quoted in newspaper coverage of Ardoyne dispute, 8–15 July 2015.

Actor	Number of times quoted
Assistant Chief Constable Stephen Martin	5
Sinn Féin MLA Gerry Kelly	3
Father Gary Donegan	3
PSNI Chief Constable George Hamilton	2
Ivan Lewis MP (Shadow Secretary of State for Northern Ireland)	2
Police Federation Chairman Mark Lindsay	2
Leigha Clawson	1
DUP MP Nigel Dodds	2
Alliance MLA Stewart Dickson	2
District Judge Amanda Henderson	2
DUP MLA William Humphreys	2
PSNI Chief Inspector Andy Lemon	2
Patricia McAuley	1
Gerard Solinas (UPRG)	1
First Minister Peter Robinson	1
PSNI Duty Inspector Michael White	1
Eyewitness to Aughey attack (unnamed)	1
John Aughey's solicitor (unnamed)	1

(Continued)

Table A2.4 (continued)

Actor	Number of times quoted
GARC spokesperson (unnamed)	1
Orange Order spokesperson (unnamed)	1
PSNI spokesperson (unnamed)	1
Social media commentator (unnamed)	1

Afterword

One would be forgiven for feeling a sense of déjà vu when doom-scrolling about the latest crisis in Northern Ireland. Many of the most vocal commentators during the flag protests have continued to dominate the partisan, polarised debates about the region's post-Brexit future. At the time of writing, online platforms have amplified 'hot takes' on the Windsor Framework (WF), the agreement between the UK Government and the European Union (EU) to (finally) resolve the issues caused by checks on goods being transported between Great Britain and Northern Ireland. The Democratic Unionist Party (DUP) have consistently blocked efforts to restore the powersharing executive in protest at the Northern Ireland Proto-col (NIP), which created a de facto 'Irish Sea Border' after the UK's departure from the EU in December 2020. Despite claims from UK Prime Minister Rishi Sunak that the WF will make the region the "world's most exciting economic zone"[1], it remains to be seen whether it will be enough to convince the DUP to go back into the Executive. Prominent loyalist commentators such as Jamie Bryson have already called on the DUP to reject the deal on the basis that "Northern Ireland's constitutional position remains diminished" due to it falling under the jurisdiction of the European Court of Justice.[2] The Stormont Brake, a mechanism whereby 30 MLAs from a mini-mum of two parties can raise concerns about how Northern Ireland is affected by changes to EU law[3] has been criticised by DUP MP Sammy Wilson for being a "delaying mechanism" rather than a brake.[4] Meanwhile, the other parties in Stormont continue to criti-cise the DUP for failing to take their seats in the Executive despite the worst cost of living crisis in living memory, with some suggesting that their reluctance to do so has more to do with having to serve

under a Sinn Féin First Minister than post-Brexit trading arrange-
ments.[5]

As alluded to in this book, democratic dysfunction remains a defining feature of the powersharing institutions created under the 1998
Belfast Agreement (the Agreement). Although the 'New Decade,
New Approach' deal in January 2020 committed all the parties to
reducing the use of the Petition of Concern to "exceptional circumstances and as a last resort"[6], there remain concerns about the way this
mechanism was used to block legislation in policy areas such as equal
marriage. Moreover, the consociationalist framework of governance
means that either of the two largest political parties have the ability
to collapse the institutions when it is politically expedient for them to
do so. Both the DUP and Sinn Féin have withdrawn support for the
powersharing Executive in recent years. As discussed in the Introduction, the 'cash for ash' scandal and the DUP's refusal to legislate for an
Irish language act were cited by Sinn Féin as reasons why they
wouldn't restore Stormont during its three year suspension from 2017
to 2020.[7] Inevitably this meant there were accusations of hypocrisy
levelled at the party for their condemnation of the DUP for refusing
to re-enter the Executive until their concerns about the NIP had
been addressed.[8] Yet, irrespective of who is to blame for the current
impasse, it should be noted that Stormont has been without a func-
tioning government for over a third of its lifespan.[9] Despite NHS
waiting times and economic inactivity being among the worst in the
UK, Stormont MLAs were still being paid an annual salary of
£37,337 (after a £14000 pay cut implemented by NI Secretary of
State Chris Heaton-Harris) nearly two years after the DUP walked
out of the Executive.[10] This absence of leadership and democratic
deficit has clearly contributed to the toxic political debates seen on
online platforms in recent years.

Social media remains toxic for public figures and activists

'Offline' events have continued to be linked to an intensification of
cyber hate and harassment in Northern Ireland. Predictably, activism
related to the constitutional future of the contested polity has often
generated a social media backlash from those who hold oppositional
views. For example, there was much online anger among loyalist commentators about the activities of 'Ireland's Future' (IF), a civic

nationalist non-profit which has campaigned for Irish reunification since 2017. James Nesbitt, a well-known actor from a Protestant background, was subject to much online abuse for having expressed an openness towards a united Ireland at an IF organised conference in Dublin in October 2022. The PSNI characterised graffiti targeting Nesbitt in the predominantly unionist town of Portrush as a hate crime.[11] A month later they confirmed that they were investigating social media posts attacking Colin Harvey, one of IF's board members and a prominent spokesperson for the organisation.[12] Threatening tweets, such as "We used to behead traitors like this", were sent to the law professor throughout the calendar year of 2022; there was also an orchestrated campaign by loyalists questioning his academic credentials and calling on Queen's University Belfast to sanction him for his participation in the campaign.[13] Activist Moore Holmes tweeted that Harvey's "unpredictable & unrestrained outbursts on Twitter" were "seriously & irreversibly damaging his credibility".[14] Commentator Jamie Bryson condemned the "unacceptable and abusive comments" directed at Harvey, whilst accusing his allies in the press ("the nationalist network") of protecting the "republican activist" from scrutiny by presenting 'legitimate challenges' as a form of abuse or intimidation.[15] He claimed that he received hundreds of abusive tweets per day but not received the same level of sympathy and support offered to Harvey by groups like Amnesty International. While critics characterised this as a form of whataboutery, loyalists were being abused online for voicing their opposition to the 'Irish Sea Border', which they claimed threatened Northern Ireland's position within the UK. For example, community worker Stacey Graham reported that she had to take a break from Twitter after being subjected to a campaign of misogynistic abuse online following her speech at an anti-NIP rally in December 2019.[16] Congruent with the findings of this book, those campaigning around such polarising, contentious issues often appear to pay a heavy price for their activism on social media.

There have also been many 'Twitterstorms' in response to the historic social media posts of elected representatives (perhaps too many to mention here). A slew of politicians from across the sectarian divide have been forced to apologise for offensive social media posts flagged by other users. In January 2022, for example, the Ulster Unionist Party (UUP) leader Doug Beattie had to issue an "unreserved apology" for tweets posed a decade earlier that made derogatory remarks about women, members of the travelling community, and Islam.[17] The same month three Sinn Féin MLAs (Jemma Dolan, Sinead Ennis, and Emma Sheerin) had to issue similar *mea culpas* for historic social media posts that used sectarian slurs about Protestants and offensive language about people with disabilities.[18] It is beyond the scope of this book to consider what sanctions, if any, politicians should face for social media utterances shared before they held public office. However, it should be noted that there was much whataboutery invoked by those seeking to defend these politicians; there were also no resignations despite the initial social media furore and subsequent media scrutiny of these controversies. One interpretation of this might be that it demonstrates Northern Ireland Twitter's status as an echo chamber, although clearly not a hermetically sealed one given the often antagonistic exchanges outlined in Chapter 3. As discussed in this book, this small but highly active group of politically motivated tweeters are not representative of the majority of social media users in the region, most of whom probably have little to no interest in the social media utterances of politicians. Much of the public anger at these remarks was probably generated by the media coverage of these tweets, demonstrating once again Twitter's disproportionate influence on public discourse due to the presence of journalists and politicians on the site (Šimunjak, 2022). It is doubtful whether these offensive social media posts would have been the subject of such contestation if they hadn't been reported in regional newspapers and television outlets. Yet, an unintended consequence of these Twitterstorms has been that parties such as Sinn Féin have forensically cleaned the social media accounts of their elected representatives. Political commentators such as Slugger O'Toole founder Mick Fealty have been among those to express concern at the lack of media coverage of 'Operation Delete Tweets', arguing that "journalism's gift to democracy is to show politicians their weaknesses"[19].

Although it remains difficult to ascertain its full scale, research has suggested that cyber hate remains prevalent on social media platforms. A report commissioned by advocacy group 'HOPE not hate' found that anti-Semitism could be "easily found" on most social media sites, with memes increasingly used to promote more "internet-friendly forms" of holocaust denial (Mulhall, 2021:8). The same can be said for online misogyny, with one in five women in the UK reporting that they have suffered online abuse or harassment[20]. In addition to the indirect effects of online incivility discussed earlier, such cyber hate has been identified as one of the many barriers to women's participation in the post-conflict society (Turner and Swaine, 2021). Politicians have reported a rise in abusive remarks being directed at them on social media. For example, DUP MLA Diane Dodds filed a police report after an anonymous social media account mocked the death of her disabled son Andrew in January 2022.[21] Alliance leader Naomi Long, one of the subjects of Amnesty's 2018 'Toxic Twitter' report, has continued to be on the receiving end of misogynistic trolling online. In March 2023 she shared some of the sexist tweets she had received that month whilst calling for the platform to "up their game" on protecting users from such abuse.[22] Both Dodds and Long criticised online platforms for not doing more to prevent anonymous accounts harassing public figures. While Long's proposed all-party forum on the issue has not been established at the time of writing, it would appear this issue will be on the policy agenda if the Stormont Executive is reconvened any time soon.

Whether local politicians have the power to address such online harms remains to be seen. Recent legislation such as the EU Digital Services Act (DSA) and the UK Online Safety Bill has introduced new financial penalties for very large online platforms that fail to take stronger action on harmful content. Critics have argued that the discretionary nature of the DSA provides 'wriggle room' for social media companies who do not want to recognise their responsibility for amplifying disinformation.[23] Take, for example, the case of Twitter under the leadership of Elon Musk since his takeover in October 2022. Despite bold claims that he would rid the site of bots and trolls, the tech entrepreneur's tenure has been associated with a rise in hate speech, misinformation and other online harms. This can be at least partially explained by Musk's 'free speech absolutism' which favours the downgrading of hateful content rather than its removal. In March 2023, Twitter insiders briefed the press about how they were no longer capable of protecting users from trolling and online abuse.[24] The site's rebranding as 'X' in July 2023 has seen Musk double down on his 'freedom of speech, not freedom of reach' approach towards content moderation.[25] Research by the Centre for Countering Digital Hate (CCDH) found that X failed to take action on 86 percent of posts containing hate speech, including comments mocking

Holocaust victims and other racist content.[26] In response, X issued a statement accusing CCDH of making false claims about these posts, whilst acknowledging that their new content moderation policy meant that the company would restrict the audience for some violative posts rather than remove them permanently.[27] Musk has went so far as to file a lawsuit against CCDH alleging that the non-profit had unlawfully accessed company data and selectively picked posts to show a rise in hate speech on the platform.[28]

While it is beyond the scope of this book to speculate on either the outcome of this lawsuit or the longevity of the platform under Musk's leadership, X appears to be even more toxic for political discourse than its predecessor. The prevalence of such online incivility might have negative effects on attitudes towards outgroups in divided societies such as Northern Ireland, especially during contentious events which mobilise affective publics online. Yet, as discussed throughout this book, these publics tend to be highly politicised and should not be taken as a proxy for public opinion *per se*.

'Brexit riots' demonstrate importance of social media in protests and related violence

In the first edition of *Digital Contention*, I argued that online mis-and disinformation during contentious public demonstrations were a consequence of the failure of the powersharing institutions to satisfactorily address these issues. That is not to underestimate the role of platforms like Facebook in protests in Northern Ireland, nor their responsibility to better regulate content that had the potential to spark violence. Online platforms were clearly being used to organise and publicise protests, as well as some instances of intercommunal violence involving predominantly young men near sectarian interfaces. However, the impact of social media on these events was often overstated, with much online activity following rather than preceding events, and involving distant onlookers instead of those able to influence events on the ground. There was also little sign that people were changing their minds about issues such as parading rights, flags or emblems as a result of being exposed to different viewpoints on sites like Facebook and Twitter. It was reasonable to presume that conversations on private messaging apps like WhatsApp were reinforcing these divisions rather than promoting conflictual consensus on these divisive issues.

Similar observations can be made about how online platforms have been used during public demonstrations and related violence since 2016. Probably the most significant mass mobilisation since the flag protests were the so-called 'Brexit riots' in April 2021. These demonstrations and related violence in Northern Ireland were nominally a manifestation of loyalist anger at the Brexit Withdrawal Agreement signed by the United Kingdom (UK) Government in December 2020. Many social media users argued that Brexit had jeopardised peace in Northern Ireland through its creation of an 'Irish Sea Border', which meant certain goods had to be checked before being transported between Great Britain and Northern Ireland (Gillespie, 2020). Meanwhile, loyalist activists condemned the NIP for undermining their position within the United Kingdom; Jamie Bryson characterised the protests as articulating "all of the key issues of the last two decades" including controversies over loyalist band parades being rerouted by the Parades Commission, a "two-tier" policing "designed to criminalise loyalism" and increased dissatisfaction with the Agreement itself (Bryson, 2021). In protest, the Loyalist Communities Council (LCC), an umbrella group representing paramilitary groups such as the Ulster Volunteer Force (UVF) and Red Hand Commandos (RHC), announced they no longer supported the Agreement, although they did urge supporters to keep their anti-NIP demonstrations "peaceful and democratic"[29]. Tensions were further raised after the PSNI announced they would not prosecute Sinn Féin members, including then Deputy First Minister Michelle O'Neill, for breaching COVID-19 regulations at the funeral of senior republican Bobby Storey in June 2020. Moore Holmes (2021) argued this was further evidence of how loyalists were "treated heavy-handedly" compared to the "light touch approach to Republicanism". The fallout from the PSNI Storey announcement, and ongoing LCC agitation against the NIP, would be blamed for four consecutive nights of loyalist rioting in the Waterside district of Derry (30 March–2 April). A subsequent anti-NIP protest in South Belfast on 2 April saw rioters throw petrol bombs and other missiles at the PSNI, with civil unrest spreading to other loyalist districts within Belfast and Carrickfergus. PSNI Assistant Chief Constable Jonathan Roberts characterised the disorder as being "at a scale not seen for years"[30].

Social media played a key role in mediating the civil unrest in April 2021. Messages calling for loyalists to "shut down Northern Ireland" reverberated around Facebook, Twitter, and WhatsApp (Creighton, 2021). Journalist David Blevins argued that "putting out the fire on the street" was difficult "while someone, somewhere is pouring petrol from a keyboard"[31]. 'False flag' social media accounts were blamed for the rioting at Lanark Way in West Belfast. Messages entitled "Calling of Arms", urging loyalist youths to "earn their strips" [sic], were shared on Facebook and WhatsApp in the wake of the Sandy Row violence; Bryson blamed anonymous republican accounts for spreading these "malicious and false" messages.[32] The LCC sought to distance itself from the violence in a statement warning unionists and loyalists "to remain vigilant to the dangers of fake and anonymous social media accounts, and we urge our people not to get drawn into violent confrontations" (Scott, 2021). Interviews with participants revealed that they had received messages via these platforms containing places and times at which riots were expected to occur, with paramilitaries often blamed for actively encouraging this violence (Walsh, 2021).

Congruent with the research findings presented earlier, social media facilitated the emergence of affective publics during the April 2021 riots. Videos recorded by eyewitnesses on smartphones, including footage of a bus being petrol bombed close to the Lanark Way interface, provided a focal point for the ire of online commentators on apps such as TikTok (Fox, 2021). Bryson (2021) responded angrily to claims that the teenage rioters did not understand the complexities of the NIP, claiming that these (online) commentators spent "their days eating avocados and sipping lattes" and held outdated stereotypical views of loyalism. Meanwhile, tweeters in Great Britain framed the violence as inevitable given the UK Government's pursuit of a 'hard' Brexit, which risked the future of the peace process by imposing a border in the Irish Sea. For example, The Guardian columnist Jonathan Freedland accused Johnson and his fellow Brexiteers of being "careless of the heartbreak and grief that had scarred" Northern Ireland.[33] These competing narratives on the violence were widely circulated on social media during this period.

My own study of the #brexitriots hashtag suggested that many of those commenting on the violence on Twitter knew little about the Northern Irish context and perpetuated stereotypical views of loyalists as 'chavs' and 'idiots'. Few mentioned the LCC or paramilitary involvement in the rioting. Rather, this was a hashtag dominated by pro-Remain, left-wing tweeters, the vast majority of whom were based in England, whose focus was firmly on Brexit rather than the delicate peace in Northern Ireland. They were broadly connected by affective statements expressing anger at how the peace process had been endangered by the lies told by the UK Government about the 'Irish Sea Border'. Then Prime Minister Boris Johnson was, in particular, singled out for being a bad faith actor who had misled the DUP and unionists in order to secure his desired form of 'hard' Brexit. This arguably demonstrated a continued lack of 'political empathy' towards Northern Ireland and a 'colonial' view of communal relations in the divided society that made no allowances for the views of marginalised communities, such as the loyalists protesting against the NIP. In effect, tweeters in Great Britain reinforced the communicative deficit that contributed to the loyalist rioting (Goulding and McCrory, 2021). However, it should be acknowledged that many of these reductive analyses were likely challenged by other tweeters who were more familiar with these issues, or on platforms that are harder for researchers like myself to collect data from.

I wish to conclude here on a (slightly more) positive note. In my Media and Conflict Transformation in Deeply Divided Societies course at the University of Glasgow this year, I asked my students to critique Johann Galtung's assertion that quicker forms of communication have the potential to bring former enemies closer together and create more positive forms of peace. Responses were inevitably mixed. While there was general agreement that online platforms empowered marginalised communities in these contexts, concerns remained about whether they were being listened to by political elites. Cyber hate, misinformation and disinformation were identified as potential barriers towards using sites like Facebook and Twitter/X to promote positive intergroup contact. Malinformation, as demonstrated by dissident republicans using WhatsApp to share the personal details of an estimated 10,000 police in August 2023[34], was also identified as having negative impacts on peacebuilding. Yet, one of my students struck a more upbeat note, arguing that online platforms were creating opportunities for freedom of expression in areas such as LGBTQ+ rights that transcended sectarian boundaries. When reflecting back on two decades of research on this topic, it is debatable whether these new forms of activism would have become so embedded in a post-conflict society like Northern Ireland without the communicative affordances of ICTs. However, as discussed earlier in this book, platform architectures alone cannot address the negative stereotyping of outgroups. A pre-requisite for resolving digital contention in deeply divided societies like Northern Ireland is the political leadership that deals with the legacy of conflict.

References

Bryson, J. (2021) A Perfect Storm – the growing discontent across grassroots unionism, *Unionist Voice*, 6 April, available at: https://unionistvoice.com/news/a-perfect-storm-the-growing-discontent-across-grassroots-unionism/ (accessed 1 April 2022).

Creighton, S. (2021) Northern Ireland needs leadership. Without it, the violence could get worse, *The Guardian*, 7 April, available at: https://www.theguardian.com/commentisfree/2021/apr/07/northern-ireland-leadership-violence-worse (accessed 14 April 2021).

Fox, C. (2021) What's behind the recent violence in Northern Ireland? *CNN*, 10 April, available at: https://edition.cnn.com/2021/04/09/uk/northern-ireland-violence-explainer-gbr-intl/index.html (accessed 6 April 2022).

Gillespie, P. (2020) Unionisms in the UK's Brexit crisis, *Irish Political Studies*, 35(3), 509–530, DOI: 10.1080/07907184.2020.1816394

Holmes, M. (2021) Opinion: Loyalist confidence in policing and justice is rock-bottom, *Unionist Voice*, 1 April.

Mulhall, J. (2021) *Antisemitism in the Digital Age: Online antisemitic hate, holocaust denial, conspiracy ideologies and terrorism in Europe*, collaborative report by Amadeu Antonio Foundation, Expo Foundation and HOPE not hate.

Scott, S. (2021) Belfast riots: Loyalist Communities Council issue statement after days of violence, *Belfast Live*, 9 April, available at: https://www.belfastlive.co.uk/news/belfast-news/belfast-riots-loyalist-communities-council-20351387 (accessed 14 April 2021).

Turner, C., and Swaine, A. (2021) At the Nexus of Participation and Protection: Protection-Related Barriers to Women's Participation in Northern Ireland," International Peace Institute, available at: https://www.ipinst.org/wp-content/uploads/2021/06/Womens-Participation-Northern-Ireland-2-Final.pdf (accessed 18 March 2023).

Walsh, C. (2021) Beyond the Spark: Young people's perspectives on the 2021 Northern Ireland Riots, report commissioned by Department of Justice (NI), 6 October, available at: https://pure.qub.ac.uk/en/publications/beyond-the-spark-young-peoples-perspectives-on-the-2021-northern- (accessed 5 November 2021).

Notes

1 Sunak was widely mocked for this admission, with critics of Brexit noting that they no longer had access to the EU Single Market enjoyed by Northern Ireland. For more on his speech, see here: https://www.inde pendent.co.uk/news/uk/politics/sunak-brexit-deal-northern-ireland-b2 291089.html (accessed 18 March 2023).

2 Bryson referred to legal opinion from John Larkin KC suggesting the Framework did not restore Northern Ireland's position within the UK. For more, see here: https://unionistvoice.com/news/jamie-bryson-union ism-should-not-endorse-the-windsor-framework/ (accessed 18 March 2023).

3 An explainer can be read here: https://www.instituteforgovernment.org. uk/explainer/stormont-brake-windsor-framework (accessed 18 March 2023).

4 Wilson suggested the Framework was not a very good deal for unionists. His statement can be read here: https://www.itv.com/news/utv/2023-03-01/wilson-hits-out-at-sunak-deal-and-kings-involvement (accessed 18 March 2023).

5 https://www.belfasttelegraph.co.uk/news/politics/serving-under-sinn-fein-first-minister-at-stormont-dups-real-reason-behind-boycott-claims-oneill/42105732.html (accessed 18 March 2023).

6 New Decade, New Approach can be read in full here: https://assets.pub lishing.service.gov.uk/government/uploads/system/uploads/attachment _data/file/856998/2020-01-08_a_new_decade__a_new_approach.pdf (accessed 18 March 2023).

7 https://www.bbc.co.uk/news/uk-northern-ireland-politics-50822912 (accessed 18 March 2023).

8 O'Neill called the DUP boycott of Stormont a 'stunt' and rejected these allegations of hypocrisy. For more on this, see: https://www.breakingne ws.ie/ireland/sinn-fein-rejects-hypocrisy-claims-over-its-criticism-of -dup-devolution-threat-1182441.html (accessed 18 March 2023).

9 https://www.bbc.co.uk/news/uk-northern-ireland-60249249 (accessed 18 March 2023).

10 There have been calls for their pay to be stopped completely until the Executive restarts. For more on this, see: https://www.bbc.co.uk/news/uk -northern-ireland-63880069 (accessed 18 March 2023).

11 https://www.irishmirror.ie/showbiz/celebrity-news/james-nesbitt-hit -hate-crime-28288910# (accessed 18 March 2023).

12 https://www.irishnews.com/paywall/tsb/irishnews/news/northernireland news/2022/11/01/news/police_probe_online_threats_and_abuse _aimed_at_qub_s_professor_colin_harvey-2881215/content.html (accessed 18 March 2023).

13 https://humanrightsfirst.org/library/calls-for-solidarity-as-attacks-on-colin-harvey-intensify/ (accessed 18 March 2023).

14 https://twitter.com/mooreholmes24/status/1562167194317897728?lang=en (accessed 18 March 2023).

15 https://unionistvoice.com/news/colin-harvey-and-other-nationalist-activists-cannot-be-allowed-to-dominate-the-public-arena/ (accessed 18 March 2023).

16 Graham disclosed this in an interview for Unionist Voice, which can be read here: https://unionistvoice.com/news/exclusive-loyalist-stacey-graham-responds-to-vile-social-media-trolling-campaign/ (accessed 18 March 2023).

17 https://www.belfasttelegraph.co.uk/news/northern-ireland/doug-beatties-tweets-what-he-said-then-and-his-explanations-now/41275822.html (accessed 18 March 2023).

18 https://www.bbc.co.uk/news/uk-northern-ireland-60145127 (accessed 18 March 2023).

19 Fealty was critical of the local media for focusing on the Doug Beattie Twitterstorm at the expense of the forensic cleaning of SF social media accounts. For more, see: https://sluggerotoole.com/2022/01/27/sinn-feins-operation-delete-tweets-goes-into-overdrive-under-cover-of-a-media-blackout/ (18 March 2023).

20 The research was conducted by IPSO Mori for Amnesty International in June 2017. For a summary of the key findings, see here: https://www.amnesty.org.uk/online-abuse-women-widespread (accessed 10 December 2021).

21 For more on this, see: https://www.itv.com/news/utv/2022-01-04/dup-mla-calls-on-social-media-companies-to-deal-with-online-trolls (accessed 18 March 2023).

22 https://www.bbc.co.uk/news/uk-northern-ireland-64854493 (accessed 18 March 2023).

23 For more on this, see here: https://www.maynoothuniversity.ie/research/spotlight-research/what-are-twitters-legal-obligations-stopping-disinformation (accessed 4 October 2023).

24 This followed reports that hate speech had increased on the platform in the wake of Elon Musk's takeover of the tech giant. For more, see: https://www.bbc.co.uk/news/technology-64804007 (accessed 10 March 2023).

25 This policy was updated in April 2023 and can be read here: https://blog.twitter.com/en_us/topics/product/2023/freedom-of-speech-not-reach-an-update-on-our-enforcement-philosophy (accessed 25 October 2023).

26 The research was conducted in September 2023. It can be read here: https://counterhate.com/wp-content/uploads/2023/09/230907-X-Content-Moderation-Report_final_CCDH.pdf (accessed 26 October 2023).

27 The full statement can be read here: https://twitter.com/safety/status/1701787700855017542?s=61&t=Z6m9aBJcXD860L-eXySg_g (accessed 21 October 2023).

28 Details of the lawsuit can be read here: https://www.cnbc.com/2023/08/01/x-sues-ccdh-for-showing-hate-speech-rise-on-twitter-after-musk-deal.html (accessed 10 September 2023).

29 The LCC wrote letters to the UK Prime Minister outlining their position on the NIP. For more on their statement, see here: https://www.theguardian.com/uk-news/2021/mar/04/brexit-northern-ireland-loyalist-armies-renounce-good-friday-agreement (accessed 1 June 2022).

30 His full statement can be read here: https://www.psni.police.uk/news/Latest-News/080421-sustained-disorder-in-belfast/ (accessed 1 June 2022).

31 Blevin's analysis can be read here: https://news.sky.com/story/northern-ireland-the-role-of-social-media-in-stirring-up-unrest-12270775 (accessed 1 June 2022).

32 Bryson's post can be viewed here: https://www.facebook.com/photo?fbid=10216481083134519&set=a.1536977919301 (accessed 14 April 2021).

33 This was one of the most frequently shared op-eds in the #brexitriots tweets I collected during this period. For more, see: https://www.theguardian.com/commentisfree/2021/apr/09/boris-johnson-brexit-belfast-violence-eu-good-friday-agreement (accessed 1 June 2022).

34 Byrne faced significant criticism for the data scandal and also a High court ruling that two PSNI officers had been unlawfully disciplined for their conduct during an event to commemorate the victims of the 1992 Sean Graham bookmakers attack in South Belfast. For more, see: https://www.thejournal.ie/psni-chief-constable-questions-data-breach-6139986-Aug2023/ (accessed 1 October 2023).

Bibliography

Alan in Belfast (2014) "'If you ask me one thing I could have done without in the last twelve months it's social media' – Jamie Bryson." *Slugger O'Toole*, 4 January 2016. http://sluggerotoole.com/2014/01/04/if-you-ask-me-one-thing-i-could-have-done-without-in-the-last-twelve-months-its-social-media-jamie-bryson/ (accessed 10 August 2014).

Alhabash, S. and A. McAlister (2015) "Redefining virality in less broad strokes: Predicting viral behavioral intentions from motivations and uses of Facebook and Twitter". *New Media & Society* 17: 1317–1339. doi: 10.1177/1461444814523726.

Allan, S. (2013) *Citizen Witnessing: Revisioning Journalism in Times of Crisis*. Cambridge: Polity Press.

Allcott, H. and M. Gentzkow (2017) "Social media and fake news in the 2016 election". *Journal of Economic Perspectives* 31 (2): 211–236. doi: 10.1257/jep.31.2.211.

Allport, G. (1954) *The Nature of Prejudice*. Cambridge, MA: Perseus Books.

Amichai-Hamburger, Y. (2008) "The contact hypothesis reconsidered: Interacting via Internet: Theoretical and Practical Aspects". In A. Barak (ed.) *Psychological Aspects of Cyberspace. Theory, Research, Applications*. Cambridge: Cambridge University Press, pp. 209–227.

Amichai-Hamburger, Y., B. S. Hasler and T. Shani-Sherman (2015) "Structured and unstructured intergroup contact in the digital age". *Computers in Human Behavior* 52: 515–522. doi: 10.1016/j.chb.2015.02.022.

Amichai-Hamburger, Y. and Z. Hayat (2013) "Internet and personality". In Y. Amichai-Hamburger (ed.), *The Social Net: Understanding our Online Behavior*. New York: Oxford University Press, pp. 1–20.

Amichai-Hamburger, Y. and K. Y. A. McKenna (2006) "The contact hypothesis reconsidered: Interacting via the Internet". *Journal of Computer-Mediated Communication* 11 (3): 7. doi: 10.1111/j.1083-6101.2006.00037.x.

Andrejevic, M. (2012) "Exploitation in the data mine". In C. Fuchs, K. Boersma, A. Albrechtsund and M. Sandoval (eds) *Internet and*

Surveillance: The Challenges of Web 2.0 and Social Media. London: Routledge, pp. 71–88.

Anstead, N. and B. O'Loughlin (2011) "The emerging viewertariat and BBC Question Time: Television debate and real time commenting online". *Press/Politics* 16 (4): 440–462. doi: 10.1177/1940161211415519.

Aughey, A. (2007) *The Politics of Northern Ireland: Beyond the Good Friday Agreement*. London: Taylor and Francis.

Baker, P. (2001) "Moral panic and alternative identity construction in Usenet". *Journal of Computer-Mediated Communication* 7(1).

Bakir, V. (2010) *Sousveillance, Media and Strategic Political Communication*. London: Continuum.

Bakshy, E., S. Messing and L. A. Adamic (2015) "Exposure to ideologically diverse news and opinion on Facebook". *Science* 348 (6239): 1130–1132. doi: 10.1126/science.aaa1160.

Barlow, F. K., S. Paolini, A. Pedersen, M. J. Hornsey, H. R. M. Radke, J. Harwood, M. Rubin, and C. G. Sibley (2012) "The contact caveat: Negative contact predicts increased prejudice more than positive contact predicts reduced prejudice". *Personality and Social Psychology Bulletin* 38: 1629–1643. doi: 10.1177/0146167212457953.

Bartlett, J. (2018) *The People vs Tech: How the Internet is Killing Democracy (and How We Save It)*. London: Penguin.

Bayeri, P. S. and L. Stoynov (2016) "Revenge by photoshop: Memefying police acts in the public dialogue about injustice". *New Media & Society* 18 (6): 1006–1026. doi: 10.1177/1461444814554747.

Beier, J. M. (2007) "Grave misgivings: Allegory, catharsis, composition". *Security Dialogue* 38 (2): 251–269.

Benkler, Y., R. M. Faris and H. Roberts (2018) *Network Propaganda: Manipulation, Disinformation and Radicalization in American Politics*. Oxford: Oxford University Press.

Bennett, W. L. and A. Segerberg (2013) *The Logic of Connective Action Digital Media and the Personalization of Contentious Politics*. Cambridge: Cambridge University Press.

Bew, P. and G. Gillespie (1993) *Northern Ireland: A Chronology of the Troubles, 1968–93*. London: Gill & Macmillan Ltd.

Black, R. (2012) "In pictures: Thousands gather for City Hall flag protest". *News Letter*, 9 December 2012.

Bode, L., S. Edgerly, C. Wells, I. Gabay, C. Franklin, L. Friedland and D. V. Shah (2018) "Participation in contentious politics: Rethinking the roles of news, social media, and conversation amid divisiveness". *Journal of Information Technology & Politics* 15 (3): 215–229. doi: 10.1080/19331681.2018.1485607.

Bonilla, Y. and J. Rosa (2015) "#Ferguson: Digital protest, hashtag ethnography and the racial politics of social media in the United States". *American Ethnologist* 00: 4–16. doi: 10.1111/amet.12112.

Bowman, S. and C. Willis (2003) "We media: How audiences are shaping the future of news and information". *The Media Center at the American Press Institute*, www.hypergene.net/wemedia/ (accessed 10 September 2012).

Boulianne, S. (2015) "Social media use and participation: A meta-analysis of current research". *Information, Communication & Society* 18 (5): 524–538. doi: 10.1080/1369118X.2015.1008542.

Boulianne, S. (2019) "Revolution in the making? Social media effects across the globe". *Information, Communication & Society* 22 (1): 39–54. doi: 10.1080/1369118X.2017.1353641.

Boulianne, S. and Y. Theocharis (2018) "Young people, digital media and engagement: A meta-analysis of research". *Social Science Computer Review* 1: 1–17. doi: 10.1177/0894439318814190.

Braun, V. and V. Clarke (2013) *Successful Qualitative Research: A Practical Guide for Beginners*. London: Sage.

Brewer, J. (2010) *Peace Processes: A Sociological Approach*. Cambridge: Polity.

Bruns, A. (2019) *Are Filter Bubbles Real?* Cambridge: Polity.

Bruns, A. and J. Burgess (2015) "Twitter hashtags from ad hoc to calculated publics". In N. Rambukkana (ed.) *Hashtag Publics: The Power and Politics of Discursive Networks*. New York: Peter Lang, pp. 13–28.

Bruns, A., J. Burgess, K. Crawford and F. Shaw (2012) *#qldfloods and @QPS-Media: Crisis Communication on Twitter in the 2011 South East Queensland Floods*. Brisbane, Australia: ARC Centre of Excellence for Creative Industries & Innovation.

Bruns, A., B. Moon, A. Paul and F. Münch (2016) "Towards a typology of hashtag publics: A large-scale comparative study of user engagement across trending topics". *Communication Research and Practice* 2 (1): 20–46.

Buetow, S. (2010) "Thematic analysis and its reconceptualization as 'saliency analysis'". *Journal of Health Services Research Policy* 15: 123–125.

Burgess, J. and A. Bruns (2015) "Easy data, hard data: The politics and pragmatics of Twitter research after the computational turn". In G. Langlois, J. Redden and G. Elmer (eds) *Compromised Data: From Social Media to Big Data*. London: Bloomsbury Publishing, pp. 93–111.

Burgess, J. and J. Green (2018) *YouTube: Online Video and Participatory Culture*. London: John Wiley & Sons.

Bush, K. and C. Duggan (2014) "How can research contribute to peacebuilding?". *Peacebuilding* 2 (3): 303–321. doi: 10.1080/21647259.2014.887617.

Byrne, J. and C. Gormley-Heenan (2014) "Beyond the walls: Dismantling Belfast's conflict architecture". *City* 18 (4–5): 447–454. doi: 10.1080/13604813.2014.939465.

Cao, B. and L. Wan-Ying (2017) "Revisiting the contact hypothesis: Effects of different modes of computer-mediated communication on intergroup relationships". *International Journal of Intercultural Relations* 58: 23–30. doi: 10.1016/j.ijintrel.2017.03.003.

Carey, J. (1992) *A Cultural Approach to Communication from Communication as Culture*. New York: Routledge.

Carswell, S. (2019) "Russians suspected of spreading fake news about Northern Ireland". *Irish Times*, 24 June 2019, www.irishtimes.com/news/ireland/ irish-news/russians-suspected-of-spreading-fake-news-about-northern-ireland-1.3935137 (accessed 26 June 2019).

Castells, M. (2009) *Communication Power*. Oxford: Oxford University Press.

Centre for Young Men's Studies (2009) *Stuck in the Middle: Some Young Men's Attitudes and Experience of Violence, Conflict and Safety*. Coleraine, NI: University of Ulster Publications.

Chadwick, A. (2011) "The political information cycle in a hybrid news system: The British prime minister and the 'bullygate' affair". *The International Journal of Press/Politics* 16(1):3–29. doi:10.1177/1940161210384730.

Chadwick, A. (2012) "Web 2.0: New challenges for study of e-democracy in an era of informational exuberance". In S. Coleman and P. Shane (eds) *Connecting Democracy: Online Consultation and the Flow of Political Information*. London: MIT Press, pp. 45–75.

Chadwick, A. (2013). *The Hybrid Media System: Politics and Power*. New York: Oxford University Press.

Chadwick, A., C. Vaccari and B. O'Loughlin (2018) "Do tabloids poison the well of social media? Explaining democratically dysfunctional news sharing". *New Media & Society* 20 (11): 4255–4274. doi: 10.1177/ 1461444818769689.

Cho, H. and J. Lee (2008) "Collaborative information seeking in intercultural computer- mediated communication groups: Testing the influence of social context using social network analysis". *Communication Research* 35 (4): 548–573. doi: 10.1177/0093650208315982.

Couldry, N. (2012) *Media, Society, World: Social Theory and Digital Media Practice*. Cambridge: Polity Press.

Cox, A. (2006) "Making mischief on the web". *Time*, December 2006. http:// content.time.com/time/magazine/article/0,9171,1570701,00.html

Dahlgren, P. (2005) "The Internet, public spheres and political communication". *Political Communication* 2: 147–162. doi: 10.1080/10584600590933160.

Dayan, D. and E. Katz (1992) *Media Events: The Live Broadcasting of History*. Cambridge, MA: Harvard University Press.

Dean, J. (2009) *Democracy and Other Neoliberal Fantasies: Communicative Capitalism and Left Politics*. Durham, NC: Duke University Press.

Della Porta, D. (2015) *Social Movements in Times of Austerity*. Oxford: Polity Press.

Denisova, A. (2016) "European memes, the hilarious antidote to the shock and uncertainty of Brexit". *Global Voices*, 5 July 2016. https://globalvoices. org/2016/07/05/european-memes-the-hilarious-antidote-to-the-shock-and-uncertainty-of-brexit/ (accessed 4 May 2020).

Diani, M. (2000) "Social movement networks virtual and real". *Information, Communication & Society* 3 (3): 386–401. doi: 10.1080/136911800510 33333.

Dixon, P. (2012) "The politics of conflict: A constructivist critique of consociational and civil society theories". *Nations and Nationalism* 18 (1): 98–121.

Donnelly, C. (2013) "Twaddell: A camp called Malice". *Slugger O'Toole*, 29 August 2013. https://sluggerotoole.com/2013/08/29/twaddell-a-camp-called-malice/comment-page-1/ (accessed 4 May 2020).

Dovidio, J. F., S. L. Gaertner and T. Saguy (2009) "Commonality and the complexity of 'we': Social attitudes and social changes". *Personality and Social Psychology Review* 13 (3): 3–20. doi: 10.1177/1088868308326751.

Dovidio, J. F., A. Love, F. M. H. Schellhaas and M. Hewstone (2017) "Reducing intergroup bias through intergroup contact: Twenty years of progress and future directions". *Group Processes & Intergroup Relations* 20 (5): 606–620. doi: 10.1177/1368430217712052.

Draper, N. A. and J. Turow (2019) "The corporate cultivation of digital resignation". *New Media & Society* 21 (4): 1824–1839. doi: 10.1177/ 1461444819833331.

Dubois, E. and G. Blank (2018) "The echo chamber is overstated: The moderating effect of political interest and diverse media". *Information, Communication & Society* 5: 729–745. doi: 10.1080/1369118X.2018.1428656.

Earl, J. and R. K. Garrett (2019) "The new information frontier: Toward a more nuanced view of social movement communication". In C. Flesher Fominaya and K. Gillan (eds) *Technology, Media and Social Movements*. Abingdon, Oxon: Routledge, pp. 97–111.

Edwards, A. and C. McGrattan (2010) *The Northern Ireland Conflict (Beginners Guide)*. London: Oneworld.

Emerson, N. (2013) "Respect are culture". *The Sunday Times*, 1 September 2013. http://loyalistsagainstdemocracy.blogspot.co.uk/2013/09/real-online-wonder-of-year.html (accessed 10 August 2017).

European Commission (2018) *Summary Report of the Public Consultation on Fake News and Online Disinformation*. https://ec.europa.eu/digital-single-market/en/news/summary-report-public- consultation-fake-news-and-online-disinformation (accessed 10 September 2018).

Fealty, M. (2005) "Glossary: What is whataboutery?". *Slugger O'Toole*, 9 February 2005. http://sluggerotoole.com/2005/02/09/glossary_what_is_ whataboutery/ (accessed 10 August 2014).

Fealty, M. (2013) "IPSOS/MORI poll on Good Friday Agreement: Scepticism on Stormont's 'progress' on sectarianism". *Slugger O'Toole*, 23 May 2013. http://sluggerotoole.com/2013/05/23/ipsosmori-poll-on-good-friday-agreement-scepticism-on-stormonts-progress-on-sectarianism/ (accessed 10 August 2014).

Ferguson, A. (2016) "Man behind Loyalists Against Democracy social media phenomenon reveals identity". *Irish News*, 27 September 2016, available at: www.irishnews.com/news/2016/09/27/news/revealed-the-man-behind-loyalists-against-democracy-710477/

Fischer, M. and K. Mohrman (2016) "Black deaths matter? Sousveillance and the invisibility of black life". *Ada: A Journal of Gender, New Media, and Technology 10*. doi: 10.7264/N3F47MDV.

Fishkin, J. (2009) *When the People Speak: Deliberative Democracy and Public Consultation*. Oxford: Oxford University Press.

Fominaya, C. F. and G. Gillan (2017) "Navigating the technology-media-movements complex". *Social Movement Studies* 16 (4): 383–402. doi: 10.1080/14742837.2017.1338943.

Freelon, D., C. D. McIlwain and M. D. Clark (2016a) *Beyond the Hashtags: #Ferguson, #Blacklivesmatter, and the Online Struggle for Offline Justice*. Washington DC: Center for Media & Social Impact, American University. http://cmsimpact.org/wp-content/uploads/2016/03/beyond_the_hashtags_2016.pdf (accessed 4 May 2020).

Freelon, D., C. D. McIlwain and M. D. Clark (2016b) "Quantifying the power and consequence of social media protest". *New Media & Society* 20 (3): 990–1011. doi: 10.1177/1461444816676646.

Froomkin, M. A. (2003) "Habermas@Discourse.net: Toward a critical theory of cyberspace". *Harvard Law Review* 116 (3). doi: 10.2139/ssrn.363840.

Fuchs, C. (2014) *Social Media: A Critical Introduction*. London: SAGE.

Gabriel, F. (2014) "Sexting, selfies and self-harm: Young people, social media and the performance of self-development". *Media International Australia* 151 (1): 104–112. doi: 10.1177/1329878X1415100114.

Galtung, J. (1967) *Theories of Peace: A Synthetic Approach to Peacebuilding*. Oslo: International Peace Research Institute.

Gamson, W. A. (1990) *The Strategy of Social Protest*. Belmont, CA: Wadsworth Pub Co.

Gauntlett, D. (2011) *Making is Connecting. The Social Meaning of Creativity, from DIY and Knitting to YouTube and Web 2.0*. Cambridge: Polity Press.

Gerbaudo P. (2012) *Tweets and the Streets: Social Media and Contemporary Activism*. London: Pluto Press.

Gerbaudo, P. (2015) "Protest avatars as memetic signifiers: Political profile pictures and the construction of collective identity on social media in the 2011 protest wave". *Information, Communication & Society* 18 (8): 916–929. doi: 10.1080/1369118X.2015.1043316.

Gerbaudo, P. (2017) "Social media teams as digital vanguards: The question of leadership in the management of key Facebook and Twitter accounts of Occupy Wall Street, Indignados and UK Uncut". *Information, Communication & Society* 20 (2): 185–202. doi: 10.1080/1369118X.2016.1161817.

Gerbaudo, P. and E. Treré (2015) "In search of the 'we' of social media activism: Introduction to the special issue on social media and protest identities". *Information, Communication & Society* 18 (8): 865–871. doi: 10.1080/1369118X.2015.1043319.

Gillespie, T. (2018) *Custodians of the Internet: Platforms, Content Moderation, and the Hidden Decisions That Shape Social Media.* New Haven, CT: Yale University Press.

Gleason, B. (2013). "#Occupy Wall Street: Exploring informal learning about a social movement on Twitter". *American Behavioral Scientist* 57 (7): 966–982. doi: 10.1177/0002764213479372.

Gordon, F. (2018) *Children, Young People and the Press in a Transitioning Society: Representations, Reactions and Criminalisation.* London: Palgrave Macmillan.

Graham, T. and S. Wright (2014) "Discursive equality and everyday talk online: The impact of 'superparticipants'". *Journal of Computer-Mediated Communication* 19 (3): 625–642. doi: 10.1111/jcc4.12016.

Guelke, A. (2014) "Northern Ireland's flags crisis and the enduring legacy of the settler–native divide". *Nationalism and Ethnic Politics* 20 (1): 133–151. doi: 10.1080/13537113.2014.879770.

Guerrini, F. (2013) "Newsrooms beware: UGC is a double-edged sword." *Journalism.co.uk*, 10 October 2013. www.journalism.co.uk/news-commentary/-user-generated-content-is-double-edged-sword-/s6/a554367/ (accessed 4 May 2020).

Haggerty, K. D. and R. V. Ericson (2000) "The surveillant assemblage". *British Journal of Sociology* 51 (4): 605–622. doi: 10.1177/1474885115608783.

Hall, R. (2011) "Police hurt in violent anti-Tesco protests". *BBC News*, 22 April 2011. http://bbc.co.uk/news/uk-england-bristol-13167041 (accessed 10 May 2011).

Hamber, B. and G. Kelly (2004) "A working definition of reconciliation". *SEUPB & Democratic Dialogue.* http://brandonhamber.com/pubs_papers. htm (accessed 4 May 2020).

Hampton, K. N., R. Rainie, W. Lu, M. Dwyer, I. Shin and K. Purcell (2014) *Social Media and the 'Spiral of Silence'.* Washington, DC: Pew Research Center.

Hands, J. (2011) @ *is for Activism: Dissent, Resistance and Rebellion in a Digital Culture*. Cambridge: Polity Press.

Hanitzsch, T. (2004) "Journalists as peacekeeping force? Peace journalism and mass communication theory". *Journalism Studies* 5 (4): 483–495. doi: 10.1080/14616700412331296419.

Harcup, T. (2016) "Alternative journalism as monitorial citizenship?". *Digital Journalism* 4 (5): 639–657. doi: 10.1080/21670811.2015.1063077.

Hardaker, C. (2010) "Trolling in asynchronous computer-mediated communication: From user discussions to academic definitions". *Journal of Politeness Research* 6: 215–242. doi: 10.1515/JPLR.2010.011.

Hartley, J. (2010) "Silly citizenship". *Critical Discourse Studies* 7 (4): 233–248. doi: 10.1080/17405904.2010.511826.

Hartley, J. (2012) *Digital Futures for Cultural and Media Studies*. Oxford: Wiley-Blackwell.

Harwood, J. (2010) "The contact space: A novel framework for intergroup contact research". *Journal of Language and Social Psychology* 29: 147–177. doi: 10.1177/0261927X09359520.

Hayward, K. and M. Komarova (2014) "The limits of local accommodation: Why contentious events remain prone to conflict in Northern Ireland". *Studies in Conflict & Terrorism* 37 (9): 777–791. doi: 10.1080/1057610X. 2014.931214.

Hayward, K. and C. McManus (2019) "Neither/nor: The rejection of unionist and nationalist identities in post-Agreement Northern Ireland". *Capital & Class* 43 (1): 139–155. doi: 10.1177/0309816818818312.

Hearty, K. (2017) "Discourses of political policing in post-Patten Northern Ireland". *Critical Criminology* 26: 129–142. doi: 10.1007/s10612-017-9376-5.

Hewstone, M., E. Cairns, A. Voci and S. Paolini (2006) "Inter-group contact in a divided society: Challenging segregation in Northern Ireland". In D. Abrams, M. A. Hogg and J. M. Marques (eds) *The Social Psychology of Inclusion and Exclusion*. Philadelphia, PA: Psychology Press, pp. 265–292.

Highfield, T. (2016a) *Social Media and Everyday Politics*. Cambridge: Polity Press.

Highfield, T. (2016b) "News via Voldemort: Parody accounts in topical discussions on Twitter". *New Media & Society* 18 (9): 2028–2045.

Highfield, T. and T. Leaver (2016) "Instagrammatics and digital methods: Studying visual social media, from selfies and GIFs to memes and emoji". *Communication Research and Practice* 2 (1): 47–62. doi: 10.1080/22041451. 2016.1155332.

Hintz, A., L. Dencik and K. Wahl-Jorgensen (2018) *Digital Citizenship in a Datafied Society*. Cambridge: Polity Press.

Hoey, P. (2017) "Evaluating the role of the internet and mainstream news journalism in the development of the Northern Ireland peace process". In J. Tong and S. Lo (eds) *Digital Technology and Journalism: An International Comparative Perspective.* London: Palgrave Macmillan, pp. 141–163.

Hoey, P. (2018) *Shinners, Dissos and Dissenters: Irish Republican Media Activism since the Good Friday Agreement.* Manchester: Manchester University Press.

Holbert, R. L. (2013) "Developing a normative approach to political satire: An empirical perspective". *International Journal of Communication* 7: 305–323.

Hoskins, A. and J. Tulloch (2016) *Risk and Hyperconnectivity: Media and Memories of Neoliberalism.* Oxford: Oxford University Press.

Howard, P. N. and M. Hussein (2013) *Democracy's Fourth Wave: Digital Media and the Arab Spring.* Oxford: Oxford University Press.

Hughes, J., A. Campbell and R. Jenkins (2011) "Contact, trust and social capital in Northern Ireland: A qualitative study of three mixed communities". *Ethnic and Racial Studies* 34 (6): 967–985. doi: 10.1080/01419870. 2010.526234.

INTERCOMM and J. Byrne (2013) *Flags and Protests: Exploring the Views, Perceptions and Experiences of People Directly and Indirectly Affected by the Flag Protests.* Coleraine, NI: University of Ulster Publications.

Isin, E. and R. Ruppert (2015) *Being Digital Citizens.* London: Rowman and Littlefield International.

Jackson, S. and B. Foucault Welles (2016) "#Ferguson is everywhere: Initiators in emerging counterpublic networks". *Information, Communication & Society* 19 (3): 397–418. doi: 10.1080/1369118X.2015.1106571.

Jarman, N. and C. O'Halloran (2001) "Recreational rioting: Young people, interface areas and violence". *Child Care and Practice* 7: 2–16. doi: 10.1080/13575270108413230.

Jenkins, H., S. Ford and J. Green (2013) *Spreadable Media: Creating Value and Meaning in a Networked Culture.* New York: New York University Press.

John, N. A. (2019) "Social media bullshit: What we don't know about Facebook.com/peace and why we should care". *Social Media + Society* (January–March 2019): 1–16. doi: 10.1177/2056305119829863.

Jones, C. (2014) "Loyalists Against Democracy are leading the fight against dumb Northern Irish politics". *Vice,* 31 July 2014, available at: www.vice. com/en_uk/article/av9zn8/lad-northern-ireland-satire-flag-protests-852

Jones, O. (2011) *Chavs: The Demonisation of the Working Class.* London: Verso.

Kanas, A., P. Scheepers and C. Sterkens (2017) "Positive and negative contact and attitudes towards the religious out-group: Testing the contact hypothesis in conflict and non-conflict regions of Indonesia and the Philippines". *Social Science Research* 63: 95–110. doi: 10.1016/j.ssresearch. 2016.09.019.

Kane, A. (2012) "Confidence requires more than a flag". Eamonnmallie.com, 14 December 2012. http://eamonnmallie.com/2012/12/confidence-requires-more-than-a-flag/ (accessed 10 August 2014).

Karpf, D. (2012) *The MoveOn Effect: The Unexpected Transformation of American Political Advocacy*. Oxford: Oxford University Press.

Karpf, D. (2016) *Analytic Activism: Digital Listening and the New Political Strategy*. Oxford: Oxford University Press.

Karpf, D. (2020) "Two provocations for the study of digital politics in time". *Journal of Information Technology & Politics* 17 (2): 87–96. doi: 10.1080/19331681. 2019.1705222.

Kavada, A. (2015) "Creating the collective: Social media, the Occupy Movement and its constitution as a collective actor". *Information, Communication & Society* 18 (8): 872–886. doi: 10.1080/1369118X.2015.1043318.

Komarova, M. (2010) "Imagining a 'shared future': Post-conflict discourses on peace-building". In K. Hayward and C. O'Donnell (eds) *Political Discourse and Conflict Resolution. Debating Peace in Northern Ireland*. London: Taylor and Francis, pp. 143–159.

Koopman, R. (2004) "Movements and media: Selection processes and evolutionary dynamics in the public sphere". *Theory and Society* 33: 367–391.

Kozinets, R. V. (2010) *Netnography: Doing Ethnographic Research Online*. London: SAGE.

Kumar, A. and H. A. Semetko (2017) "Citizens advancing change and emerging digital third space". Conference paper, International Studies Association annual conference, 23 February 2017, Baltimore, MD.

Kwak, D. H., C. E. San Miguel and D. L. Carreon (2012) "Political legitimacy and public confidence in police: An analysis of attitudes toward Mexican police". *Policing: An International Journal of Police Strategies & Management* 35 (1): 124–146. doi: 10.1177/1461355719852645.

Lederach, J. P. (1997) *Building Peace: Sustainable Reconciliation in Divided Societies*. Washington, DC: United States Institute for Peace.

Lehner, S. and C. McGrattan (2018) "Written evidence submitted to Northern Ireland Affairs Committee's inquiry into devolution and democracy in NI-dealing with the deficit". http://data.parliament.uk/writtenevidence/ committeeevidence.svc/evidencedocument/northern-ireland-affairs-committee/devolution-and-democracy-in-northern-ireland-dealing-with-the-deficit/written/75847.html (accessed 15 May 2019).

Lemert, J. B. (1981) *Does Mass Communication Change Public Opinion After All? A New Approach to Effects Analysis*. Chicago, IL: Nelson-Hall.

Leonard, M. (2010) "What's recreational about 'recreational rioting'? Children on the streets in Belfast". *Children and Society* 24: 38–49. doi: 10.1111/j.1099-0860.2008.00190.x.

Lippmann, W. (1922) *Public Opinion*. Chicago, IL: Transaction.

Loader, B., A. Vromen and M. Xenos (2016) "Performing for the young networked citizen?: Celebrity politics, social networking and the political engagement of young people". *Media, Culture & Society* 38 (3): 400–419. doi: 10.1177/0163443715608261.

Long, S. A. (2018) "Online loyalist resistance: Struggles for recognition in contested Northern Ireland". *Irish Political Studies* 33 (1): 43–67. doi: 10.1080/07907184.2017.1301433

Lotan, G., E. Graeff, M. Ananny, D. Gaffney, I. Pearce and D. Boyd (2011) "The revolutions were tweeted: Information flows during the 2011 Tunisian and Egyptian Revolutions". *International Journal of Communication* 5: 1375–1405.

Loyalists Against Democracy (2013) "LAD is dead. Long live LAD". http://loyalistsagainstdemocracy.blogspot.co.uk/2013/10/lad-is-dead-long-live-lad.html (accessed 10 August 2014).

LSE Commission on Truth, Trust and Technology (2018) *Tackling the Information Crisis: A Policy Framework for Media System Resilience.* London: LSE Press.

Lunt, P. and S. Livingstone (2013) "Media studies' fascination with the concept of the public sphere: Critical reflections and emerging debates". *Media, Culture & Society* 35 (1): 87–96. doi: 10.1177/0163443712464562.

Luskin, R. C., I. O. O'Flynn, J. Fishkin and D. Russell (2014) "Deliberating across deep divides". *Political Studies* 62 (1): 116–135. doi: 10.1111/j.1467-9248.2012.01005.x.

MacGinty, R. (2009) "The liberal peace at home and abroad: Northern Ireland and liberal internationalism". *British Journal of Politics and International Relations* 11: 690–708. doi: 10.1111/j.1467-856X.2009.00385.x.

McCann, D. (2014a) "@LADFLEG: 'We are pro-Union and pro-Loyalist'". *Slugger O'Toole*, 30 June 2014. http://sluggerotoole.com/2014/06/30/lad-fleg-we-are-pro-union-and-pro-loyalist/ (accessed 10 August 2014).

McCann, D. (2014b) "McCann meets … @LADFLEG Part 2". *Slugger O'Toole*, 20 February 2014. http://sluggerotoole.com/2014/02/20/mccann-meets-ladfleg-part-2/ (accessed 4 May 2020).

McDonald, H. (2013) "Belfast union flag dispute is lightning rod for loyalist dissatisfaction". *The Guardian*, 6 January 2013. www.theguardian.com/uk/2013/jan/06/belfast-union-flag-dispute-loyalist (accessed 4 May 2020).

McGarry, J. and B. O'Leary (1995) *Explaining Northern Ireland.* Oxford: Blackwell.

McGookin, S. (2018) "Lucidtalk poll: Local media – old and new – face issues of trust and performance". *Northern Slant*, 12 March 2018. www.northernslant.com/lucidtalk-poll-local-media-old-new-face-issues-trust-performance/ (accessed 4 May 2020).

McGrattan, C. (2013) *Memory, Politics and Identity: Haunted by History.* Basingstoke: Palgrave Macmillan.

McGrattan, C. (2014) "Peace building and the politics of responsibility: Governing Northern Ireland". *Peace & Change* 39 (4). doi: 10.1111/pech.12092.

McLaughlin, G. and S. Baker (2010) *The Propaganda of Peace: The Role of the Media and Culture in the Northern Ireland Peace Process*. Bristol: Intellect.

Magee, D. (2013a) "Exposing bigotry or exposing their own bigotry? Loyalists Against Democracy: Part 1", 13 October 2013. http://dgmagee.wordpress.com/2013/10/13/exposing-bigotry-or-exposing-their-own-bigotry-loyalists-against-democracy-part-1/ (accessed 4 May 2020).

Magee, D. (2013b) "Exposing bigotry or exposing their own bigotry? Loyalists Against Democracy: Part 2", 14 October 2013. http://dgmagee.wordpress.com/2013/10/14/exposing-bigotry-or-exposing-their-own-bigotry-loyalists-against-democracy-part-2/ (accessed 4 May 2020).

Magill, C. and B. Hamber (2011) "If they don't start listening to us, the future is going to look the same as the past: Young people and reconciliation in Northern Ireland and Bosnia and Herzegovina". *Youth and Society* 43 (2): 509–527. doi: 10.1177/0044118X10383644.

Mahrt, M. and M. Scharkow (2013) "The value of big data in digital media research". *Journal of Broadcasting & Electronic Media* 57 (1): 20–33. doi: 10.1080/08838151.2012.761700.

Malik, M., H. Lamba, C. Nakos and J. Pfeffer (2015) "Population bias in geotagged tweets". In *Standards and Practices in Large-Scale Social Media Research: Papers from the 2015 ICWSM Workshop*. AAAI Publications.

Mamadouh, V. (2003) "11 September and popular geopolitics: A study of websites run for and by Dutch Moroccans". *Geopolitics* 8 (3): 191–216. https://hdl.handle.net/11245/1.419675 (accessed 4 May 2020).

Manley, J. (2014) "'Satanic Islam' pastor gets Robinson support", *Irish News*, 28 May 2014.

Mann, S. (2004) "'Sousveillance': Inverse surveillance in multimedia imaging". *Multimedia:* 620–627. doi: 10.1145/1027527.1027673.

Mann, S. (2013) "Veillance and reciprocal transparency: Surveillance versus sousveillance, AR glass, lifelogging, and wearable computing". http://wearcam.org/veillance/veillance.pdf (accessed 10 April 2019).

Mann, S. (2017) "Big data is a big lie without little data: Humanistic intelligence as a human right". *Big Data & Society* 11 (1/2): 1–10. doi: 10.1177/2053951717691550.

Mann, S. and J. Ferenbok (2013) "New media and the power politics of sousveillance in a surveillance dominated world". *Surveillance & Society* 11 (2): 18–34. doi: 10.24908/ss.v11i1/2.4456.

Mann, S., J. Nolan and B. Wellman (2003) "Sousveillance: Inventing and using wearable computing devices for data collection in surveillance environments". *Surveillance & Society* 1 (3): 331–355. doi: 10.24908/ss.v1i3.3344.

Margetts, H., P. John, S. Hale and T. Yasseri (2016) *Political Turbulence: How Social Media Shapes Collective Action*. Princeton, NJ: Princeton University Press.

Markham, A., E. Buchanan and AoIR Ethics Working Committee (2012) "Ethical decision making and internet research". www.aoir.org/reports/ethics.pdf (accessed 11 October 2014).

Marwick, A. and R. Lewis (2017) *Media Manipulation and Disinformation Online*. New York: Data and Society Research Institute.

Mattoni, A. (2019) "A situated understanding of digital technologies in social movements. Media ecology and media practices approach". In C. Flesher Fominaya and K. Gillan (eds) *Technology, Media and Social Movements*. Abingdon, Oxon: Routledge, pp. 112–124.

Meban, A. (2013) "Interview with Loyalists Against Democracy – will @LADFLEG's second year in existence be their difficult second album?" *Slugger O'Toole*, 9 December 2013. http://sluggerotoole.com/2013/12/09/loyalists-against-democracy-will-ladflegs-second-year-in-existence-be-their-difficult-second-album/

Meikle, G. (2016) *Social Media: Communication, Sharing and Visibility*. London: Routledge.

Melaugh, M. (2013) "A background note on the protests and violence related to the Union Flag at Belfast City Hall, December 2012 – January 2013". *Conflict Archive on the Internet (CAIN)*, 8 February 2013. http://cain.ulst.ac.uk/issues/identity/flag-2012.htm (accessed 10 August 2014).

Meraz, S. and Z. Papacharissi (2013) "Networked gatekeeping and networked framing on #Egypt". *The International Journal of Press/Politics* 18 (2): 138–166. doi: 10.1177/1940161212474472.

Mercea, D. (2012) "Digital prefigurative participation: The entwinement of online communication and offline participation in protest events". *New Media & Society* 14 (1): 153–169. doi: 10.1177/1461444811429103.

Mercea, D. and M. T. Bastos (2016) "Being a serial transnational activist". *Journal of Computer-Mediated Communication* 21 (2): 140–155. doi: 10.1111/jcc4.12150.

Mercea, D. and K. E. Yilmaz (2018) "Movement social learning on Twitter: The case of the People's Assembly". *The Sociological Review* 66 (1): 20–40. doi: 10.1177/0038026117710536.

Miller, C., S. Ginnis, R. Stobart, A. Krasodomski-Jones and M. Clemence (2015) *The Road to Representivity: A Demos and Ipsos MORI Report on Sociological Research using Twitter*. London: Demos.

Morozov, E. (2011) *The Net Delusion: How Not to Liberate the World*. London: Allen Lane.

Morozov, E. (2013) *To Save Everything, Click Here: Technology, Solutionism, and the Urge to Fix Problems that Don't Exist*. London: Penguin.

Morris, A. D. and S. Staggenborg (2004) "Leadership in social movements". In D. A. Snow, S. A. Soule and H. Kriesi (eds) *The Blackwell Companion to Social Movements*. Oxford: Blackwell Publishing, pp. 171–196.

Morrow, D. (2014) *Mixed Messages: Community Relations in 2014: Research Update 105*. Belfast: ARK.

Mossberger, K., C. J. Tolbert and R. S. McNeal (2008) *Digital Citizenship: The Internet, Society and Participation*. Cambridge, MA: MIT Press.

Mouffe, C. (2013) *Agonistics: Thinking the World Politically*. London: Verso Books.

Muldoon, O., N. McNamara, P. Devine and K. Trew (2008) "Beyond gross divisions: National and religious identity combinations". www.ark.ac.uk/publications/updates/update58.pdf (accessed 15 June 2019).

Mulvenna, G. (2013) "LAD won't fix anything Special Feature: Loyalists Against Democracy". *The Gown*, 29 October 2013. http://issuu.com/thegown/docs/the_gown_october_2013 (accessed 10 November 2014).

Murakami Wood, D. (2015) "Vanishing surveillance: Ghost hunting in the ubiquitous surveillance society". In H. Steiner and K. Veel (eds) *Invisibility Studies: Surveillance, Transparency and the Hidden in Contemporary Culture*. New York: Peter Lang, pp. 281–301.

Murtagh, B., B. Graham and P. Shirlow (2008) "Authenticity and stakeholder planning in the segregated city". *Progress in Planning* 69: 41–49.

Murthy, D. (2013) *Twitter: Social Communication in the Twitter Age*. Cambridge: Polity Press.

Nagle, A. (2017) *Kill All Normies: Online Culture Wars from 4chan and Tumblr to Trump and the Alt-Right*. Winchester, UK: Zero Books.

Nahon, K. and J. Hemsley (2013) *Going Viral*. Cambridge: Polity Press.

Neill, W. J. V. (2004) *Urban Planning and Cultural Identity*. London: Routledge.

Neumayer, C., M. Mortensen and T. Poell (2019) "Introduction: Social media materialities and protest". In M. Mortensen, C. Neumayer and T. Poell (eds) *Social Media Materialities and Protest*. London: Routledge, pp. 1–14.

Newman, N. and R. Fletcher (2017) *Bias, Bullshit and Lies: Audience Perspectives on Low Trust in the Media*. Oxford: Reuters Institute for the Study of Journalism.

Nolan, P. (2014) *Northern Ireland Peace Monitoring Report 3*. Belfast: Northern Ireland Community Relations Council.

Nolan, P. and R. Wilson (2017) *Beyond Voting*. Belfast: Building Change Trust. http://civicactivism.buildingchangetrust.org/beyond-voting/Introduction (accessed 4 May 2020).

Nolan, P., D. Bryan, C. Dwyer, K. Hayward, K. Radford and P. Shirlow (2014) *The Flag Dispute: Anatomy of a Protest*. Belfast: Queens University Publications.

Novosel, T. (2013) *Northern Ireland's Lost Opportunity: The Frustrated Promise of Political Loyalism*. London: Pluto.

O'Dochartaigh, N. (2007) "Conflict, territory and new technologies: Online interaction at a Belfast interface". *Political Geography* 26: 474–491. doi: 10.1016/j.polgeo.2007.01.001.

Ofcom (2015) *The Communications Market Report: Northern Ireland*, 6 August 2015. www.ofcom.org.uk/research-and-data/multi-sector-research/cmr/cm15/northern-ireland (accessed 4 May 2020).

Ofcom (2017a) *Internet Use and Attitudes: 2017 Metrics Bulletin*, 3 August 2017. www.ofcom.org.uk/__data/assets/pdf_file/0018/105507/internet-use-attitudes-bulletin-2017.pdf (accessed 4 May 2020).

Ofcom (2017b) *The Communications Market Report: Northern Ireland*, 3 August 2017. www.ofcom.org.uk/research-and-data/multi-sector-research/cmr/cmr-2017/northern-ireland (accessed 4 May 2020).

O'Loughlin, B., C. Vaccari, B. A. Ozgul and J. Dennis (2017) "Twitter and global political crises cycles of insecurity in #PrayforParis and #PrayforSyria". *Middle East Journal of Culture and Communication* 10: 175–203. doi: 10.1163/18739865-01002006.

O'Rawe, M. (2010) "Security sector reform and identity in divided societies: Lessons from Northern Ireland". In P. Arthur (ed.) *Identities in Transition: Challenges for Transitional Justice in Divided Societies*. Cambridge: Cambridge University Press, pp. 87–117.

O'Reilly, T. (2005) "What is Web 2.0: Design patterns and business models for the next generation of software". http://oreilly.com/web2/archive/what-is-web-20.html (accessed 10 September 2014).

O'Reilly, T. and S. Milstein (2012) *The Twitter Book*. Sebastopol, CA: O'Reilly Media.

Paolini, S., M. Hewstone, E. Cairns and A. Voci (2004) "Effects of direct and indirect cross- group friendships on judgments of Catholics and Protestants in Northern Ireland: The mediating role of an anxiety-reduction mechanism". *Personality and Social Psychology Bulletin* 30: 770–786. doi: 10.1177/0146167203262848.

Papacharissi, Z. (2014) *Affective Publics: Sentiment, Technology and Politics*. Oxford: Oxford University Press.

Papacharissi, Z. (2016) "Affective publics and structures of storytelling: Sentiment, events and mediality". *Information, Communication & Society* 19 (3): 307–324.

Parades Commission for Northern Ireland (2013) *Annual Report and Financial Statements Parades Commission for Northern Ireland for the Year Ended 31st March 2012*. www.gov.uk/government/publications/annual-report-and-financial-statements-parades-commission-for-northern-ireland-for-the-year-ended-31st-march-2012 (accessed 1 April 2017).

Pennington, K. and O. Lynch (2015) "Counterterrorism, community policing and the flags protests: An examination of police perceptions of Northern Ireland's Operation Dulcet". *Studies in Conflict & Terrorism* 38 (7): 543–559.

Petersen, L., G. Havarneanu, P. Reilly, E. Serafinelli and R. Bossu (2018) "November 2015 Paris terrorist attacks and social media use: Preliminary findings from authorities, critical infrastructure operators and journalists". In K. Boersma and B. Tomaszewski (eds) *Proceedings of the 15th ISCRAM Conference*. Rochester, NY: Rochester Institute of Technology, pp. 629–638.

Pettigrew, T. F. and L. R. Tropp (2006) "A meta-analytical test of the intergroup contact theory". *Journal of Personality and Social Psychology* 90: 751–783.

Pettigrew, T., L. R. Tropp, U. Wagner and O. Christ (2011) "Recent advances in intergroup contact theory". *International Journal of Intercultural Relations* 35: 271–280. doi: 10.1016/j.ijintrel.2011.03.001.

Phillips, W. (2015) *This is Why We Can't Have Nice Things: Mapping the Relationship between Online Trolling and Mainstream Culture*. Cambridge, MA: MIT Press.

Pickerill, J. (2003) *Cyberprotest: Environmental Activism Online*. Manchester: Manchester University Press.

Poell, T., R. Abdulla, B. Rieder, R. Woltering and L. Zack (2016) "Protest leadership in the age of social media". *Information, Communication & Society* 19 (7): 994–1014. https://hdl.handle.net/11245/1.534282 (accessed 4 May 2020).

People's Republic of Stokes Croft (2012) "No Tesco in Stokes Croft campaign update" PRSC.org.uk, 17 April 2012. https://prsc.org.uk/no-tesco-in-stokes-croft-campaign-update/.

Purvis, D. and Working Group (2011) *Educational Disadvantage and the Protestant Working Class: A Call to Action*. Belfast: Northern Ireland Assembly.

Reilly, P. (2008). "Googling terrorists: Are Northern Irish terrorists visible on Internet search engines?". In A. Spink and M. Zimmer (eds) *Search Engines: Interdisciplinary Perspectives*. New York: Springer, pp. 151–177.

Reilly, P. (2011a) *Framing The Troubles Online: Northern Irish Political Groups and Website Strategy*. Manchester: Manchester University Press.

Reilly, P. (2011b) "'Anti-social' networking in Northern Ireland: Policy responses to young people's use of social media for organising anti-social behaviour". *Policy and Internet* 3 (1): Article 7.

Reilly, P. (2012) "Community worker perspectives on the use of new media to promote conflict transformation in Belfast". *Urban Studies* 49 (15): 3385–3401.

Reilly, P. (2013) "Ourselves alone (but making connections): The social media strategies of Sinn Féin". In P. Nixon, R. Rawal and D. Mercea (eds) *Chasing the Promise of Internet Politics*. London: Routledge, pp. 157–168.

Reilly, P. (2014) "The 'Battle of Stokes Croft' on YouTube: The development of an ethical stance for the study of online comments". *SAGE Research Methods Cases*. doi: 10.4135/978144627305013509209.

Reilly, P. (2015) "Every little helps? YouTube, sousveillance and the 'anti-Tesco' riot in Bristol". *New Media & Society* 17 (5): 755–771.

Reilly, P. (2016) "Tweeting for peace? Twitter and the Ardoyne parade dispute, July 2014". *First Monday* 21 (11).

Reilly, P. (2018) "Sinn Féin's MP's resignation demonstrates the dangers of social media for politicians", *Democratic Audit*, 26 January 2018. www.democraticaudit.com/2018/01/26/sinn-fein-mps-resignation-demonstrates-the-dangers-of-social-media-for-politicians/ (accessed 4 May 2020).

Reilly, P. and D. Atanasova (2016) *A Strategy for Communication between Key Agencies and Members of the Public during Crisis Situations*. http://casceff.eu/media2/2016/05/D3.3-Communication-strategy.pdf (accessed 4 May 2020).

Reilly, P. and F. Trevisan (2016) "Researching protest on Facebook: Developing an ethical stance for the study of Northern Irish flag protest pages". *Information, Communication & Society* 19 (3): 419–435.

Reis, L. A. (1995) "The Rodney King beating: Beyond fair use: A broadcaster's right to air copyrighted videotape as part of a newscast". *John Marshall Journal of Computer & Information Law* 13 (2): 269–311.

Richmond, O. P. and I. Tellidis (2012) "The complex relationship between peacebuilding and terrorism approaches: Towards post-terrorism and a post-liberal peace?". *Terrorism and Political Violence* 24 (1): 120–143. doi: 10.1080/09546553.2011.628720.

Schaefer, B. P. and K. F. Steinmetz (2014) "Watching the watchers and McLuhan's tetrad: The limits of cop-watching in the internet age". *Surveillance & Society* 12 (4): 502–515. doi: 10.24908/ss.v12i4.5028.

Schudson, M. (1998) *The Good Citizen: A History of American Civil Life*. New York: Free Press.

Schwab, A. K., C. Sagioglou and T. Greitemeyer (2019) "Getting connected: Intergroup contact on Facebook". *The Journal of Social Psychology* 159 (3): 344–348. doi: 10.1080/00224545.2018.1489367.

Shifman, L. (2015) *Memes in Digital Culture*. Cambridge, MA: MIT Press.

Shirlow, P. and B. Murtagh (2006) *Belfast: Segregation, Violence and the City*. London: Pluto Press.

Shirlow, P. and K. McEvoy (2008) *Beyond the Wire: Former Prisoners and Conflict Transformation in Northern Ireland*. London: Pluto Press.

Simpson, E. (2013) "A response to Brian John Spencer, Loyalists Against Democracy". http://loyalistsagainstdemocracy.blogspot.co.uk/2013/12/a-response-to-brian-john-spencer.html (accessed 4 May 2020).

Simpson, P. (2003) *On the Discourse of Satire: Towards a Stylistic Model of Satirical Humor*. Amsterdam: John Benjamins Publishing Company.

Singh, A. (2017) "Anticipatory citizen surveillance of the police". *Surveillance & Society* 15 (5): 676–688. doi: 10.24908/ss.v15i5.6418.

Smith, W. (2014) "A wrong turn", 21 April 2014. http://winkiesmith.blogspot.co.uk/2014_04_01_archive.html (accessed 4 May 2020).

Smithey, L. (2013) *Unionists, Loyalists, and Conflict Transformation in Northern Ireland*. Oxford: Oxford University Press.

Snow, D. A., S. A. Soule and H. Kriesi (2004) "Mapping the terrain". In D. A. Snow, S. A. Soule and H. Kriesi (eds) *The Blackwell Companion to Social Movements*. Oxford: Blackwell, pp. 3–16.

Soares, A.H.G.M. (2015) "The parodic/sincere political satire of Loyalists Against Democracy (LAD) and its digital remixing of Northern Ireland". *Queen's Political Review* 3 (2): 36–53.

Spencer, B. (2013a) "Loyalists Against Democracy – unveiling and assailing sectarianism", 14 October 2013. http://eamonnmallie.com/2013/10/loyalists-against-democracy-unveiling-and-assailing-sectarianism/ (accessed 4 May 2020).

Spencer, B. (2013b) "Stand up for Northern Ireland's Tahrir Square", *Huffington Post*, 11 October 2013. www.huffingtonpost.co.uk/brian-john-spencer/northern-ireland_b_4069544.html (accessed 10 May 2019).

Stanley, J. and B. Steinhardt (2003) *Bigger Monster, Weaker Chains: The Growth of an American Surveillance Society*. Washington: Technology and Liberty Program, American Civil Liberties Union.

Sumiala, J., K. Valaskivi, M. Tikka and J. Huhtamaki (2018) *Hybrid Media Events: The Charlie Hebdo Attacks and the Global Circulation of Terrorist Violence*. Bingley, UK: Emerald.

Tellidis, I. and S. Kappler (2016) "Information and communication technologies in peacebuilding: Implications, opportunities and challenges". *Cooperation and Conflict* 51 (1): 75–93. doi: 10.1177/0010836715603752.

Thelwall, M., P. Sud and F. Vis (2012) "Commenting on YouTube videos: From Guatemalan rock to El Big Bang". *Journal of the American Society for Information Science and Technology* 63: 616–629. doi: 10.1002/asi.21679.

Tilly, C. (2008) *Contentious Performances*. Cambridge: Cambridge University Press.

Tilly, C. and S. Tarrow (2015) *Contentious Politics*. Oxford: Oxford University Press.

Tomlinson, M., G. Kelly and P. Hillyard (2013) "Northern Ireland: Faring badly". http://poverty.ac.uk/pse-research/northern-ireland-faring-badly (accessed 1 April 2017).

Treré, E. (2019) *Hybrid Media Activism: Ecologies, Imaginaries, Algorithms*. Abingdon, Oxon: Routledge.

Treré, E. and A. Mattoni (2016) "Media ecologies and protest movements: Main perspectives and key lessons". *Information, Communication & Society* 19 (3): 290–306.

Trevisan, F. and P. Reilly (2014) "Ethical dilemmas in researching social media campaigns on sensitive personal issues: Lessons from the study of British disability dissent networks". *Information, Communication & Society* 17 (9): 1131–1146.

Tufekci, Z. (2013) "'Not this one': Social movements, the attention economy, and microcelebrity networked activism". *American Behavioral Scientist* 257: 848–870. doi: 10.1177/0002764213479369.

Tufekci, Z. (2017) *Twitter and Tear Gas: The Power and Fragility of Networked Protest*. London: Yale University Press.

Tufekci, Z. and C. Wilson (2012). "Social media and the decision to participate in political protest: Observations from Tahrir Square". *Journal of Communication* 62: 363–379. doi: 10.1111/j.1460-2466.2012.01629.x.

Tyler, I. (2013) *Revolting Subjects: Social Abjection and Resistance in Neoliberal Britain*. London: Zed Books.

Tyler, T. R. (2006) "Psychological perspectives on legitimacy and legitimation". *Annual Review of Psychology* 57 (1): 375–400. doi: 10.1146/annurev. psych.57.102904.190038.

Tyler, T. R. and J. Fagan (2008) "Legitimacy and cooperation: Why do people help the police fight crime in their communities?" *Ohio State Journal of Criminal Law* 6: 231–275.

Vaccari, C., A. Chadwick and B. O'Loughlin (2015) "Dual screening the political: Media events, social media, and citizen engagement". *Journal of Communication* 65 (6): 1041–1061. doi: 10.1111/jcom.12187.

Vaidhyanathan, S. (2018) *Anti-Social Media: How Facebook Disconnects Us and Undermines Democracy*. Oxford: Oxford University Press.

Valenzuela, S. (2013) "Unpacking the use of social media for protest behavior: The roles of information, opinion expression, and activism". *American Behavioral Scientist* 57: 920–942. doi: 10.1177/0002764213479375.

Valeriani, A. and C. Vaccari (2016) "Accidental exposure to politics on social media as online participation equalizer in Germany, Italy, and the United Kingdom". *New Media & Society* 18 (9): 1857–1874. doi: 10.1177/ 1461444815616223.

Van Dijck, J. (2013) *The Culture of Connectivity: A Critical History of Social Media*. Oxford: Oxford University Press.

Van Zoonen, L., F. Vis and S. Mihelj (2011) "YouTube interactions between agonism, antagonism and dialogue: Video responses to the anti-Islam film Fitna". *New Media & Society* 13: 1283–1300. doi: 10.1177/ 1461444811405020.

Vezzali, L., M. Hewstone, D. Capozza, D. Giovannini and R. Wolfer (2014) "Improving intergroup relations with extended and vicarious forms of indirect contact". *European Review of Social Psychology* 25 (1): 314–389. doi: 10.1080/10463283.2014.982948.

Vicari, S. (2017) "Twitter and non-elites: Interpreting power dynamics in the life story of the (#)BRCA Twitter stream". *Social Media & Society* (July–September): 1–14. doi: 10.1177/2056305117733224.

Vromen, A. (2017) *Digital Citizenship and Political Engagement: The Challenge from Online Campaigning and Advocacy Organisations*. London: Palgrave Macmillan.

Wang, Z., J. B. Walther and J. T. Hancock (2009) "Social identification and interpersonal communication in computer-mediated communication: What you do versus who you are in virtual groups". *Human Communication Research* 35: 59–85.

Wardle, C. (2017) "Fake news. It's complicated", *First Draft News*. https://firstdraftnews.com:443/fake-news-complicated/ (accessed 10 May 2019).

Weltevrede, E., E. Helmond and C. Gerlitz (2014) "The politics of real-time: A device perspective on social media platforms and search engines". *Theory Culture Society* 31 (6): 125–150. doi: 10.1177/0263276414537318.

Westerman, D. and P. Spence (2013) "Social media as information source: Recency of updates and credibility of information". *Journal of Computer-Mediated Communication* 19: 17–183. doi: 10.1111/jcc4.12041.

White, L. (2019) "The Troubles with Twitter: We meet Belfast Child, On This Day the IRA, Irish Border and MLAs and the Like". *Belfast Telegraph*, 13 April 2019. www.belfasttelegraph.co.uk/life/features/the-troubles-with-twitter-we-meet-belfast-child-on-this-day-the-ira-irish-border-and-mlas-and-the-like-38009949.html (accessed 10 May 2019).

Whiteman, N. (2012) *Undoing Ethics: Rethinking Practice in Online Research*. New York: Springer.

Wolfsfeld, G. (2018) "The role of the media in violent conflicts in the digital age: Israeli and Palestinian leaders' perceptions". *Media, War & Conflict* 11 (1): 107–124. doi: 10.1177/1750635217727312.

Wolfsfeld, G., E. Segev and T. Sheafer (2013) "Social media and the Arab Spring: Politics comes first". *International Journal of Press/Politics* 18 (2): 115–137. doi: 10.1177/1940161212471716.

Worden, R. E. and S. J. McLean (2017) "Research on police legitimacy: The state of the art". *Policing: An International Journal of Police Strategies & Management* 4 (3): 480–513.

Young, O. (2014) *New Media and Young People in Interface Areas of Belfast*. Belfast: NICRC.

Zimmer, M. (2010) "'But the data is already public': On the ethics of research in Facebook". *Ethics and Information Technology* 12 (4): 313–325. doi: 10.1007/s10676-010-9227-5.

Zuboff, S. (2018) *The Age of Surveillance Capitalism: The Fight for a Human Future at the New Frontier of Power*. New York: Public Affairs.

Zuckerman, E. (2015) "Cute cats to the rescue? Participatory media and political expression". In D. Allen and J. Light (eds) *From Voice to Influence: Understanding Citizenship in the Digital Age*. Chicago, IL: University of Chicago Press, pp. 131–154.

Index

Adams, David 40
Adams, Gerry 146, 148
Alliance Party of Northern Ireland
    48, 67, 83, 90, 94, 96, 150, 169,
    198
  offices attacked 94, 150
  subject of leaflet campaign
    90, 94
Allister, Jim 56, 68, 93, 148,
    173, 194
Amnesty International 13, 66
  #Toxic Twitter report 197–198
An Garda Síochána 54, 66, 185
An Phoblacht 52
Andersonstown News 70
Anglo-Irish Agreement
  protests 29
'Arab Spring' 9, 18, 24, 33, 45
Ardoyne 44, 67, 69, 90, 110, 121,
    139, 156–162, 165–166,
    169–172, 175–178
Ardoyne Republican (Blogger) 167,
    174
Aughey, John 162–163, 175–176

#BackinBelfast 19, 74
Baggott, Matt 49, 55, 103, 110
'Battle of Stokes Croft' 108
BBC Newsline 165
BBC Spotlight 27, 89, 149

Bebo 5, 34, 45
  and 'recreational rioting' 5
Belfast Agreement/Good Friday
    Agreement 3, 26, 28, 39, 51, 52,
    78, 109, 185, 189, 198
Belfast City Council 26, 47, 48, 60,
    79, 80, 89, 194
  vote on flag protocol 48–52, 53,
    60–61, 80, 90, 93, 139–140,
    150, 194
Belfast City Hall 26–29, 44,
    47–49, 52–53, 57, 63–65,
    88–91, 96, 110, 124, 136, 141,
    156, 195
Belfast Daily 66
Belfast Telegraph 93, 103, 159–164,
    171–172, 176, 177, 195
Black Lives Matter 34, 107, 125,
    185, 200
  sharing footage of police killings
    107
Black, Rebecca 172
Blame Game, The (BBC) 145
Blanket 39–40
Blevins, David 171
Border Irish (@BorderIrish)
    195–196
Brannigan, Tim 96
Brewer, John 148
Brexit 1, 2, 187–188, 195–196

Bryson, Jamie 18–19, 30, 45, 50, 53, 126, 153
  subject of online abuse 152, 186, 193
Buchanan, Tom 151
Bunting, Jolene 194

Channel 4 89, 147
Citizens' Assembly (Northern Ireland) 191–192
citizenship 9–11
  digital 9–10, 184, 196–199
  silly 10–11, 20, 152–153, 192–196
Clarke, Breandán 90
Clawson, Phoebe 163, 176, 178
connective action 199
Conservative Party 1, 195
contact hypothesis 6–9, 190
contentious politics 18, 21, 24–26
Corr, Julie Ann 150, 173

deliberative polls 191
Democratic Unionist Party (DUP) 1, 27–30, 40–44, 48, 52, 67–68, 71, 83, 88, 93, 143, 146, 147, 149–153, 161, 169, 173, 187, 189, 193–197
Derry/Londonderry 1, 5, 81, 140
  Bloody Sunday 53, 95, 121, 135, 140
Disappeared, The (BBC) 143, 148, 150, 193
Discovertext 15, 17, 58, 81, 134, 165, 199
Dissenter, The 36
Dissolving Boundaries project 8
Dodds, Diane 149
Dodds, Nigel 161, 163
Donaldson, Sir Jeffrey 43
Dowson, Jim 50, 54–55, 92–93, 118, 122, 126–127, 139
Drumcree crisis 49, 140

East Belfast 48–49, 58, 74, 87, 90–92, 94, 97, 102–103, 110–111, 118, 120–122, 125, 134, 136, 139, 140, 147, 200
  threats against St Matthew's Church 136
  violence at Short Strand interface 49, 59
Edelman Trust 188
Edwards, Rodney 176
Emerson, Newton 131

Facebook 1–2, 5, 8, 9, 12–15, 17–18, 20, 31–33, 35, 38–39, 42–44, 47–48, 52–58, 60, 62–64, 67, 70–72, 74–75, 92, 95–96, 107, 111, 113, 126, 129, 131–142, 144, 147–148, 151–152, 164, 184–188, 190–191, 193–194, 196–201
  Peace on Facebook 9, 191
Fealty, Mick 36, 85, 94
#flegs 79–80
Ford, David 41, 52, 54
Fourthwrite 39
Frazer, Willie 30, 45, 50, 53, 55–56, 62–65, 69, 71, 74, 90, 92–93, 97, 131, 137–140, 145–147, 153
  subject of online abuse 152, 186, 193
Frontline Freelance Media 118

Gallagher, Dara 91
Garvaghy Road Residents' Coalition 4, 140
Giles, Izzy 145
Give My Head Peace 141
Greater Ardoyne Residents' Collective 174–175

Haas, Richard 145
Hamilton, George 161–162, 176

Harvey, Johnny 56, 78
Hoey, Paddy 39–40
Hume, John 87
Hutchinson, Billy 56, 68, 146

Impartial Reporter 176
Irish News 38, 53–56, 86, 103, 140,
    164, 168, 171
Irvine, Winston 149

Kells, Nigel 173
Kelly, Gerry 102, 176
Kerr, Will 103
Knox, Oscar 88, 159, 176
Kyle, John 94, 95, 150

Long, Naomi 48, 94, 198
Loyalists Against Democracy
    (LAD) 20, 47, 57, 80, 84, 98,
    129–145, 147–153, 169, 186,
    193–195, 197
Loyalist Peaceful Protester Updater
    (LPPU) 15, 18–20, 48, 52, 55,
    57– 63, 65–66, 68–71, 74,
    89–90, 97, 113, 134–140, 142,
    151–152, 185, 197, 199, 200
    backup page 18, 48, 58, 69, 138
    and J18 case 55, 57, 60, 67,
    69–71, 137, 142, 151, 199
Loyalist Perspective 133

McAllister, John 131, 149
McConnell, James 194–195
McCrea, Basil 94, 131
McDowell, Jim 136
McElduff, Barry 195
McGuinness, Martin 41, 146
McIntyre, Anthony 39, 102
McKay, Daithí 160
McKee, Lyra 1, 187
McKenzie, Tina 145
Magee, Dave 132, 137, 148

Maginness, Alban 161
Mallie, Eamonn 94
Mallon, Nichola 172
Martin, Peter 151
Martin, Stephen 162
May, Theresa 1
Meban, Alan 38, 129, 193
memes 12, 89, 96, 141, 145–147,
    174
@MLAsAndTheLike 196
Monaghan, John 164
Morris, Allison 54, 86–87, 140, 168,
    172, 198
Morrison, Sammy 148
Morrow, Maurice 151
Mouffe, Chantal 6, 197
Mulvenna, Gareth 133
Murphy, Stephen 86

*Nelson McCausland Looking at
    Things* 195
Nesbitt, Mike 93, 146–147
Net Intergroup Contact (NIC)
    platform 8
New Irish Republican Army 1
New Unionism 36
News Letter 19, 38, 53, 83, 87, 139
NI21 131, 145, 149, 197
Nolan, Aoife 91
Nolan, Stephen (BBC) 88, 131,
    148, 152
Northern Ireland Community
    Relations Council 168
Northern Ireland Conservatives 38
Northern Ireland Equality
    Commission 194
    Ashers Baking Company case
    194
Northern Ireland Executive 27–28,
    39, 43–44, 50–51, 78, 160, 187
    Good Relations Strategy 4
    Petition of Concern 196

Northern Ireland Housing Executive 27
Northern Ireland Life and Times Survey 27, 187
Northern Ireland Parades Commission 28
Northern Ireland Peace Monitoring Report 51
Northern Ireland Policing Board 49
Northern Ireland Public Processions Act 110
Northern Ireland Unionist Collective Group (NIUG) 133

Occupy Wall Street 199
Ofcom 18
O'Kane, Jake 145
online activism 31–34
    clicktivist critique 32, 45
@OnThisDayTheIRA 197
Open Unionism 38
Operation Dulcet 50, 55, 63, 110
Operation Standstill 19, 49, 57, 74, 78, 88, 124
Operation Titan 102
#OperationSitin 74, 78
Orange Order 2, 15, 20, 49, 68, 90, 91, 102, 138–139, 156–161, 163, 171, 173–177, 192, 197
O'Sullivan, Meghan 145

Paisley, Ian 29, 93
Patterson, Ruth 150
peacebuilding 3, 4, 6
    and ICTs 6–10
Pew Internet and American Life Project 178
Police Ombudsman for Northern Ireland 111, 119
Police Service of Northern Ireland (PSNI) 19–21, 28, 39, 47, 49–50, 52, 54–55, 66–67,
69–71, 88, 90–91, 95, 97, 102–103, 109–113, 118–124, 126, 135–137, 140, 146–147, 157–158, 160–163, 170–173, 176–177, 185, 192–193, 198–200
    accusations of brutality 19, 66–67, 69, 71, 90, 103–104, 111, 118–121, 125–126, 185, 198, 200–201
Polley, Owen 38–39, 40–41
Poots, Edwin 143, 147, 150, 152, 193
#PositiveNI 74, 78
Pride of Ardoyne band 163, 173
Progressive Unionist Party (PUP) 40, 68, 71, 83, 95, 145–146, 149–150, 152, 169, 170, 173
Protestant Coalition (PC) 26, 145–148, 152
Provisional Irish Republican Army (Provisional IRA) 39, 56, 81, 92, 102, 109, 138, 143, 147, 150

Real Irish Republican Army (Real IRA) 3, 124, 157
Red Sky scandal 27
Reddit 12
Reilly, Henry 149
renewable heating incentive scheme 187–188
Robinson, Iris 27
Robinson, Peter 48, 50, 65, 67, 93, 149, 195
Rowan, Brian 160
Royal Ulster Constabulary (RUC) 66, 109
Russia Today 164, 175
Ryder, Chris 91

St Andrews Agreement 109
Sharkey, Kevin (BBC) 171

'Shinnerbots' 197
Simpson, Mark (BBC) 170–171
Sinn Féin 25, 28, 30, 39–44, 47, 50,
    67–68, 71, 83, 85, 93, 102, 109,
    126, 139, 146, 148, 152, 160,
    169–170, 172, 176, 185, 187,
    189, 193, 194–195, 197
Slugger O'Toole 36–38, 45, 93
Smyth, Paul 36
Social Democratic and Labour
    Party (SDLP) 40, 42, 83, 87,
    161, 169, 173
social media 5–13
    echo chamber thesis 186
    Marxist critique 13
    parody accounts 130–131,
        142–143, 193
    and 'spiral of silence' 178, 190
    surveillance capitalism 13, 107,
        198–199
    wordplay 11, 79, 130, 145,
        152, 192
social movement theory
    25–27
Solinas, Gerard 163
sousveillance 104–108
    hierarchical and personal
        forms 105
    'Veillance Plane' 106
Spencer, Brian John 131, 167,
    170
Stalford, Christopher 151
Stevenson, Edward 160, 163
Sunday Life 53, 103, 159, 162

'Take Back the City' 79
technological solutionism 8–9
Traditional Unionist Voice (TUV)
    1, 40, 68, 71,
Trump, Donald 2, 12, 14
Twaddell peace camp 146, 158,
    163, 173

Twelfth of July parades 2, 21, 28,
    67, 90, 159, 160–165, 174, 177
Twitter 1, 2, 9, 11–15, 17, 19–20,
    31–32, 34–42, 44, 66, 74, 79, 82,
    84, 86, 92, 94, 97–98, 107, 112,
    129–132, 134, 137, 138–142,
    144–149, 151, 156, 159, 162,
    164–165, 167–168, 170, 173,
    175–179, 184 –186, 190, 192,
    194–198, 200
    and affective publics 76–77
    as ambient news environment
        75–76

UK Communications Act (2003)
    123
UK Terrorism Act (2000) 124
Ulster Defence Association (UDA)
    40, 49, 62, 65, 123, 174, 175
Ulster Defence Regiment 66
Ulster People's Forum (UPF) 26,
    47, 50, 56, 59–60, 64–65, 68,
    87, 91–93, 124, 140, 142, 152
Ulster Political Research Group
    (UPRG) 139, 161, 163, 172,
    175–176
Ulster Unionist Party (UUP) 30, 83
Ulster Volunteer Force (UVF) 5, 49,
    68, 123, 138, 146, 149, 150, 174
United Protestant Voice 174
UTV Insight 89
UTV Live Tonight 165

View, The 145
Villiers, Theresa 144, 161, 162
Vote Leave 2

Watterson, Paul 38
Webometric Analyst 112
Weir, Peter 151
whataboutery 66, 69, 70, 90,
    111, 121

Whearty, John-Paul 131
Where is my Public Servant
    (WIMPS) 36
Williamson, Claire 164
Wilson, Sammy 68
Wright, Sean 102

Young Conway Volunteers (YCV)
    28
YouTube 2, 5, 14, 15, 19, 35, 40, 79,
    88, 103–104, 108, 111–112,
    119, 123–126, 131, 174,
    184–185, 194, 200–201

EU authorised representative for GPSR:
Easy Access System Europe, Mustamäe tee 50,
10621 Tallinn, Estonia
gpsr.requests@easproject.com